SOURCES FOR THE STUDY OF GREEK RELIGION

SOCIETY OF BIBLICAL LITERATURE
Sources for Biblical Study

edited by
Burke O. Long

Number 14

SOURCES FOR THE STUDY OF GREEK RELIGION

by
David G. Rice and John E. Stambaugh

SOURCES FOR THE STUDY OF GREEK RELIGION

by

David G. Rice and John E. Stambaugh

Published by
SCHOLARS PRESS
for
The Society of Biblical Literature

SOURCES FOR THE STUDY OF GREEK RELIGION

by
David G. Rice
College of St. Scholastica
and
John E. Stambaugh
Williams College

Library of Congress Cataloging in Publication Data

Stambaugh, John E.
 Sources for the study of Greek religion.

 (Sources for Biblical study ; no. 14 ISSN 0145-2762)
 Includes bibliographical references and indexes. 1.
Greece—Religion—Collected works. I. Rice, David G.,
joint author. II. Title. III. Series.
BL782.s7   292'.08   79-18389
ISBN 0-89130-346-4
ISBN 0-89130-347-2 pbk.
10 09 08 07   13 12 11

For our teachers

JOHN V.A. FINE

AND

C. BRADFORD WELLES

TABLE OF CONTENTS

"It was Homer and Hesiod," wrote Herodotus (*Histories* II. 53), "who first compiled genealogies of the gods for the Greeks, gave the gods their titles, defined their honors and skills, and described their appearances." A source book on Greek religion almost inevitably, therefore, begins with Homer, who reflects the civilization of Bronze Age Greece combined with features from the five centuries which intervened between the Bronze Age and his own time in the eighth century B.C., and with Hesiod, who reflects more particularly the Greece of the eighth and early seventh centuries B.C., when the map of classical Greece was beginning to emerge. The basic social unit in the centuries following Homer and Hesiod was the *polis* or city-state, usually composed of several tribal groups which were in turn composed of smaller clans and families, all of which had their own special religious traditions. In the eighth, seventh and sixth centuries, the mainland Greeks were subject to new cultural influences from the Near East through the Ionian Greeks in Asia Minor and through direct contacts with Egypt and Syria. In these same centuries the Greeks launched an extensive colonization effort toward Sicily and southern Italy, and toward the Black Sea; new techniques in political organization, such as tyranny and democracy, emerged. At the same time diplomatic relations among the states were encouraged by the growth of such religious centers as Delphi and Olympia. By the beginning of the fifth century, Athens, Sparta and Corinth had emerged as the strongest of the Greek cities, and the pressure of foreign invasion from Persia helped to make the Greeks conscious of a Panhellenic unity: this unity was seldom expressed in political terms, but is marked in the religious exercises of the clan, the tribe and the state, which gave citizens a feeling of harmony, well-being and shared traditions. The end of the fifty century, however, saw serious challenges to the traditional religion:

the violence of the Peloponnesian War and the collapse of
Athens, the probing skepticism of the Sophists, the generally perceived decay of traditional standards and values,
led many to reassess their religious attitudes. In the late
fifth century and the fourth we find some professing atheism,
others constructing sophisticated philosophical systems,
others embracing mysticism or superstition or the cult of
some such nurturing god as Asclepius: all together exhibit
a tendency toward personal choice in religion, in contrast
to the group-oriented practices which seemed to dominate
earlier.

Such a general summary of the religious trends of
classical Greece has considerable validity, yet the sources
show that common religious ceremonies continued after 400
B.C., and also that individuals expressed their private devotion to a god before 400 B.C. One of the functions of a
source book about the ancient Greeks is to demonstrate the
complexity and immediacy of the subject by allowing the
Greeks to speak for themselves. In editing this collection
of sources, our intention has been to present a representative sample of familiar and unfamiliar texts illustrating
the range (rather than the totality) of the Greek religious
experience, from the most abstract speculations of Plato
and Aristotle to the most homely domestic ritual. We have
tried to provide modern, intelligible translations of the
literature and documents which the ancient world has left
us on this subject, and through them to demonstrate how the
Greeks worshipped their gods and what they themselves said
about their religious beliefs and practices.

Our primary focus is on the four centuries from Homer
to Alexander the Great, although passages from later antiquity
have been included freely when they cast some important light
on archaic and classical Greek practices. In general, however, we have not dealt explicitly with the religious attitudes of the Hellenistic and Roman periods because this has
already been done by F.C. Grant in his *Hellenistic Religions*
(Indianapolis and New York, 1953) and *Ancient Roman Religion*
(New York, 1957).

The very varied material has been organized into six chapters, dealing with (1) the traditional Olympian gods and (2) their chthonian counterparts represented by the heroes; with (3) public cult practices and (4) more private concerns of family and individual; with (5) the mystery cults and their promises; and with (6) death and the nature of the soul. The categories overlap to some extent, and some of the general sections and specific passages might easily have been put in a different part of the book. The index should, however, provide help for anyone who wants to pull together all the references to a single topic, as for example sacrificial regulations or the Orphics. Within each category, we have attempted to arrange the selections so as to illustrate the historical development of attitudes, beliefs and practices

In transliterating Greek, it has seemed reasonable, if not entirely consistent, to use a Latinized spelling for names in which this has become "normal" English usage, and in other cases to follow a more literal pattern.

It is a pleasure to be able to acknowledge the help we have received in preparing this collection of sources: suggestions as to content and format from Norman R. Petersen, Jr., Wayne A. Meeks and Harold Y. McCulloch; the typing of preliminary drafts by Rosemary Lane, Louise Gilotti, Donna Chenail and Eileen Sahady; the preparation of camera-ready copy by Marla Krystkowiak; the patient support of Patricia Rice and Paula Carew; and grants from the Faculty Welfare Committee of St. Scholastica College and the Division I research fund of Williams College. Our special debts of training, inspiration and the fostering of our interest in the documentation of ancient Greek religion are acknowledged in the dedication.

David G. Rice   John E. Stambaugh
College of St. Scholastica   Williams College
Duluth, Minnesota 55811   Williamstown, Massachusetts 01267

June, 1979

LIST OF ABBREVIATIONS

Diels-Kranz   H. Diels, *Die Fragmente der Vorsokratiker*, rev. by W. Kranz. Berlin, 5th ed. ff., 1934 ff.

FGrH   F. Jacoby, *Die Fragmente der Griechischen Historiker*. Berlin, 1923-1927; Leiden, 1940-1958.

IC   M. Guarducci, *Inscriptiones Creticae*. Rome, 1934 ff.

IG   *Inscriptiones Graecae*. Berlin, 1873 ff.

LGS   L. Ziehen, *Leges Graecorum Sacrae e Titulis Collectae*, Pars Altera. Leipzig, 1906.

LSAM   F. Sokolowski, *Lois Sacrées de l'Asie Mineure*. Paris, 1955.

LSCG   F. Sokolowski, *Lois Sacrées des Cités Grecques*, Supplément. Paris, 1962.

SEG   *Supplementum Epigraphicum Graecum*. Leiden.

SIG[3]   G. Dittenberger, *Sylloge Inscriptionum Graecarum*, 3rd ed. Leipzig, 1915-1924.

CHAPTER I. THE OLYMPIAN GODS

A. The Divine World of Homer

It was one of the many achievements of the first poets
of Greece, in particular Homer and Hesiod, to create for
the Greeks and for Western man the pantheon of deities we
call the gods of Olympus. The poets were not afraid to
create their portraits of the gods and goddesses fully,
showing in their stories not only divine power but divine
frailty and weaknesses. The Greeks depicted these creations
in plastic forms, in temples and shrines, on fresco and
sculpture, so that the gods not only symbolized the inexpli-
cable forces at work in history, but became representatives
of the best and worst of Greek civilization. The following
passages from Homer, who lived at some point prior to 700
B.C., are selected to represent the range of poetic description of the gods; Homer functioned for the Greeks in some
ways as the Bible functions for Christians, as the source
and starting point for man's curiosity about the divine.
For further reading see W.K.C. Guthrie, *The Greeks and their
Gods* (Boston, 1951); H.J. Rose, *Religion in Greece and Rome*
(New York, 1959). For the Homeric poems themselves, see
G.S. Kirk, *The Songs of Homer* (Cambridge, 1962); M.I. Finley,
The World of Odysseus (New York, 1965). A particularly
useful treatment of the intellectual history of the Greeks
may be found in Bruno Snell, *The Discovery of the Mind*
(Eng. tr., New York, 1960), especially pages 1-42.

(Homer, *Iliad* I. 493-610.)

But when the twelfth day came, then all the gods who

live forever returned to Olympus, all together, and Zeus

was their leader. But Thetis did not forget the commands

of her son, but rose from the sea and at dawn went up to

great heaven and Olympus. She found the son of Kronos, Zeus

of the wide-resounding voice, sitting apart from all the

rest of the gods, on the very topmost peak of many-ridged

Olympus. She sat before him and held his knees with her

left hand, but with her right she grasped him beneath the

chin and in supplication spoke to Zeus the lordly son of

Kronos. "O Father Zeus, if I ever aided you in word or deed

among the immortals, grant me this wish - give honor to my

son, whose life is short beyond all other men. Now Agamemnon

the leader of men has dishonored him. He has taken away his

1

prize and now holds on to it, and the king himself has com-
mitted the robbery. But you honor him, Olympian Zeus,
Counselor, and give strength to the Trojans until the
Achaeans praise my son and raise him high with honor."

She finished her speech, but Zeus the cloud-gatherer
made no response, but sat in silence for a long time. Just
as Thetis first clasped his knees, so now she held him fast
and clung to him, and spoke to him again: "Promise me right
now to grant this favor and give your nod of assent, or tell
me no, since you have nothing to fear, in order that I may
clearly know that my status is least among all the gods."

Zeus the cloudgatherer was deeply disturbed and replied: "This is a wretched affair if you will cause me to
quarrel with Hera, at the times when she provokes me with
sharp words. Even now she is accustomed to insult me among
the deathless gods and accuses me of aiding the Trojans in
the war. You must go away, lest Hera notice anything. These
things will be my concern and I will bring them to pass.
As a proof I will nod my head, that you may be confident.
This action of mine is the surest proof among the gods. For
my word is irrevocable and true and will be fulfilled, when
I nod my head."

So he spoke, and the son of Kronos nodded his dark brows,
and the ambrosial locks streamed from the immortal head of
the lord, and he shook great Olympus.

When the two of them had made their plans, Thetis jumped
into the deep sea from shining Olympus, but Zeus went to his
own home. All the gods rose from their seats to greet their
father, nor did anyone dare to await his arrival, but all of
them rose before him. He took his seat there on the throne.
But Hera was well aware that silver-footed Thetis, the daughter of the old man of the sea, had made plans with him, and
she spoke to Zeus the son of Kronos in a mocking tone, "Who
then of the gods has taken counsel with you, O crafty one?
It is always your pleasure to plan in secret and give your
judgments apart from me; never have you been willing to tell
me what you propose."

Then the father of gods and men replied, "Hera, don't
expect to know all my thoughts; they will be hard for you,
even though you are my wife. But if there is something you
ought to know, no one among gods or men will hear it before
you. But if I choose to deliberate apart from the gods, do
not in any way fret or question each and every thing."

Then the ox-eyed lady Hera replied, "Most dread son of
Kronos, what have you said? Before I have not fretted nor
questioned, but in peace you planned all you wished. But
I am very fearful lest the silver-footed Thetis, the daughter
of the old man of the sea, has spoken with you. For at dawn
she sat by your side and clasped your knees. I believe you
gave her a solemn promise to honor Achilles and destroy many
by the Achaean ships."

Then Zeus the cloud-gatherer replied, "You wily one, you
are always thinking and never do I escape you; still, you
will not be able to accomplish anything; in fact, you will
be farther from my heart, which will be a worse situation
for you. If the matter is as you have described it, that
is my business. Sit and be silent, and obey my word. For
not all the gods in Olympus will protect you, when I lay my
irresistible hands on you."

So he spoke, and the ox-eyed lady Hera was frightened.
She took her seat unwillingly, and checked her anger, but
the heavenly gods were concerned throughout the house of
Zeus. Then Hephaestus the famed artisan began to speak among
them, to do a kindness to his dear mother, white-armed Hera.
"This business will be distasteful and unendurable if the
two of you quarrel in this fashion on account of mortals,
particularly if it causes the gods to wrangle among themselves. There will no longer be joy in the feast, since
lesser matters triumph. I advise my mother, though she herself is wise, to be gracious to our father Zeus, in order
that my father not again scold us and throw the banquet into
confusion. What if the Olympian wielder of lightning should
want to throw us from our seats, for he is by far the strongest. You deal with him in gentle words, then the Olympian
will be gracious to us."

So he spoke, and stood up and placed in his mother's
hand a two-handled cup and said to her, "Endure, my mother,
and though you are angry, restrain yourself. I would not
want to see you, who are dear to me, mistreated, and then
I would not be able to save you, although I would be saddened
by the fact. The Olympian is a formidable foe. Once before
I wished to save you, and he snatched me by the foot and
hurled me from the threshold of heaven and I was carried
along the whole day and at dusk fell into Lemnos, and little
breath was still in me. There the Sintians cared for me
after my fall."

So he spoke, and the white-armed goddess Hera smiled,
and with a smile took the cup from her son's hand. Then in
turn Hephaestus poured wine for the other gods, beginning
on the right, and ladled sweet nectar from the mixing bowl.
Unquenchable laughter arose among the blessed gods, as they
saw Hephaestus bustle about in the palace.

So they feasted through the day till sunset, and no one
lacked his fill of the equal feast, nor of the lovely lyre
that Apollo played nor of the Muses, who sang in turn with
lovely voices.

But when the shining light of the sun fell, then each
one went home to bed, each in the palace made for him with
wondrous craftsmanship by famous Hephaestus the lame god.
Zeus the Olympian, the lord of lightning, went to his own
bed, where he was long accustomed to rest when sweet sleep
overcame him. There he went and slept, and Hera of the golden
throne lay beside him.

(*Iliad* III. 380-420. The duel between Paris and Menelaus,
designed to end the conflict, has been interrupted by divine
interference. The scene now shifts to Troy.)

But Aphrodite snatched Paris away easily, for she was
a goddess, and cloaked him in a thick mist, and then set him
down in his fragrant, vaulted chamber. Then she went to summon Helen. She found her on the high tower, surrounded by
crowds of Trojan women; she grasped her by her fragrant robe
and tugged it, likening her appearance to that of an old

woman who dressed wool, who, while she dwelt in Lacedaemon,
carded lovely wool, and who loved her most of all. In her
likeness the goddess Aphrodite spoke, "Come now, Alexander
[Paris] calls you to come home. He is in his chamber in
the rounded bed; he is radiant in his beauty and costume.
You would never expect that he had just returned from
fighting a man, but you would think he was going to a dance,
or was resting after just finishing a dance." Thus she
spoke, and troubled the heart in Helen's breast. And as
she recognized the goddess' lovely neck and seductive breasts
and glittering eyes, she spoke in wonder and called her by
name. "O divine one, why do you long to cajole me in this
fashion? Or will you carry me farther away among well-
settled cities, to somewhere in Phrygia or fair Maionia?
Is some man dear to you there also? Is it because Menelaus
has defeated mighty Alexander and wishes to drag me back
home, though I am hateful? Is it for this reason that you
stand beside me plotting treachery? You go and sit with
him, give up the way of the gods, never turn your feet back
to Olympus, but always snivel at his side and guard him until he makes you his wife, or slave girl. I will not go
to him - it would be most shameful - nor service his bed.
For all the Trojan women would henceforth mock me, all of
them; I put up with a confusion of sorrows in my heart."
      Then in a rage the goddess Aphrodite scolded her.
"Don't cross me, wretched girl, lest in my wrath I abandon
you, and just as much as I now love you beyond measure I
come to hate you. I will contrive bitter hatred for you on
both sides, Trojans and Greeks, and you then will perish in
a wretched death."
      So she spoke, and Helen, child of Zeus, was frightened
and went wrapped in a shining white robe, in silence, unnoticed by all the Trojan women, for a goddess guided her.

(*Iliad* VI. 286-311.)

      Hecuba entered the palace and called to her handmaidens.
They in turn gathered the noble elders among the women from
the city. Meanwhile she descended to a fragrant storage room.

There lay richly embroidered robes, the work of Sidonian
women, whom the godlike Alexander had brought back from
Sidon, having sailed across the broad sea on that journey
when he brought back the high-born Helen as well. Selecting
one of them, Hecuba carried it away as a gift to Athena; it
was the robe which was the most attractively decorated and
the largest, and it shined like a star. It lay there beneath the others. She went on her journey, and many of the
elders hastened with her.

When they came to the shrine of Athena on the acropolis,
Theano of the lovely cheeks opened the doors for them. She
was the daughter of Kisseus and the wife of Antenor the
tamer of horses. It was she whom the Trojans made priestess
of Athena. All the rest then with a cry lifted their hands
to Athena, but the fair-cheeked Theano took the robe, placed
it on the knees of lovely-haired Athena, and in her prayer
begged the daughter of mighty Zeus thus: "Mistress Athena,
defence of our country, most shining of goddesses, break the
spear of Diomedes and cast the man himself headlong before
the Scian gates, that we may immediately offer twelve yearling
heifers, unbroken, in your shrine, if you will pity the city
and the Trojan wives and their innocent children." So she
spoke in prayer, but Pallas Athena turned her head away.

(*Iliad* XIV. 153-351.)

Hera of the golden throne stood on the horn of Olympus
and looked outwards with her eyes. She saw Poseidon her own
brother and her husband's brother busy in the battle that
brings glory to men, and she rejoiced in her heart. But then
she spotted Zeus perched on the topmost peak of many-springed
Ida, and he seemed hateful to her heart. Then the ox-eyed
lady Hera debated how she might distract the mind of Zeus
the aegis-bearer. This seemed to be the best device in her
mind - to descend to Ida arrayed in her finest robes, so that
he might somehow become eager to lie with her next to her
skin in love; then she might pour over his eyes soft sleep
that takes away cares and lull his crafty mind. She went

into her chamber, which her son Hephaestus had made for her,
and shut tight the leaves in the doorposts with a secret
crossbar, which no other god could open. She went in, shut
the shining doors, then first washed all the stains from
her desirable body with ambrosia, then anointed herself
with olive oil fragrant with ambrosia, which stood by her
side filled with sweet scents. As the vial was shaken a
fragrance poured from the bronze-floored house of Zeus over
the earth and heavens. After she had thus anointed her
body, she combed her hair and arranged the shining, lovely
ambrosial locks on her immortal head and cast about her body
an ambrosial robe, which Athena had woven for her, smoothed
it, and worked into it many lovely figures. She pinned it
across her breast with a golden brooch and wrapped around
her waist a girdle with a hundred tassels. In her pierced
earlobes she placed rings of carefully wrought triple drops.
A marvelous radiance shone forth from her. The lovely goddess then covered her head with a lovely veil that shone
white like the sun. Beneath her shining feet she fastened
beautiful sandals. When she had covered her flesh with all
this beauty, she left the chamber, called Aphrodite away
from the other gods and spoke to her. "Would you do my bidding, my child, or resist it, because your heart is angry
since I support the Greeks, while you favor the Trojans?"
Aphrodite, daughter of Zeus, replied, "Hera, most revered
goddess, daughter of great Kronos, tell me what you are
thinking about; my heart bids me do it for you if I can and
it is something that can be done." Then the lady Hera spoke
to her with treachery on her mind. "Make me seductive and
desirable now, with the power that overwhelms both mortals
and immortals, for I am now going to the ends of the bountiful earth to see Ocean, the source of the gods' beginning,
and Tethys my mother, who in their own home brought me up
well and cherished me and took me from Rheia, when Zeus
drove the far-seeing Kronos beneath the earth and the bitter
sea. I plan to visit them and end their continuous discord.
For a long time now they have stayed apart from the bed of
love, since hostility has filled their hearts. If by my

words I could persuade their hearts, and lead them back to
mingle in love, then I would always be held dear and revered
by them."

Then laughter-loving Aphrodite spoke in turn, "It is
neither possible nor proper to refuse your request. For you
lie in the embrace of Zeus, who is the best among us."

From her breasts she loosed the embroidered, patterned
girdle; in it are woven all spells, and beauty, and passion,
and the persuasive endearments which snatch reason even from
the wise. This girdle she placed in her hands and called
her by name and spoke, "Take this girdle and place it in your
bosom; it is finely embroidered and on it are figured all
things. I am sure that whatever you have in mind will not
be unaccomplished."

So she spoke and the ox-eyed lady Hera smiled, and with
a smile placed it in her bosom.

Aphrodite the daughter of Zeus went to her father's
house, but Hera in a flash left the summit of Olympus, went
across Pieria and lovely Emathia and passed over the snow-
covered hills of the Thracian horsemen, over the topmost
peaks, and she did not touch the ground with her feet. From
Athos she crossed the swelling sea and came to Lemnos and
the city of the godlike Thoas. There she found Sleep, the
brother of Death, took him by the hand, called him by name,
and said, "Sleep, lord over all gods and men, if ever you
heeded my words before, heed them now. Then I will feel
grateful to you all my days. Put to sleep the shining eyes
of Zeus beneath his brows, after I have first lain with him
in love. I will give you gifts, a lovely throne, indestruct-
ible forever, a golden throne. My son, Hephaestus of the
strong arms, will make it for you artfully, and will make a
footstool for your feet, on which you may put your shining
feet whenever you feast."

Then delightful Sleep replied, "Hera, honored goddess,
daughter of great Kronos, anyone of the immortal gods I
would easily put to sleep, even the stream of river Ocean,
who is the source for all, but I would not come too close to
Zeus, nor put him to sleep, unless he himself so ordered.

Once before your command put me to grief, on that day when
that high-hearted son of Zeus sailed from Ilium, having
sacked the city of the Trojans. Then I drifted gently upon
the mind of Zeus who wields the aegis and put it to sleep.
Your mind was devising evil, and you raised the blasts of
the troublesome winds over the sea, and you drove him to
well-situated Kos with the loss of all his friends. Zeus
awoke in a rage, and beat the gods in his house, seeking me
beyond all the rest and would have buried me out of sight
of the sky in the sea, had not Night, who tames both gods
and men, saved me. In my flight I came to her, and he
stopped his pursuit, though he was still angry, lest he do
deeds displeasing to swift Night. Now you ask me to bring
about yet another impossibility."

Then ox-eyed lady Hera replied, "Why do you ponder these
matters in your heart, O Sleep? Or do you believe that Zeus
of the wide brows will defend the Trojans with the same wrath
that he displayed in the case of Heracles? Come now, I will
give you one of the younger Graces to marry and be called
your wife." So she spoke, and Sleep was pleased, and said,
"Come now and swear to me by the unimpeachable Styx, with
one hand take the prospering earth, and with the other the
shining salt sea, so that all the other gods who are around
Kronos may be witnesses that you will give to me one of the
younger graces, Pasithea, whom I have desired all my days."

So he spoke, and the white-armed goddess Hera agreed.
She swore the oath he ordered, and named all the gods who
dwell under Tartarus, who are called the Titans. When she
had completed her oath the two left Lemnos and the city of
Imbros, clothed themselves in mist, and lightly followed
their path. They came to Ida which is rich in springs, the
mother of beasts, to Lektos, where they first left the sea
and crossed on the dry land, and the tops of the woods shook
beneath their feet. Then Sleep stopped before the eyes of
Zeus spied him, and he climbed to the top of a tall pine,
which then was the tallest on Ida, which broke through the
air to the aether. On this he sat, concealed by pine branches,

in the guise of a singing bird, which lives in the mountains and the gods call *chalchis*, but men *kymindis*.

But Hera quickly climbed to the peak of Gargaros on lofty Mt. Ida. Zeus the cloud-gatherer saw her, and when he saw her love so overwhelmed his wise heart, just like the time when they first joined in love and slept together with their parents none the wiser. He stood before her and called her by name, "Hera, for what reason do you come down here from Olympus? Your horses aren't here nor your chariot, in which you might come."

Then the lady Hera replied deceptively, "I am going to see the ends of the bountiful earth, and Ocean, the source of the gods, and mother Tethys; they brought me up well in their home and cared for me. I am off to see them and I will end their quarrel, for they have stayed apart from the couch and have done so for a long time now, for anger has fallen upon their hearts. The horses stand on the lower slopes of well-watered Ida, and they will carry me over the dry land and the water. But I have come down here from Olympus on your account, lest in some fashion you be angry with me later, if I went without a word to the house of deep-flowing Ocean."

Then Zeus the cloud-gatherer replied, "Hera, there will be a later time for you to pay a visit, but now let us lie together and turn to love making, for never yet has desire for goddess or woman so filled my heart inside me and over-whelmed it, not even when I loved the wife of Ixion, who bore Perithoos, a councilor equal to the gods, nor when I bedded Danaë, the lovely-ankled daughter of Akrisione, who bore Perseus, glorious among all men, nor when I fell in love with the daughter of far-renowned Phoenix, who bore Minos and godlike Rhadamanthys, nor when I loved Semele or Alkmene in Thebes; the latter bore me the strong-hearted Heracles, but Semele bore Dionysus, who gives pleasure to men; nor when I loved queenly Demeter of the lovely hair, nor when my choice was glorious Leto, nor even yourself. So now do I desire you and sweet passion has seized me."

Then the lady Hera replied deceptively, "Most dreadful
son of Kronos, what have you said? If you now long to sleep
together on the peaks of Ida, everything would be seen.
Then what would the situation be, if someone of the immortal
gods should spy us sleeping, and told the other gods about
it? I couldn't get out of bed and go back to your house;
it would be improper. But, if you are really set on this
course and it is your desire, there is our chamber, which
my son Hephaestus made for me, and hung tight-fitting doors
on the posts. Let us go there and lie down, since the couch
is your desire."

Then Zeus the cloud-gatherer replied, "Hera, don't fear
that god or man will see. I will gather such a golden cloud
about us that not even Helios could peer through it and see
us, though his light is the strongest for seeing through
things."

So he spoke, and the son of Kronos caught his wife into
his arms, and under them the divine earth gave birth to fresh
grass, and dewy clover and crocuses and hyacinth, thick and
rich, and these held them high off the ground. On this they
lay and they drew around them a lovely golden cloud and the
glistening dew dropped around them.

So the father slept peacefully on the peaks of Gargaros,
overwhelmed by sleep and love, holding his wife in his arms.
But sweet Sleep ran to the ships of the Achaeans with a message for him who encircles and shakes the earth [Poseidon].
To him he spoke winged words, "With all your heart now support the Danaans, Poseidon, and give them glory, if only for
a while, while Zeus still sleeps, since I have wrapped him
about in swift slumber, and Hera seduced him to sleep by her
side."

(*Iliad* XV. 4-141.)

But Zeus awoke on the peaks of Ida by the side of Hera
of the golden throne, and stood upright, saw the Trojans and
Achaeans, the former driven in flight, the Argives pursuing
them, and with the Argives the Lord Poseidon. He saw Hector

lying on the plain, and about him sat his companions. He
lay senseless, and breathed with difficulty, vomiting blood,
since not the weakest of the Achaeans had struck him. Seeing
him the father of gods and men had pity, and with a dreadful
scowl spoke to Hera, "Hopeless one, deviser of evil, your
treachery has driven glorious Hector from battle, Hera, and
frightened his people. I don't know whether you may enjoy
the first fruits of this troublesome mischief, or whether
I may flog you with the lash. Don't you remember when you
hung from on high, and to your feet I attached two anvils,
and around your limbs I threw a golden unbreakable chain;
you hung amid the air and sky. The gods throughout broad
Olympus were distraught, but could not set you free, though
they stood at your side. If I caught one of them, I would
seize him and throw him from the threshold until he came to
earth, powerless. But unceasing grief for godlike Heracles
did not leave my spirit. You persuaded the storm winds with
the aid of Boreas and with such help you drove him over the
barren sea, with evil purpose, and then you carried him away
to well-landed Kos, and I rescued him from there and brought
him once again to Argos the nurse of horses, though he had
endured much travail there. I will mention these things
again, in order that you may once and for all give up your
treachery, in order that you may learn whether or not there
is any profit in love-making and the couch, whether it is
profitable to make love apart from the gods and deceive me."

So he spoke, and the ox-eyed lady Hera trembled, and
she spoke to him with winged words, "Let earth know this
now and broad heaven above, and the downward flowing water
of Styx, which is the greatest and most fearful oath among
the blessed gods, and your blessed head and our marriage bed,
by which I could never swear in vain. It is not by my device that Poseidon the earth-shaker troubles the Trojans and
Hector, and helps the Achaeans, but rather his own heart
urges and pushes him to this. He saw the Achaeans worn down
beside their ships, and pitied them, but I would rather advise him that we follow the path on which you, O dark-clouded
one, lead us."

So she spoke, and the father of gods and men smiled,
and replied with winged words, "If ever you should sit with
the immortals thinking the same as I, then Poseidon, even
if he should wish otherwise, would turn his thought to follow your mind and my heart. If this is true and you speak
without deception, go now among the tribes of the gods and
summon Iris to come here, and Apollo, whose glory is the
bow, in order that she may go among the host of the bronze-
clad Achaeans and speak to Lord Poseidon, to leave the battle
and to go back to his home, and let Phoebus Apollo stir
Hector again to battle, and breathe strength into him once
again, and make him forget the pains which now wear out his
thoughts. Let him raise strengthless fear and turn back
the Achaeans, let them flee and fall back to the many-benched
ships of Peleus' son Achilles. He will raise up his comrade
Patroclus, whom shining Hector will kill with the spear
before Ilium, after he [Patroclus] has destroyed many other
lusty spearmen, among them my shining son Sarpedon. In wrath
for Patroclus' destruction shall Achilles the godlike slay
Hector, and from that time on I will continue their retreat
from the ships, a continual retreat, until the Achaeans take
sheer Ilium through the devices of Athena. I won't stop my
anger before this point, nor will I let any of the other immortals aid the Danaans, until the prayer of the son of
Peleus has been accomplished, as I agreed to first, and
nodded my head, on that day when the goddess Thetis clasped
my knees, begging me to honor Achilles, the sacker of cities."

So he spoke, nor did Hera the white-armed goddess disobey. She went back to lofty Olympus from the mountains of
Ida. Just as when the mind of a man flashes, a man who has
crossed much of the earth and thinks with a penetrating
heart, "if only I were here, or there," and plans many things,
so with eagerness did the lady Hera rapidly wing her way to
sheer Olympus; she entered the house of Zeus and found the
immortal gods assembled. They all saw her, rose, and saluted
her with their cups. She passed the rest, but took a cup
from fair-cheeked Themis, who had been the first to come

running, and spoke to her with winged words, "Hera, why have
you come; you look terrified; has the son of Kronos, your
husband, scared you?"

The white-armed goddess Hera then replied, "Don't
question me about these things, divine Themis. You yourself
know how stubborn and haughty is his nature. You now begin
the equal feast in the house of the gods; you with all the
immortals may hear this, what sort of evil actions Zeus tells
of. Nor do I think that all our hearts will be pleased,
neither mortals nor gods, even if now one feasts in pleasure."

So speaking Lady Hera sat down, and the gods in the
house of Zeus were troubled. Hera laughed with her lips,
but her forehead above her dark brows was not at peace. In
anger she spoke among them all, "Fools we were, who try to
oppose the plan of Zeus thoughtlessly. Even now we think
to stop him by word or force, going nearby; he sits apart
nor does he care for or regard us, but says that among the
immortals he is eminently the best in strength and power,
therefore it is necessary for each of you to accept whatever
evil he sends you. Already I believe sorrow has befallen
Ares, for his son has perished in battle, the dearest of
men, Askalaphos, whom mighty Ares called his son."

So she spoke, but Ares struck both thighs with the flats
of his hands, and spoke in sorrow, "Now you must not blame
me, you who dwell on Olympus, if I go among the ships of the
Achaeans and avenge my son's death, even if it is my fate
to lie in the blood and dust among the dead, struck by Zeus'
thunderbolt."

So he spoke, and ordered Fear and Rout to yoke his
horses, and he himself put on his shining armor. Then might
have taken place a still greater, more bitter quarrel between
Zeus and the gods, had not Athena in fear for the gods jumped
out to the forecourt, leaving the throne on which she was
sitting, and took the helmet from his head, the shield from
his shoulders, snatched the huge spear from his heavy hand
and placed it aside, and then with her words soothed mighty
Ares. "Madman, crazed in your wits, this is destruction.

You hear with your ears, but thought and discipline have
perished. Didn't you hear what the white-armed goddess
Hera said, who has just now returned to Olympus from Zeus?
Or would you rather return to Olympus, having accomplished
many woeful tasks, reluctantly and under compulsion? You
will create much sorrow for the rest of us. Soon Zeus will
leave the high-hearted Trojans and Achaeans, and create
havoc among us on Olympus, and will catch us in turn, the
guilty and the innocent. I bid you give up your anger for
your son, for already someone better in strength and hand
has fallen, or will fall, and it is a hard thing to rescue
all the seed and generation of men."

So speaking she set mighty Ares on his throne.

(*Iliad* XVI. 419-462, 665-683.)

When Sarpedon saw his unbelted companions slain by the
hands of Patroclus the son of Menoitios, he cried out and
scolded the godlike Lycians. "Shame, O Lycians! Where are
you fleeing? You are swift enough now! I will stand against
this man that I may learn who it is that is strong and has
done so much harm to the Trojans, for he has loosed the knees
of many good men."

So he spoke, and leaped to the ground from his chariot
with all his armor. Patroclus on the other side, when he
saw him, jumped from his chariot. Like two vultures, with
crooked claws and curved beaks, who fight on a high rock,
screaming loudly, so did these two rush upon each other
shouting loudly. When Zeus the son of crooked-counseling
Kronos saw them he pitied them and spoke to Hera his sister
and wife. "It grieves me that Destiny has doomed Sarpedon,
the dearest of men, to fall at the hands of Patroclus the
son of Menoitios. As I think on it my heart is divided -
whether I shall snatch him still alive from the tearful
battle and place him in the rich country of Lycia, or let
him fall at the hands of the son of Menoitios."

Then the ox-eyed queen Hera replied. "Most dread son
of Kronos, what word have you spoken? This man is a mortal,

long doomed to death; do you wish to free him from wretched
death? Let it be so, but not all the other gods will praise
you. I will tell you another thing, and you ponder it in
your heart. If you return Sarpedon to his home yet living,
think whether some other god might wish to send his own son
out of the fierce conflict. Many sons of gods are fighting
around the great city of Priam; among them you will stir up
great resentment. If he is dear to you, and your heart is
griefstricken, allow him to perish in the mighty conflict
at the hands of Patroclus, but when the soul and life have
left him, send Death and gentle Sleep to bear him away until
they come to the countryside of broad Lycia. There his
brothers and kinsmen will bury with a grave and marker.
This is the lot of mortals." So she spoke, and the father
of gods and men agreed. But he poured bloody rain over the
earth, to honor his son, whom Patroclus was about to slay
in deep-soiled Troy, far from his homeland. ...

   And then Zeus the cloud-gatherer spoke to Apollo. "Come
on now, dear Phoebus, go and take Sarpedon out of range of
the weapons; wash away the dark blood, carry him far away
and wash him in the streams of the river. Anoint him with
ambrosia and put ambrosial clothes around him and send him
along with two swift escorts, Sleep and Death, twin brothers,
who will lay him quickly in the rich land of broad Lycia,
and there his brothers and kinsmen will bury him with grave
and marker, for this is the fate of men."

   So he spoke, and Apollo did not disobey his father, but
went down along the mountains of Ida into the dreadful melee
of battle, and rescued shining Sarpedon from the weapons,
carried him far away, washed him in the streams of the river,
anointed him with ambrosia, dressed him in ambrosial clothing,
and sent him along with two swift escorts, Sleep and Death,
twin brothers, who carried him away and placed him in the
rich land of broad Lycia.

(*Iliad* XIX. 74-145; Agamemnon apologizes to Achilles.)

So Achilles spoke, but the well-greaved Achaeans rejoiced to hear how the great hearted son of Peleus put off
his wrath. Among them then spoke Agamemnon, the leader of
men. He spoke from his seat, and did not rise among them.
"My friends, heroic Danaans, servants of Ares, it is a fine
thing to hear a speaker, but it is not fitting to interrupt
him. It would be a hard thing even for one well-skilled!
In the loud murmur of men who could hear or speak? A speaker,
even a clear-voiced one, is stopped. I will address the son
of Peleus, but all the rest of you Argives pay heed, and
each of you consider my words. Very often the Achaeans have
spoken words against me and criticized me. But I am not to
blame, but Zeus, and Fate and the Fury who walks unseen.
In the assembly they cast fierce blindness around me, on
that day when I myself snatched Achilles' prize from him.
But what could I do? God brings everything to completion.
Blindness is the eldest daughter of Zeus, it is she who
blinds all men, she is destructive. She has delicate feet,
nor does she step on the earth, but she walks over the heads
of men and deceives them. She has fettered many others.
Once upon a time Zeus was blinded, though men say that he
is the best of gods and men. But Hera, a woman, deceived
him by her craftiness on that day when in well-crowned Thebe
Alkmene was about to bring forth the mighty Heracles. Zeus
in prayer spoke before all the gods. 'Hear me, all you gods
and goddesses, while I speak what the heart in my chest bids
me to say. Today Eileithyia, the goddess of woman's child-
pains, will reveal to the light a man who will lord it over
all the men dwelling about him, of the race coming from my
blood.'

"Then with treacherous purpose spoke the Lady Hera.
'You will be a liar, nor will you fulfill what you say. Come
now and swear a mighty oath, Olympian, that he will be the
lord over all the men who dwell around him, he who shall on
this day fall at the feet of a woman, and he shall lord it
over the offspring of your blood.' So she spoke, and Zeus

in no way recognized her treachery, but swore a great oath,
and thereby was greatly blinded. Hera then darted away
from the peak of Olympus, swiftly came to Achaean Argos;
there she knew was the mighty wife of Sthenelos, son of
Perseus. She was carrying a son, but it was only the seventh
month. But Hera led him to the light and made him born out
of time. But she stopped the birth of Alkmene, and held
back Eileithyia. Then she went to Zeus the son of Kronos
and reported, 'Father Zeus, Lord of the shining thunderbolt,
I place this message in your heart. A great man is born,
who will lord it over the Argives, Eurystheus, son of
Sthenelos, son of Perseus, from your own seed. It is not
unfitting that he should rule over the Argives.'

"So she spoke, and sharp sorrow struck deep into his
heart; he snatched the goddess Blindness by the shining
hair of her head in the depths of his wrath, and swore
another mighty oath, that never thereafter would Blindness
return again to Olympus and the stars of heaven, she who
blinds all. So speaking he hurled her from starry heaven,
whirling her in his hand. Soon she came to the works of
men. Always thereafter Zeus groaned about her, whenever he
saw his son doing the shameful tasks commanded by Eurystheus.
So too I, when great Hector of the glancing helmet was
destroying the Argives by the sterns of their ships, I was
not able to forget Blindness, by whom I was first deluded.
But since I was blinded, and Zeus snatched away my good
sense, I am willing to make it up and to give unmeasurable
rewards. Rise up to battle, and rouse the rest of your
people. But I am the one who will provide the gifts, as
many as godlike Odysseus promised yesterday in your tent.
If you are willing, remain, though you are eager for battle,
until my followers take the gifts from my ship, so that you
may know what suitable things I will give you."

(*Iliad* XX. 47-74.)

But when the Olympians joined in the company of men,
mighty Strife, the rouser of the people, burst forth, and
Athena cried out, standing at one moment beside the ditch
dug outside the wall, but at another by the resounding sea,
and let loose her mighty battle cry. On the other side Ares
bellowed, like to a dark hurricane, now giving sharp orders
to the Trojans along the top of the citadel, now running by
the Fair Hill along the banks of Simoeis.

As the blessed gods stirred on their followers, they
too came together, and among themselves raised a bitter
quarrel. On high the father of gods and men thundered
dreadfully; from deep below Poseidon shook the boundless
earth and the steep mountain cliffs. All the roots of Ida
with her abundant waters were shaken and her peaks, and the
city of the Trojans and the ships of the Achaeans. Aidoneus,
lord of the dead below, was frightened, and in his fear
jumped from his throne and shrieked, fearing that Poseidon
who encircles the land might open the earth above him and
open the houses of the dead, which were dank and frightening
both to gods and men - the gods themselves loathe them.
Such was the clamor that arose when the gods clashed in
strife. Against the Lord Poseidon stood Phoebus Apollo,
holding his winged arrows; against Enyalios the grey-eyed
goddess Athena; against Hera stood the lady of the golden
distaff, the loud-voiced huntress Artemis, the sister of
the far-shooter. Against Leto stood the strong helper,
Hermes; against Hephaestus stood the great, deep-eddying
river which the gods call Xanthos, but men Skamandros.

(*Iliad* XXII. 167-187, 207-224.)

Among the gods the first to speak was the father of
gods and men. "Alas, I see with my eyes a beloved man pursued around the walls; my heart mourns for Hector, who has
burned many thighs of oxen for me on the peaks of Ida on
many occasions, and at other times on the citadel of the
city. But now the godlike Achilles pursues him on swift feet

around the city of Priam. Come on now, you gods, take
thought and consider whether to rescue this man from death,
or to subdue him at the hands of Achilles son of Peleus,
though he is good."

Then the goddess bright-eyed Athena spoke, "O Father,
lord of the gleaming thunderbolt, dark clouded one, what
have you said! This is a mortal, long doomed by fate; do
you wish to preserve him from death, the bringer of woe?
Do so, but all the rest of the gods shall not approve."

Then Zeus the cloud-gatherer replied, "Take heart,
Thrice-born, my child. I am saying nothing with set purpose, and I wish to be gentle to you. Act now as your mind
urges, hold back no more."

So he spoke, and stirred on Athena who was already
eager. She went darting down the peaks of Olympus. ...

But when for the fourth time they came to the springs,
then the father raised his golden scales and in them placed
two portions of long-woeful death - one for Achilles, one
for Hector the tamer of horses. Taking it in the middle he
held it in balance; the fated day for Hector sank, and went
down towards death, and Phoebus Apollo left him. But the
bright-eyed goddess Athena came to the son of Peleus, stood
near and spoke winged words. "Beloved of Zeus, glorious
Achilles, now I think we two shall bring back great glory
to the ships of the Achaeans, after we have killed Hector,
though he is insatiable for battle. No longer does he have
the means to escape, even if the far-shooter Apollo should
suffer much, and roll in supplication before our father Zeus
of the aegis. You now stand here and catch your breath; I
will go to the man and persuade him to fight hand to hand."

B.   The Gods of Classical Greece

The Theogony *of Hesiod*

The epic poetry of Homer provides a powerful description
of Greece during the late Bronze Age. The poems, composed
probably between 800 and 700 B.C., do not represent a "pure"
Mycenaean tradition, however, but are rather a composite of
some four hundred years of historical development. Hesiod
presents a more systematic account of the generations of
gods and goddesses in his *Theogony*. His date is usually
given as a little later than Homer's, perhaps around 700
B.C., but he too seems to have included a great deal of
traditional material, some of it perhaps influenced by similar tales of the civilizations of the Sumerians and Akkadians
in Mesopotamia, the Hittites in Asia Minor, and the
Phoenicians in Palestine. See J.B. Pritchard, *Ancient Near
Eastern Texts* (Princeton, 1950), pp. 60-72, 120-126;
P. Walcot, *Hesiod and the Near East* (Cardiff, 1966);
F. Solmsen, *Hesiod and Aeschylus* (Ithaca, 1949), pp. 3-75.
Whatever their derivation, the genealogical relationships
of the gods as Hesiod defined them became a standard basis
of classical Greek myth.

(Hesiod, *Theogony*, 116-210, 453-506.)

First of all was born Chaos, and then wide-breasted

Gaia [Earth], to be the absolutely secure foundation of all

the immortals who hold the peaks of snowy Olympus; and then

divine Tartaros in the depths of the wide-pathed earth, and

Eros, who is the loveliest of the immortals and weakens the

strength of limbs, who overwhelms the mind in the breasts

of all the gods and men and their wise counsel. From Chaos

was born Erebos, the black one, and Night. From Night again

Aither and Day, when Night conceived them and bore them,

mingling in love with Erebos. But Gaia gave birth to one

equal to herself, strong Ouranos [Heaven], in order that he

might cover her completely and be an absolutely secure seat

for the blessed gods. Then she bore the high hills, wild

places beloved of the gods (of the nymphs, who dwell in the

woody mountain glens). And she produced the barren sea,

Pontos, foaming in his swell, but without sweet love. Then

she lay with Ouranos and produced deep-sounding Ocean, and

21

Kois, Krios, Hyperion, Iapetos, and Theia, Rheia, Themis
and Mnemosyne, and Phoebe with the golden crown and lovely
Tethys, and after them her youngest was Kronos of the crooked
counsels, the most dreadful of her children; he hated his
strong father. She also bore the Cyclopes, who have proud
hearts, Brontes and Steropes and Arges the stubborn-hearted
(who made the thunder and lightning, and gave them to Zeus).
They were like the gods in all other respects, but only one
eye was set in the middle of their foreheads. (Cyclopes was
their eponymous name, because of the one circular eye in
their foreheads.) Strength and power and skill were present
in their labors (they were raised as mortals with human
voice, though born of gods). Other children were born to
Gaia and Ouranos, three mighty and powerful sons, indescrib-
able, Kottos and Briareos and Gyes, insolent children. Each
of them had a hundred unapproachable arms springing from his
shoulders, and on the shoulders of each grew fifty heads,
hanging from their shoulders over their strong limbs. Stubborn and mighty was the strength of their huge forms. Of
all the children born to Gaia and Ouranos, they were the
most dreadful, and they hated their father from the beginning.

When anyone of them first began to come forth, Ouranos
would push him back into the womb of Gaia, and would not
allow them to come into the light, and Ouranos rejoiced in
his wicked work. But great Gaia groaned within, as she was
constrained, and devised a wicked, treacherous attack. She
quickly created the element of gray flint, and shaped from
it a great sickle, and explained it to her children. She
spoke in deep distress, vexed in her heart. "My children,
though also born of a sinful father, if you are willing to
obey me, we will punish your father for his cruel outrage.
For he was the first to devise wicked deeds." So she spoke,
and fear took them all, nor did anyone speak. Then crooked-
counseling Kronos took heart, and replied to his gracious
mother, "Mother, I promise to undertake this deed, since I
do not at all pay reverence to my shameless father. He was

the first to devise treacherous deeds." So he spoke, and
vast Gaia rejoiced greatly; she took him and secreted him
in ambush, placed in his hands the jagged sickle, and revealed to him all her treachery. Huge Ouranos came, bringing
Night; in his longing he stretched out all over Gaia and
spread himself out fully. Then Kronos from his ambush
seized him with his left hand and with his right hand he
held the enormous sickle with its jagged teeth, swung it and
sheared off the genitals of his father and cast them back-
wards to fall wherever they might. They did not leave his
hands without effect, but all the bloody drops were gathered
by Gaia and, when the seasons moved around she gave birth
to the Erinyes [Furies] and the mighty, tall Giants, gleaming
in their armor and holding long spears in their hands; and
the nymphs, the ones who are called the Nymphs of the Ash
Tree on the boundless earth. But the members themselves,
when he first cut them off with the flint, he threw from
the mainland into the surging sea. They were carried for a
long time by the sea, and a white foam spread from the immortal flesh and in it a maiden was born. She first came
near holy Cythera, and from there she came to sea-girt
Cyprus; she came forth a modest, lovely goddess, and beneath
her shapely feet the grass bloomed. The gods call her
Aphrodite and men do too because she was nurtured in the
foam;[1] they called her Cythereia because she went to Cythera,
and Cyprogeneia, because she came forth from billowing Cyprus,
and Philommedea, because she came from members [mēdea]. With
her were Eros and lovely Himeros [Desire] to be her followers,
when first she was born and entered the community of the gods.
This is the privilege she had from the beginning and this is
the role she plays among men and deathless gods - the whispers
of maidens, the smiles, the deceptions, sweet delight and
love and flattery.

Then in bitterness of reproach their father Ouranos gave
to the sons which he himself had borne the name of Titans
[Stretchers] for they stretched their powers outrageously
and accomplished a monstrous task, and they would be punished
for that deed afterwards. ...

When Rheia was subdued by Kronos, she bore glorious
children, Hestia and Demeter and Hera of the golden sandals
and Hades the mighty, who dwells beneath the earth and has
a pitiless heart; also [Poseidon] the earth shaker; and
Zeus who devises counsels, the father of gods and men, and
the broad earth was shaken by his thunder. These the mighty
Kronos swallowed down, as each one came forth from the womb
of its holy mother to her knees; Kronos thought that thus
no one of the proud children of Ouranos' line would ever
hold the position of king among the immortals. For he had
learned from Gaia and starry Ouranos that it had been ordained that although he was strong he would be beaten by
his son and through the plans of great Zeus. Therefore he
was not careless, but kept watch, waited for his children
and swallowed them. Insufferable woe consumed Rheia. But
when she was about to give birth to the father of gods and
men, Zeus, then she begged her own parents Gaia and starry
Ouranos, to devise with her some plan whereby she might
escape his notice when she gave birth, and the vengeance
both of his father and his children be on Kronos, the children whom mighty Kronos of the crooked counsel swallowed.
They listened with pleasure to their daughter and explained
to her all that destiny had decreed for King Kronos and for
his son powerful in spirit; they sent her to Lyktos in the
fertile land of Crete, when she was about to give birth to
the youngest of her children, great Zeus. Great Gaia took
him inside her in wide Crete to nurture and cherish. To that
place she came bearing him through the swift black night,
first to Lyktos. Taking him in her arms she laid him in the
cave of a cliff, beneath the depths of sacred Earth, in
Mount Aigaion, thickly covered with woods. Then carrying
a great stone wrapped in swaddling clothes she presented it
to her mighty lord, the son of Ouranos, the former king of
the gods. He took this stone in turn into his hands, and
stuffed it down into his stomach, the fool. For he did not
recognize that instead of the stone his son, invincible and
unshakable, had been left, who was destined by force and his
hands to defeat him and deprive him of his title, and then
lord it over the immortals.

When the strength and shining limbs of the Lord grew
powerful with the circling of the years, great Kronos, fooled
by the thoughtful suggestions of Gaia, vomited up his offspring, overwhelmed by the cleverness and strength of his
son. First he vomited up the stone, having swallowed it
most recently; this stone Zeus planted in the wide-wayed
earth, in holy Pytho, in the hollows beneath Mount Parnassos,
to be a portent and wonder thereafter for mortals.

He freed then the brothers of his father from their
grievous bonds, the sons of Ouranos, whom his father chained
in his witlessness, who remembered and were grateful for his
benevolence. They gave him the thunder and the lightning
which smokes and the flash, which to this point great Gaia
had hidden. Relying then on these he rules both men and
gods.

Zeus

The awesome Zeus of Homer, the king of gods and men
whose very nod could shake Olympus, was depicted by Hesiod
in equally awesome terms, as the victor in a physical
struggle over the earlier generation of gods. In the fifth
century the nature of this greatest of gods was the subject
of meditation and speculation, as shown in the following
passages. Aeschylus in his hymn to Zeus in the *Agamemnon*
recalls the Hesiodic account in celebrating the intellectual
understanding of life's mysteries which comes from Zeus. On
the other hand, in *Prometheus Bound* Aeschylus (assuming he
was indeed the author) emphasizes the immaturity of a Zeus
who relies on physical force to subdue his enemies in the
older generation of Titans; cf. F. Solmsen, *Hesiod and
Aeschylus* (Ithaca, 1949), pp. 124-177; H. Lloyd-Jones, *The
Justice of Zeus* (Berkeley, 1971), esp. pp. 79-103. In the
460's a great temple of Zeus was built at the panhellenic
shrine of Olympia, and later in the fifth century it was
equipped with a new and imposing statue of Zeus by Pheidias,
the foremost sculptor of Greece, who had just completed the
great statue of Athena in the Parthenon at Athens. The
descriptions of the statue in Strabo and Pausanias indicate
its influence, which at least to these writers of the Roman
period was as much religious as artistic. Finally, a very
different view of Zeus is introduced by the fourth-century
Cretan *Hymn of the Kouretes*, in which Zeus is addressed as
the "greatest Kouros [Boy]," reborn as an eternal youth; this
recalls Hesiod's account of Zeus's infancy in Crete, and seems
to reflect a native, non-Greek fertility cult in which a
vegetation god was annually reborn and to which the name of
Zeus was later attached. See J. Harrison, *Themis* (Cambridge,

1912), pp. 1-74; M.P. Nilsson, *Minoan-Mycenaean Religion* (Lund, 1927), pp. 475-483; W.K.C. Guthrie, *The Greeks and Their Gods* (Boston, 1950), pp. 42-51; R.F. Willetts, *Cretan Cults and Festivals* (New York, 1962), pp. 199-220.

(Aeschylus, *Agamemnon*, 160-182.)

Chorus: Zeus, whoever he is, if this name pleases him when he is invoked, by this name I address him. I have reflected carefully on all things, but I am unable to compare him to anyone save Zeus, if it is necessary to cast truly this vain burden from my mind.

Not even he who before was great [Ouranos], swelling in strength, sufficient in every battle, shall be mentioned as ever having existed. But he who was born afterwards [Kronos] is gone, for he met his victor in three falls. But the man who eagerly celebrates Zeus as victor will hit understanding four-square.

It was Zeus who put me on the road to understanding, who provided the law that understanding comes through suffering. In sleep, pain flows into one's heart, a pain that brings remembrance. And discretion comes, even to those who are unwilling. There is, it seems, a grace that comes from the gods enthroned on the dread helmsman's bench, a constraining grace.

(Aeschylus, *Prometheus Bound*, 160-168, 188-193, 199-205, 528-535.)

Chorus: Who of the gods is so hard-hearted that this gives him pleasure? Who will not feel sympathy with your troubles - except, of course, Zeus. He always puts on in his wrath an inflexible mind and brings to ruin the race of Ouranos; he will not stop until either his heart has its fill, or someone with cunning hand takes from him that rule which is hard to capture. ...

Prometheus: I know that he is harsh, that he keeps what is just by his own side, Zeus does. Nevertheless, his mood will soften one day, when there is alleviation of this pain. He will soften his hard anger and will come eagerly to a pact of

friendship with me, equally eager. ... At first, when the
daimones began their quarrel and strife rose up among them,
one faction wanted to expel Kronos from his throne, in order
(I suppose) that Zeus might reign; but others were eager for
the opposite, in order that Zeus might never rule over the
gods. On this side I tried to give the best advice, but did
not succeed in persuading the Titans, the children of Ouranos
and Earth. Scorning my wily tricks, they supposed in their
notions about their strength that they would win the mastery
with no effort at all. My mother - not Themis alone but
also Gaia, one person with many names - foretold to me how
the future would come out, how those who prevailed would
have to gain the power not by might or strength, but by
craftiness. I explained all this, but they regarded the
whole thing as worth not even a glance. So it seemed to me
that in the circumstances the best at the moment was to take
my mother and willingly take my stand by Zeus, equally willing. And thanks to my plans the deep, dark recess of Tartaros
contains Kronos the ancient-born, attended by his allies.
Even though helped in this way on my initiative, the monarch
of the gods has repaid me with these toilsome punishments.
This affliction is engrained in monarchy, to put no trust
in friends. ...
Chorus: May he who governs all things, Zeus, never put his
power in opposition to my intent. May I never fail to celebrate the gods with sacred feasts, with cattle slaughtered
beside the quenchless flow of Father Ocean. May I never
utter a sinful word. May this rather remain in my mind,
and never melt away.

(Pausanias, *Description of Greece* V. 11.1, an account of
Pheidias' statue of Zeus at Olympia.)

The god is seated on a throne; he is made of gold and
ivory. There is a crown on his head like twigs of olive.
In his right hand he holds a Nike of ivory and gold; she has
a ribbon and wreath on her head. In the god's left hand is
a staff blossoming with all kinds of precious metals. The

bird sitting on the sceptre is an eagle. The sandals of
the god are made of gold and his cloak is made of the same
material. On the cloak are carved animals and the blossoms
of lilies.

(Strabo, *Geography* VIII. 353-354.)

It remains for me to speak about the Olympia and the
transfer of everything into the hands of the Eleans. The
temple is in Pisatis, less than 300 stades from Elis. In
front is situated a grove of wild olives, in which is the
stadium. Past the temple flows the Alphaeus, flowing from
Arcadia to the Triphylian sea between the west and the
south. From the beginning the temple was famed because of
the oracle of Olympian Zeus, and when it failed the reputation of the temple remained no less, and in fact increased,
to the extent that we know it, because of the festival
assembly and the Olympic games. A crown was the prize of
victory, and the games were recognized as sacred and superior
to all others. The temple was made lovely by the number of
the votive offerings, which were offered from all parts of
Greece. Among them was the beaten-gold statue of Zeus,
offered by Cypselus, the tyrant of Corinth. The greatest
of them was the statue of Zeus which Pheidias the son of
Charmides the Athenian made of ivory. It was of such a
size that, although the temple was very large, the artist
seems to have missed the symmetry. For he made Zeus seated,
but nearly touching the roof with his head, so that he
created the impression that if Zeus rose up and stood straight
he would take off the roof of the temple. Some have recorded the measurements of the statue, and Callimachus has
set them forth in iambic poetry. Panainos the painter, a
nephew and collaborator of Pheidias, aided him a great deal
in decorating the statue with colors, and particularly in
reference to its clothing. Many wonderful paintings can be
seen around the temple, and they are his work. Concerning
Pheidias they recall that when Panainos asked him after what
model he would make the statue of Zeus, he replied that he

would model it according to the likeness described by Homer
in these words, "So he spoke, and the son of Kronos nodded
his dark brows, and the ambrosial locks flowed from the
immortal head of the lord, and he shook great Olympus."[2]
This description seems excellent, both for other reasons
and because of the brows, for the poet compels the intellect
to create a mighty person and great power worthy of Zeus.

(*IC* III. 2.2, the *Hymn of the Kouretes*; a fragmentary
inscription from Palaikastro, Crete, dating about 300 B.C.,
though its content is probably older.)

Hail, Greatest Kouros, Kronian one, receive my greeting,
thou Almighty of Radiance; thou art come, leading thy
daimones; do thou come for the year to Dikte, and rejoice
in this hymn, which we pluck on the strings, blending with
the flutes, and which we sing, standing about thy well-
fenced altar.

Hail, Greatest Kouros, Kronian one, receive my greeting,
thou Almighty of Radiance; thou art come, leading thy
daimones; do thou come for the year to Dikte, and rejoice
in this hymn; for there [the Kouretes] took thee, the immortal child, from Rhea on their shields, and circling with
their feet hid thee away.

[Hail, Greatest Kouros, etc. ... of the] beautiful Dawn.

Hail, Greatest Kouros, Kronian one, receive my greeting,
thou Almighty of Radiance; thou art come, leading thy
daimones; do thou come for the year to Dikte, and rejoice
in this hymn; the Seasons grew teeming year by year, and
Justice took hold of man, and Peace the lover of prosperity
took charge of all living things.

Hail, Greatest Kouros, Kronian one, receive my greeting,
thou Almighty of Radiance; thou art come, leading thy
daimones; do thou come for the year to Dikte, and rejoice
in this hymn; [do thou leap into the cattle] herds, and leap
into the fleece-bearing [flocks, and into the supplies] of
grain leap, and also into the fruit-[bearing households.]

Hail, Greatest Kouros, Kronian one, receive my greeting,
thou Almighty of Radiance; thou art come, leading thy
daimones; do thou come for the year to Dikte, and rejoice
in this hymn; do thou leap also into our cities, leap also
into the sea-faring ships, leap also into the y[oung ci]ti-
zens, leap also into Themis the fa[mous.]

Hail, Greatest Kouros, Kronian one, receive my greeting,
thou Almighty of Radiance; thou art come, leading thy
daimones; do thou come for the year to Dikte, and rejoice
in this hymn.

C. Criticism of the Traditional Theology

The Pre-Socratics

The stories of Homer and the epic poets, the cosmology of Hesiod did not satisfy all Greeks. In Ionia Thales, Anaximander and Anaximenes examined material phenomena and attempted to describe the world in completely rational terms. This strain of thought was soon challenged by the Pythagorean and Eleatic schools of thought, which were located in Italy. The Ionians had begun with dissatisfaction about the old explanations; the Italian schools were motivated by religious concerns, though it may be argued that their end results were no less materialistic than the Ionians'. Further readings on the first scientific thinkers of Greece may be found in G.S. Kirk and J.E. Raven, *The Presocratic Philosophers* (Cambridge, 1957); E.A. Havelock, *The Liberal Temper in Greek Politics* (London, 1957) and *A Preface to Plato* (Cambridge, Mass., 1963); W.K.C. Guthrie, *A History of Greek Philosophy*, vol. I and II (Cambridge, 1962 and 1965).

(Xenophanes of Colophon, 6th century B.C.; fragments published in H. Diels and W. Kranz, *Die Fragmente der Vorsokratiker*, Berlin, 1934.)

(11)   Homer and Hesiod have attributed to the gods all things that are shameful and a reproach: thievery, adultery, and deception of each other.

(12)   They have spoken as much as possible concerning the wicked deeds of the gods: stealing, committing adultery, deceiving each other.

(14)   Mortals believe that the gods were created, and have their own clothing, voice and body.

(23)   There is one god, greatest among gods and men, like to men neither in body nor in soul.

(24)   He sees as a whole, he knows wholly, and hears wholly.

(25)   But without toil he sets all into motion, by the thought in his mind.

(26)   Always he remains in the same place, not moving at all, nor is it appropriate to change his position from one place to another.

(34) In respect to the truth no man has there been or will
be who knows about the gods and the things which I mention.
Even if a man happened to speak the truth, nevertheless he
doesn't know it. Seeming is created over everything.

(Heraclitus of Ephesus, 6th century B.C.; fragments in
Diels-Kranz.)

(5) They purify themselves of blood by blood; they are
crazy, as if one having stepped into mud were to wash with
mud. Such a man would be thought mad, if someone noticed
him doing such a thing. Furthermore they pray to these
statues as if one were to have a conversation with houses,
nor do they recognize in the case of gods or heroes what
sort of beings they really are.
(15) If they were not processing for Dionysus and singing
the hymn to the private parts they would be acting most
disgracefully; but Hades and Dionysus, for whom they are
inspired and celebrate the Lenaean rites, are the same being.
(119) Character is a *daimon* for man.

(Anaxagoras of Clazomenae, c. 500-c. 428 B.C., in Simplicius,
Commentary on Aristotle's *Physics*, 164, 24; frag. 12 in
Diels-Kranz.)

     Other things contain a part of everything, but mind is
infinite and self-ruling and is mixed with nothing, but is
alone by itself. If it were not by itself, but were mixed
with something else, it would share in all things if it were
mixed with anything. In everything there is a portion of
everything, as we have said before. The things mixed in
would hinder it, so that it could hold sway over nothing in
the same way as it does being alone by itself. It is the
finest of all things and the purest, and has complete knowledge of all things, and is most powerful. All things which
have a soul, both greater and lesser, are all ruled by mind.
Mind ruled over the revolution of the universe, so that
everything would revolve at the beginning. It began to ro-
tate in a small area, then over a greater one, and will ro-
tate over a still wider area. The things mixed together,

and things separated off and divided, these are all known
by mind. Whatever would be, and whatever existed then but
does no longer, whatever exists and will exist, all of these
mind arranged, and this revolution, in which now the stars,
sun, moon, the air and the aither that are cut off, this was
arranged by mind. This revolution caused the separation.
The dense is separated from the rare, the hot from the cold,
the dry from the wet. There are many portions of many things,
nothing is absolutely distinguished or separated, the one
from the other, except mind. Mind is all alike, both greater
and less. Nothing else is like it, but each thing is and
was most clearly that which it most contained.

The Sophists

As the Greeks began the fifth century they were faced
with a great challenge in foreign affairs - the Persian
invasion, first of Ionia, then of Greece. Greek victories
at Marathon in the first campaign (490 B.C.), at Salamis
and Plataea in the second (480-479 B.C.) not only repelled
the invaders but forged in the Greeks a sense of national
consciousness. This consciousness was not, however, expressed in political unification, but rather in the creation
of two great alliance systems, the Spartan and the Athenian,
whose quarrels were to dominate the last sixty years of the
fifth century and severely cripple the city-state. Against
this background of power politics took place some of the
finest creations of the human intellect, notably in Athens.
One has only to think of Aeschylus, Sophocles, Euripides,
Aristophanes; of Thucydides, Herodotus, and Xenophon; of
Socrates and Plato; of the Parthenon and Erechtheum to
appreciate the Greek contribution to western civilization.
It was a restless time, and it is not surprising that one
manifestation of this restlessness should appear in new
educational theories, which challenged old beliefs, but did
not often offer new beliefs to replace the old. If man truly
was the measure of all things, as Protagoras contended, the
fifth century shows man in both his most creative and most
destructive aspects. For reading about these new educators,
the Sophists, see W.K.C. Guthrie, A History of Greek Philosophy, vol. III, pt. 1 (Cambridge, 1968); E.R. Dodds, The
Greeks and the Irrational (Berkeley, 1951), pp. 179-195;
W. Jaeger, Paideia, vol. I (Oxford, 1939), pp. 283-329.

(Protagoras of Abdera, c. 485-c. 415 B.C., in Sextus
Empiricus, *Pyrrhonism* I. 216; frag. A14 in Diels-Kranz.)

Protagoras also wants man to be the measure of all
things, of existing things, that they exist, of non-existent
things, that they do not exist; by "measure" he means the
criterion, and by "things" the object, so that he is saying
that man is the criterion of all things, of things that are
that they are, of things that are not that they are not.
For this reason he puts forward only what appears to each
individual, and so he introduces relativity. Wherefore he
seems to have some knowledge in common with the Pythagoreans,
but he differs from them, and we will present the differences
when we have accurately analyzed his views.

(Protagoras, in Diogenes Laertius, *Lives of the Philosophers*
IX. 51-52; frags. A1 and B4 in Diels-Kranz.)

Protagoras used to say that the soul was nothing without the senses (Plato also speaks thus in the *Theatetus*) and
that everything is true. Elsewhere he begins "Concerning
the gods I can not say that they exist - by human reasoning.
Many things impede knowledge, the absurdity of the question
and the short span of human life." For this introduction
he was expelled by the Athenians; they burned his books in
the marketplace after a herald's inquiry had been made of
all who had them.

The Tragedians

The speculations and questionings of the philosophers
and sophists found reflection in the works of several of the
writers of tragedy in the late fifth century. A fragment
of the *Sisyphus* of Critias sets the rationalistic tone,
and this is picked up in the selections from Euripides'
Trojan Women. In the *Hippolytus*, Euripides portrays the
behavior of Aphrodite toward Artemis' favorite, Hippolytus,
as petty, while emphasizing the irresistibility of the erotic
impulse represented by Aphrodite; and in the *Ion*, Apollo's
temple attendant at Delphi questions the moral propriety of
Apollo's actions, as portrayed in the myth.

(Critias, *Sisyphus*, in Sextus Empiricus, *Adv. Math.* IX.
403-404; frag. 1 in A. Nauck, *Tragicorum Graecorum Fragmenta*.
Leipzig, 1889, pp. 771-772; frag. B25 in Diels-Kranz.)

There was a time when the life of men was rude and
bestial and subject to force, when there was no reward for
the good, and there was no punishment for the bad. Then,
it seems to me, men made laws as punishers, and justice became a tyrant, to hold wanton violence in subjection. If
anyone committed an offense, he was punished. Consequently,
the laws prevented them from doing violent deeds out in the
open, but in secret they did commit them. So then, I believe, some smart and clever man invented the gods for
mortals, so that they might serve as a terror to the bad,
whenever they do or say or think anything wrong. Next The
Divine was introduced, to be a *daimon* blooming with boundless
life, perceptively hearing, seeing, thinking and noticing
all things, assuming a divine nature, one who will hear
everything said among mortals, and will be able to see
everything that is done. Even if you devise some evil thing
in silence, you will not evade the gods' attention, for it
is their attribute to be mindful.

Then he introduced a most palatable teaching, and with
words like these he used a deceitful tale to obscure the
truth: in order to make the most striking impression on
men, he said that the gods dwell right here, and he derived
the fears that beset men (as well as the blessings which aid
them in their wretched life) from the heavens, where he saw
the lightning flashes, the terrible claps of thunder, the
star-filled radiance of the sky - the beautiful tapestry of
Chronos [Time], the skilled craftsman. Thence shines the
red-hot gleam of the stars, and thence proceeds to earth the
dampening rain. With such terrible fears he surrounded men;
with his fancy tale he gave the *daimon* a home in a conspicuous place, and stifled lawlessness with fears.

In this way, then, I think that someone first persuaded
men to believe that the race of *daimones* exists.

(Euripides, *Trojan Women*, 969-990.)

Hecuba: First I shall stand as an ally to the goddesses
and I will show that this woman [Helen] does not speak
justly. I don't believe that Hera and the virgin Athena
could come to such a depth of folly that the former would
peddle Argos to barbarians or Pallas permit Athens to be
the slave of Phrygians. They came to Ida for fun and a
beauty contest. Why should Hera be so concerned with the
prize for beauty? To take a husband mightier than Zeus?
Or has Athena sought some god for her husband, she who requested the gift of virginity from her father and flees the
wedding couch? Do not make the gods appear stupid in covering over your own sin, for you will not persuade wise people.
You said that Cypris [Aphrodite] - these comments make me
laugh a lot - came with my son to the house of Menelaus.
Could she not have remained quietly in heaven and caught
up you and Amyclae and brought you to Ilium?

My son was outstanding in his handsomeness, and you
at the first sight of him went Cyprian. All lust is Aphrodite
for mortals, since the name of the goddess rightly begins
with the name of folly.[3]... I am just making an argument -
you gave account to men for your lawless beddings, you and
Poseidon and Zeus who rules heaven, by paying the penalty
for your ways you would empty your temples. You do wrong
in pursuing pleasures before you take thought. No longer
is it just to reproach men, if we imitate the deeds that
seem acceptable to the gods, but rather those who teach this
kind of behavior.

(Euripides, *Hippolytus*, 1-8, 1325-1341, 1416-1438.)

Aphrodite: I am powerful among men and not without fame, I
am called the goddess Cypris, and I am mighty in heaven.
All who dwell within the boundaries of Atlas and Ocean and
see the light of the sun, of these the ones who revere my
name I favor, but I bring down those who are proud against
me. For this is the custom even among the gods, that they
rejoice when honored by men. ...

Artemis [*to Theseus, Hippolytus' father, as Hippolytus lies dying*]: You have done sinful deeds, but it is still possible even for you to win pardon. Cypris wanted the matter to turn out in this way and satisfied her anger. This is the custom of the gods, that no one is willing to counter the desire of another; we always stand aloof. Know this well that, if I didn't fear Zeus, I would never have come to this depth of embarrassment, to allow the man dearest to me among mortals to perish. As regards your sin, first ignorance excuses you, secondly your wife by her death destroyed the possibility of testing her words, and so you were persuaded. These evils have shattered you most of all, Theseus, but they are grief to me. For the gods do not rejoice when pious people perish, but we destroy the wicked, their children and their house. ...

Artemis [*to the dying Hippolytus*]: Let it be. You will not be without honor in the gloom below the earth because of the zeal of the goddess Cypris. This wrath against your body because of your piety and good heart shall cost her. With my own hand I will take vengeance upon someone of hers, who is especially dear to her, with these unerring arrows. To you, O wretched Hippolytus, in recompense for these evils I will give the greatest honors in Troezene. Unwedded maidens before their marriage will cut off their hair in memory of you; through the long ages you will reap a plentiful mourning of tears. Always will the songs of the maidens remember you, you will not fall without name, nor will the love of Phaedra for you be forgotten in silence. [*to Theseus*] You, son of old Aegeus, take your son in your arms and draw him close to you. Unwillingly you destroyed him. It is natural for men to err when the gods so decree it. I beg you, Hippolytus, do not hate your father; it was your fate to die thus.

And now, farewell; it is not proper for me to look upon the dead nor my eye to be defiled by dying gasps. I see that you are already at this point.

(Euripides, *Ion*, 433-451.)

What concern is the daughter of Erechtheus to me?
None at all. I will go and pour the holy water from golden
pitchers into the stoups. Yet Phoebus must be brought to
account for what she suffers.[4] Imagine bedding maidens by
force and then betraying them! To leave children born in
secret to die, without caring! Don't do it. Rather, since
you are powerful, pursue virtue. Whoever among mortals is
born evil, the gods punish. How then is it just for you,
who have decreed the laws for men, yourselves to incur a
reputation as a breaker of the laws? But - it would be
impossible, but I will say it for the sake of argument - if
you had to pay the penalty in human terms for forcible se-
duction, you [Apollo] and Poseidon and Zeus who rules over
heaven, you would have to empty out your temples to pay the
fines. When you chase after pleasure and get ahead of
responsible consideration, you are acting unjustly; now,
if we are imitating the fine deeds of the gods, it is no
longer just to reproach us men, but rather those who taught
us to act this way.

D. The Orphic Cosmogony

Orphism was a religious movement among the Greeks dating well back into the archaic period. It differed from most other Greek religious expression in that it was a revealed religion, with a founder (the poet Orpheus) and a body of doctrine expressed in verse. Unfortunately these verses are lost, and much of our knowledge depends upon later sources. Thus Apollonius, a writer of the third century B.C., summarized the Orphic cosmogony as it was known to him. Earlier sources give other details - Plato's summary in the fourth century helps us understand some of the learned commentary on an Orphic text which is preserved on a papyrus of the late fourth century, and it also suggests that the choral passage quoted from Aristophanes' *Birds* is at least partly inspired by some Orphic texts. The sources indicate that early Orphism owed some debt to Hesiod, but apparently the Orphics applied speculation and analysis in an attempt to improve the traditional account. For example, on the basis of the final selection, from Plato's *Laws*, it is usually argued that the Orphic cosmogony includes an account of the genesis of man from the ashes of the Titans who had eaten the flesh of Dionysus, which would imply that man partakes of a dual nature, sinful and divine. Other sources, such as Pindar (cf. p. 000 below), indicate that the Orphics believed in metempsychosis and had a highly developed view of the afterlife. Euripides and Aristophanes (cf. p. 000 below) emphasized that the Orphics refused to kill animals or eat meat, and that they participated in some sort of initiation rites. For general accounts of Orphism, see M.P. Nilsson, "Early Orphism and kindred religious movements," *Harvard Theological Review* 28 (1935) 181-230; W.K.C. Guthrie, *Orpheus and Greek Religion* (London, 1935) and *The Greeks and their Gods* (Boston, 1950), pp. 307-332; I. Linforth, *The Arts of Orpheus* (Berkeley, 1941). On the newly discovered (and only partially published) papyrus from Derveni, see S.G. Kapsomenos in the *Bulletin of the American Society of Papyrologists* 2 (1964-65) 3-14; W. Burkert in *Antike und Abendland* 14 (1968) 93-114; E. Turner, *Greek Manuscripts of the Ancient World* (Princeton, 1971), #51, pp. 92-93. On the passage from Aristophanes, see J.R.T. Pollard, "The 'Birds' of Aristophanes: v. The Wind Egg," *American Journal of Philology* 69 (1948) 373-376.

(Apollonius Rhodius, *Argonautica* I. 494-511.)

And Orpheus in his left hand lifted up his lyre and made trial of his song. He sang how the earth, heaven and sea, which were formerly joined together in one form, were separated from each other after deadly strife. He sang of

how stars and the moon and the paths of the sun always hold
a fixed place in the sky; how the mountains rose, how the
resounding rivers with their nymphs were created, and all
things that crawl. Then he sang how Ophion and Eurynome,
the daughter of Ocean, first ruled the peak of snowy Olympus,
how through physical force he yielded his power to Kronos,
and she to Rhea, and how they then fell into the waves of
Ocean; in the meantime Kronos and Rhea ruled over the blessed
Titan gods, while Zeus still a child, still thinking the
thoughts of a child, lived in the Diktaion cave. The earth-
born Cyclops had not yet outfitted him with the bolt, the
thunder and lightning. These things gave Zeus his fame.

(Plato, *Timaeus*, 40 d.)

Concerning the other *daimones* it is beyond our power
to know or describe their origin, but it is necessary for
us to accept the accounts of those ancients who claimed to
be the children of the gods, as they say, and surely they
must have known who there own ancestors were. It is impossible to distrust the children of the gods, although they
give their account without probable or necessary demonstra-
tions, still, since they say that they are relating family
accounts, we must follow custom and believe them. So,
according to them, the generation of the gods is to be accepted and proclaimed in the following fashion. Ocean and
Tethys were the children of Ge [Earth] and Ouranos [Sky];
from them came Phorkys and Kronos and Rhea, and all that
generation; from Kronos and Rhea came Zeus and Hera and all
that we know are called their brothers, and others who were
children of these.

(*Commentary* on a cosmogonic poem, the "Derveni Papyrus."
The phrases in quotation marks are parts of the poem, the
rest is the work of the fourth-century editor.)

--"Nor does the cold rush upon the cold." By saying
"rush" he shows that in the air small particles were moving
and rushing about. And as they were rushing they were con-
densed toward each other.

--"Until this point they were rushing," i.e., until each (particle) went to its usual place.

--"Heavenly Aphrodite and Zeus" and "to aphroditize and rush" and "Peitho [Persuasion] and Harmonia." The nomenclature applies to the same god. When a man mingles with a woman he is said to "aphroditize" according to the saying, as for example "When the things which now exist have mingled with each other." Aphrodite is called Persuasion because she has yielded the things which exist to each other; "to yield" and "to persuade" is the same thing. She is called "Harmony" because she has brought into harmony many of the things which exist.

(Aristophanes, *Birds*, 688-702.)

Pay heed now to us, the immortals, always existing, heavenly, unaging, thinking eternal thoughts, that you may hear accurately from us about the heavenly bodies, the origin of birds, the birth of gods, rivers, Erebos and Chaos. ... There was Chaos first, and Night, dark Erebos and wide Tartaros; there was no earth, nor air, nor sky, but Night, she of the dark wings, bore first of all a wind-egg,[5] nesting in the limitless bosom of Erebos, and in the fullness of time there hatched from it, swift as the whirl-wind, Eros, he who inspires passion, on whose back glisten golden wings. He mated with winged, dark Chaos in wide Tartaros, and he hatched our race [the birds] and brought us first into the light. The race of the immortals did not exist before Eros commingled all things. But when different things had commingled with others, the sky came into being, and earth, and the immortal race of the blessed gods.

(Plato, *Laws* III. 701b-c.)

...The last stage of all is not to have any concern for oaths, pledges, or any of the gods, and to display and imitate what is called the ancient Titanic nature; they constantly revert to the same condition again, and lead a difficult life without any relief from troubles.

E. The Search for a Rational Theology:
Plato and Aristotle

The Peloponnesian War (431-404 B.C.) brought into
active conflict the two major alliance systems of Greece -
the Spartan Alliance and the Athenian Empire. The course
of that war as described by Thucydides and Xenophon is a
powerful lesson in the effects of total prolonged war upon
society. By the end of the war the Greek cities were bank-
rupt and exhausted and, while Sparta emerged the victor,
the first three decades of the fourth century are marked by
continual challenges to her position as *hegemon* or leader
of the Greeks. Sparta won the war with Persian aid, and
Persia was not loathe to use her financial resources to try
to play the Greeks off against one another during the next
century. The spirit of national confidence won at Marathon
and Salamis was lost forever, and the political history of
Greece in the fourth century is a dreary tale of bickering
and squabbles, until Philip of Macedonia and his son
Alexander the Great put an end to this strife, and in the
process completed the destruction of Greek political freedom. In the intellectual realm the great creation of fifth
century tragedy and comedy did not see successors in the
fourth century. Comedy in particular became comedy of
manners, with none of the political invective characteristic
of Aristophanic comedy. The law courts predominated in
Athenian life, so the art of rhetoric became a dominant
feature of the education of young Athenians. Experiments
in new forms of political organization were made, but proved
in almost every case to be short-lived. As Greeks found less
and less stimulation in daily political adventure in their
city states, they turned to literature - letters, speeches,
memoir, biography and autobiography, history as means of
self expression. The pupils of Socrates also sought to
memorialize their master's efforts. First Plato, then
Aristotle, to mention only the most familiar figures, sought
to examine in some methodologically consistent fashion the
universal questions asked by humanity. In particular they
sought some understanding of the role of the gods or god in
the universe - the search for a rational theology to supple-
ment or replace the old myths and rituals. The following
selections are meant only as a sample of the range of their
thought; see also the selections from Plato on mystic contemplation, p. 000 below and on the afterlife, p. 000 below.
For further reading see W.K.C. Guthrie, *A History of Greek
Philosophy* IV and V (Cambridge, 1975, 1978) and *The Greeks
and their Gods* (Boston, 1950); H.J. Rose, *Religion in Greece
and Rome* (New York, 1959).

(Plato, *Laws* IV. 716c.)

Athenian Stranger: Therefore what sort of action is dear
to and in conformity with God? One kind of action, which
is expressed in one ancient saying, that "like is dear to
like in moderation," but immoderate things are not of value
either to each other or to moderate things. God then will
be in our judgment the measure of all things in the very
highest degree, and much more so than any human being, as
they say. That man therefore who wishes to become dear to
such a god as that must become as like to that being as is
possible. According to this argument the temperate man among
us is dear to God, for he is like Him, and he that is in-
temperate is unlike Him and an enemy and unjust. So too
with everything else by the same argument.

(Plato, *Laws* V. 729C.)

...If a man honors and respects his family and all who
join in the worship of the family gods and all who share
the same blood, that man would secure the gods of birth to
bless his creation of children.

(Plato, *Laws* V. 738b-d.)

...Concerning gods and temples, which temples it is
necessary to set up in the state for each and to what gods
or *daimones* they are to be dedicated, no man with sense will
try to alter what has been proclaimed by Delphi or Dodona
or Ammon or some old traditions which are persuasive where
they are persuasive - stories of divine appearances or so-
called divine revelation - and have led to the establishment
of sacrifices and rituals, whether these are indigenous or
brought from Etruria or Cyprus or from some other place, and
by these sayings they consecrated oracles and statues and
altars and temples, and for each of them they allotted sacred
precincts. None of these provisions should be altered in the
slightest degree by the lawgiver; to each district he must
allot a god or a spirit or some hero; in the assignment of

the land to them first he must assign precincts and whatever
goes with them, so that when assemblies of each district
take place at appropriate times they may provide a sufficient
number of what is necessary and appropriate and the people
may mingle with each other at the sacrifices and become
familiar and intimate with each other. There is nothing more
beneficial to the state than this mutual acquaintenance. ...

(Plato, *Laws* IX. 854b-c.)

Strange fellow, the evil which now moves you to rob
a temple is neither human nor divine, but is an impulse
born from ancient and unexpiated crimes in men. It brings
destruction and you must guard against it with all your
strength. Learn now what is the way to guard against it.
Whenever any such temptation seizes you, go to the rites
which take away guilt, go as a supplicant to the shrines
of the gods who deliver men from curses, go into the fellowship of those reputed to be good among you, and learn by
hearing, and proclaim it yourself, that it is necessary for
every man to honor what is beautiful and good, but avoid
the company of evil men and don't turn back. If you act in
such a fashion and your desire thereby abates, very good;
but if not, consider death a more noble solution and abandon
life.

(Plato, *Laws* X. 909d-910d.)

Let us lay down the following general law: No one is
permitted to establish shrines in private houses. Whenever
it occurs to anyone to perform a sacrifice, he shall go to
the public shrines to perform it, and hand over the offerings
to the priests and priestesses, whose duty it is to consecrate
these things. Then he shall join in the prayers, and anyone he chooses shall pray along with him. The reasons for
such a proceeding shall be these: it is no light thing to
set up shrines and gods, and such an action requires considerable deliberation; it is customary, especially for all

women, and also for all kinds of sick, endangered or
troubled people, no matter what their trouble or what their
good luck, to consecrate whatever is at hand, to make
prayers and sacrifices, and to vow dedications to gods,
daimones and children of gods; they see portents and dreams,
and when they wake up in terror, they try to produce a cure
for each of them, as they also do when they recall many
visions: they build altars and shrines in open spaces or
wherever anything has happened, and fill up all the houses
and all the villages. So for all these reasons we must
enact the aforesaid law. An additional reason is on account
of sacrilegious people, to forbid them from committing their
thieveries and then building shrines and altars in their own
homes in the expectation of propitiating the gods with secret
sacrifices and prayers; in the process they increase their
wrong infinitely, and incur the gods' blame both on themselves and on those who (though they are better people) give
them permission. God will not blame the lawgiver; let this
be the law: "Let no one possess shrines of the gods in a
private house; if anyone is shown to possess and to worship
before a shrine other than the public one, and if he has
done no great wrong, whether man or woman, let the one who
notices the offense report it to the guardians of the law,
and let them give orders that the private shrines be carried
to the public ones, and let those who don't obey be punished
until the shrines are taken away. If anyone is convicted
of impiety not of a childish sort but that of an adult,
either by dedicating a shrine on private grounds or by offering sacrifice to the gods on public grounds whatsoever,
let him be punished with death for not sacrificing in a state
of purity. The lawgivers shall decide what is childish behavior or not, and they will bring the defendants into the
court, and they shall inflict the penalty appropriate for
their impiety."

(Plato, *Timaeus*, 71d-72c.)

...Remembering the command of their father who ordered
them to make mankind as good as possible, those who made us
corrected the bad part of us by placing therein the organ
of divination, in order that it might apprehend the truth
to some extent. This is a sufficient proof that God gave
the art of divination to human folly - no one achieves inspired and truthful divination when rational, but only when
his rationality is fettered by sleep or by disease or is
altered by some sort of divine possession. It is the practice
of a clear-thinking man to recollect and reflect upon the
things spoken in a dream or in a waking vision by the mantic
and inspired nature, and in addition all the phantasms that
were seen, and to analyze in all cases by reason in what
respect they signify something and for whom they foretell
good or evil in future or past or present. But it is not
incumbent upon one in a state of possession and still re-
maining in it to judge what is seen or spoken by him; for
it was well said long ago that to do and to know the things
pertaining to oneself and the self is appropriate only for
someone of sound mind. Hence it is the custom to assign the
tribe of prophets the task of analyzing these inspired divi-
nations. These men are called "diviners" by some who are
totally unaware that they are interpreters of the dark voice
and apparition, but are in no way diviners; rather, they
would most correctly be called prophets of things divined.

(Plato, *Timaeus*, 29d-30c.)

Let us state for what reason the Artificer made becoming and the All. He was good, and in the good no enmity
arises concerning anything. Since he was without enmity,
he wished that everything resemble himself to the extent
possible. If we accept this principle as the supreme origi-
nating principle of becoming and the cosmos, based on the
testimony of wise men, we should be wholly correct. God
wished that all be good and nothing evil, in so far as possible. When he took over all that could be perceived and

realized that it was not at rest, but in disorderly and
disruptive motion, he brought it into order from disorder,
thinking the former situation to be entirely better than
the latter. For it was not proper or possible for him who
was the best to do anything but the fairest. In his re-
flections on all creatures visible by nature he perceived
that nothing irrational would be fairer than the rational,
if taken as a whole. He also realized that reason apart
from the soul was not possible in anything. For this reason
he created reason within soul, and soul within body, when
he created the All, in order that the work he was performing
might be most fair and most good. So according to the
likely account it is necessary to say that the cosmos is a
living being endowed with soul and reason and in truth has
come into being because of the providence [forethought] of
God.

(Aristotle, *Physics*, 258b10-259a13.)

Since it is necessary that motion be eternal and not
cease, it is necessary that there be a prime mover, whether
one or many, which is eternal and which, being unmoved, first
causes movement. The belief that all unmoved movers are
eternal does not pertain to our present argument, but that
it is necessary that there exist something in itself not
moved regarding all external change, both necessary and ac-
cidental, but is capable of moving something else, is clear
to those considering as follows.

Let us hypothesize, if anyone wishes, that there are
things which sometimes exist and sometimes do not exist
without generation or destruction (it is necessary to believe that if something without parts at one time exists and
at another does not exist, that any such thing without change
is entirely such when it is and when it is not). Furthermore,
of the principles which are unmoved yet cause movements let
us grant that some of these at one time exist and at another
time do not exist. But this is impossible in all cases. For
it is clear that there must be some cause in reference to

those things that move themselves, for they at one time
exist, at another time are not in existence. Since nothing
without parts moves, that which moves itself must have as a
whole magnitude. But such a mover has not been proven by
our arguments. The pure cause of generation and destruction
can not be discerned from the unmoved movers which are not
eternal, nor among those who produce motion in these things
and others in other things. Of this continuous and eternal
process neither can any one of these or all of them be the
cause. That this process be such is eternal and necessary,
but the totality of these movements is limitless, and all
do not exist together. It is clear, therefore, that even
if often some of these unmoved movers that impart motion
perish, and many of the things that move themselves perish
and are followed by others that come into being, and one
unmoved thing moves another, and another another, nevertheless there is something that embraces all, and is apart from
each of them, and is the cause of some things existing and
some things not existing and the process of change. This
causes the motion of those things which in turn cause the
movement of other things. If therefore motion is eternal,
the prime mover must be eternal also, if there is one, but
if there is more than one, then there will be a plurality
of eternal movements. It is necessary to believe that there
is one rather than many and a limited rather than limitless
number. For if the same consequences result the finite
should always be assumed, for in the things of nature it is
necessary that the limited and better be found, if possible.
A single principle is adequate which as the first of the unmoved movers and eternal will be the source of motion for
the rest.

(Aristotle, *Metaphysics*, 1072b25-31.)

If God always enjoys the happiness we enjoy upon occasion, this is marvelous; if His happiness is still greater,
than that is even more wonderful. It is the case. Life is
the beginning. For the actuality of thought is life, and

life is God. The essential activity of God is life in its
best and eternal form. Therefore we say that God is a being
eternal and most good, so that life and continuous eternal
existence belong to God, for this is God.

CHAPTER II. HEROES

A. The Ranks of the Gods

The Greeks did not restrict their worship to the deities
of Mt. Olympus or the forces of nature. They also venerated
dead men and women on the grounds that the character and
quality of their life had earned for them a special, super-
human status. These people could be either real or imaginary
and, with the exception of Heracles, their worship tended
to be a local phenomenon, usually centered at their supposed
burial place.[6] While Homer does not record any hero-cults,
the practice seems to have gone back to the Mycenaean period,
and is frequently mentioned in classical and Hellenistic
literature. One type of hero includes Theseus and Orestes;
these might be people who actually lived, who were worshipped
by their family, clan or tribal group, or city; or they might
be characters from the epic poems, whose worship was taken
over by some city in hopes that the hero might prove to be
a powerful protector. Another group includes actual historical figures, such as Lysander or Brasidas among the Spartans,
and the poet Sophocles among the Athenians. Other heroes,
such as Asclepius, may originally have been considered actual
gods, who for some reason or other had fallen to a lesser
status. For further reading, see E. Rohde, *Psyche* (Eng. tr.
New York, 1925); L.G. Farnell, *Greek Hero-Cults and Ideas
of Immortality* (Oxford, 1921); A.D. Nock, "The Cult of
Heroes," *Harvard Theological Review* 37 (1944) 141-174.

(*Epinomis*, 984d-985b, from a spurious work attributed to
Plato, offers an interesting analysis of the heavenly hier-
archy.)

In reference to the gods - Zeus, Hera, and all the rest
- let one rank them as he wishes in accordance with law,
provided that he holds fast to a fixed principle. But as
for the visible gods, it must be said that the greatest and
most worthy of honor and most clear-sighted are the stars
and the bodies that exist with them; after them and beneath
them in order are the *daimones* and the creatures of the air,
which hold the third and middle place and are the source of
interpretation, and it is necessary to honor them particularly
in our prayers in order to secure favorable mediation. Of
these living creatures, the one of aether and the one of air
which is next in rank, each is wholly transparent - although

51

they may be close to us, they cannot be seen by us. They
possess a marvelous mind, for they are a race quick to learn
and remember; let us say that they can know all our thoughts,
and the good and beautiful in us they praise wondrously, but
that which is truly evil they loathe. They experience pain,
but a god who has the nature of divinity is beyond the concerns of pain and pleasure, and shares fully in wisdom and
knowledge. Since the universe is full of living creatures,
they all act as interpreters of all things to each other
and to the highest gods, for the middle group of the living
creatures can be borne over the earth and the whole universe
lightly. The fifth substance, water, one might conjecture
correctly that it is a demigod, and that sometimes it is
visible and at other times it is invisible and conceals
itself, and perplexes us by its indistinct appearance.

B. The Mythical Heroes

The following selections are designed to illustrate
the category of heroes drawn from the legends of the Greeks
themselves. We begin with Hesiod's account of the heroic
age as background, then move to specific cases. If these
heroes ever existed, they began as mortals, but mortals
seen as particularly favored or appointed by the gods to
perform outstanding deeds.

(Hesiod, *Works and Days*, 121-126, 156-173.)

But when earth had covered this generation [the golden
race], they are called through the plans of great Zeus
daimones who dwell on the earth; they are good, they deliver
men from harm, they are guardians of men, they watch over
judgments and cruel deeds, they are clothed in mist and roam
everywhere on the earth. They are givers of wealth - for
they share this royal right. ...

But when earth had covered this generation [the bronze
race] Zeus the son of Kronos created another race, the
fourth, on the fruitful earth, a more just and better race,
a god-like race of heroic men, who are called demi-gods, the
race which comes before ours on the boundless earth. Evil
war and the terrible cry of battle destroyed a part of them,
some before seven-gated Thebes, in the land of Cadmus, as
they contended for the flocks of Oedipus; some others were
brought in ships across the great gulf of the sea to Troy
for the sake of fair-haired Helen. There the end of death
covered some. To others Zeus the son of Kronos gave a
source of income and a place to dwell apart from mortal men
and settled them at the ends of the earth. Now they dwell
with hearts free from care in the islands of the blessed by
the deep-eddying Ocean - happy heroes, for whom the life-
giving earth bears fruit sweet as honey, which flourishes
three times in one year.

53

Theseus

Our first example, Theseus, was honored especially in
Athens as a local hero and bringer of security. Plutarch
in his *Life* collects the legends about Theseus' heroic ex-
ploits and his beneficences to the Athenians, and in this
excerpt he describes the recovery of the supposed bones of
Theseus by the general Cimon in 476/5 B.C., their return
to Athens and the establishment of a cult in Theseus' honor.
See in general A.G. Ward (ed.), *The Quest for Theseus* (New
York, 1970), and J. Boardman, "Heracles, Peisistratos and
Sons," *Revue Archéologique* (1972), pp. 57-72.

(Plutarch, *Life of Theseus*, 35-36.)

...Afterwards the Athenians chose to honor Theseus as
an hero. For not just a few of those who fought at Marathon
against the Medes thought that they saw the ghost of Theseus
in arms charging before them against the Persians.

After the wars against the Medes, in the archonship of
Phaedo, when the Athenians were consulting the Delphic
oracle, the priestess ordered them to take up the bones of
Theseus [on the island of Siphnos] and bury them reverently
and guard them. It was a problem to find the grave and
collect the bones, because the Dolopians, who then inhabited
the island, were unfriendly and barbarous. Cimon however
took the island, as I mentioned in my account of his life,
and was eager to discover the grave. He saw an eagle plucking
away at a certain place with his beak and scratching at the
ground with his talons. By some sort of divine providence
he considered the matter, recognized the meaning, and dug at
that spot. In the grave were found the coffin of an unusually large man, a bronze spear and sword lying by its side.
These articles were brought back by Cimon on his trireme.
The Athenians were thrilled, and received them with brilliant
processions and sacrifices as if the man himself were returning to the city. Now he lies at peace in the middle of the
city by the present gymnasium, and the tomb functions as a
place of refuge for household slaves and the humble who fear
the more powerful, for Theseus was their protector and helper
and received graciously the requests of the needy. Of the
sacrifices paid in his honor the chief and most solemn occurs

on the eighth day of Pyanepsion, which commemorates his
return from Crete with the young men. In addition, they
sacrifice to him on the eighth day of each month.

Orestes

Theseus was not the only mythical hero whose relics
were enshrined and venerated by a city-state. A similar
story is told in the following account in Herodotus'
Histories of how the Spartans defeated their neighbors in
Tegea by gaining possession of the bones of Orestes. Such
recoveries may well have involved the discovery of a tholos
or chamber tomb from the Mycenaean Bronze Age, the true
"heroic" age of Greece.

(Herodotus, *The Histories* I. 67-68.)

In the prior war with Tegea the Spartans were consis-
tently and badly beaten, but in the time of Croesus and the
reign of Anaxandrides and Ariston in Sparta, the Spartans
had now become dominant in the war, and did so in the following fashion. Since they were always being defeated by
the Tegeans, they sent messengers and inquired which god
they should propitiate to gain the upper hand over the
Tegeans. The Pythian priestess told them in an oracle that
they must bring back home the bones of Orestes, son of
Agamemnon. Since they were unable to find his tomb, they
again sent messengers to the god to discover the place where
Orestes lay. To the questions of the messengers the Pythia
replied:

> There is a certain Tegea on the level plain of Arcadia
> Two winds blow there by sharp necessity
> Blow is met by blow, and grief lies upon grief
> There the fertile earth conceals the son of Agamemnon.
> Bring him home and you will be lord over Tegea.

When the Spartans heard this they were no less hampered in
their search, but continued to look everywhere, until Lichas,
one of the Spartiates called "Benefactors," discovered them.
The Benefactors are from the citizen body, and pass out of

the rank of knights, five in number each year, always the
eldest. It was necessary for them during the following
year in which they go out from the cavalry not to linger
if dispatched on business for the Spartiate commonwealth.

Lichas, one of these men, found the tomb in Tegea, and
he employed both good luck and wisdom. Since there was at
that time free access to Tegea, he went to a blacksmith's
shop and saw iron being worked, and wondered at what he saw
being accomplished. When the smith saw how astonished he
was, he stopped what he was doing and said, "O Spartan
stranger, if only you had seen what I saw, then you would
have something to wonder about, whereas now you are struck
with wonder on seeing iron being worked. I wanted to dig
a well in this courtyard, and as I was digging I hit a
coffin seven cubits long. I did not believe that there had
ever been men larger than us, so I opened the coffin and
found within it a corpse as long as it was. I measured it
and buried the corpse again." The smith thus told what he
had seen, but Lichas considered what he said and decided,
in light of the Oracle, that this must be Orestes. He
reasoned as follows: the two bellows were the winds, the
hammer and anvil were the blow and counterblow, the forged
iron the woe lying on woe, for he reasoned on the basis that
the discovery of iron was a source of woe for men. Having
made his analysis he returned to Sparta and told the whole
story to the Spartiates. They fabricated a charge and
brought it against him, then banished him. He went to Tegea
and told the smith about his troubles and offered to rent
the courtyard from the smith. At first he wasn't willing,
but in time Lichas persuaded him. He took up residence
there, opened the grave, collected the bones and carried
them off to Sparta. From that time on the Spartans did con-
siderably better in battle, whenever they made trial of
each other, for they had already conquered much of the
Peloponnese by this time.

Thersander

The following passage gives another example of a
mythical hero honored for his help in battle.

(Pausanias, *Description of Greece* IX. 5.7.)

The Argives captured Thebes and gave it to Thersander,
the son of Polyneikes. When the soldiers of Agamemnon on
their way to Troy lost their course and the disastrous
battle of Mysia took place, then it also happened that
Thersander perished at the hands of Telephus. He had demonstrated that he was the best Greek in battle; his tomb may
be found in the city of Elaia, as you are journeying to the
plain of Kaikos. It is a stone standing in the open part
of the marketplace; the natives say they offer sacrifice
to him as a hero.

Oedipus

At Kolonos, a village on the outskirts of Athens, was
a hero-shrine to Oedipus, the famous king of Thebes. In a
sequel to his tragedy about Oedipus' discovery of his par-
ricide and incest, Sophocles describes how the blind, exiled
king has come to Athens and been granted asylum by its king
Theseus. The play's climax is reported in the following
way by a messenger, as he describes the heroically haunting
circumstances of Oedipus' death.

(Sophocles, *Oedipus at Kolonos*, 1590-1666.)

When he had come to the sheer path, planted with bronze
steps in the earth, he stood still on one of the many branch-
ing paths, near the hollow bowl, at the site where Perithous
and Theseus made their perpetual agreement. He took his
stand in the middle, between this point and the rock of
Thorikos, and sat between the hollow, wild-pear tree and
the stone tomb. There he loosened his squalid clothes, then
called to his daughters and commanded them to fetch some
flowing water, with which he might wash and make an offering.
The two of them obeyed their father's commands, went to a
hill in sight, the hill of Demeter, who makes all fresh and
green. In a short time they returned, and then washed and
dressed him as custom dictates.

When he was satisfied that all had been done, and there
was no part of his desire neglected, then Zeus of the underworld thundered, and the girls trembled as they heard it.
They fell before the knees of their father and wept, and
did not cease beating their breasts nor uttering mournful
cries.

When he heard their bitter, sudden cry, he enfolded
them in his arms and said, "Children, on this day your father
will be with you no longer. Everything that belonged to me
has been destroyed, and no longer need the burden of my care
rest heavily on you, and I know it was heavy, children. One
small word compensates for all these toils; no one loved you
more than I did, and now for the rest of your days you must
carry on your life without me." And so in close embrace
they all wept. But when they came to the end of their
wailing, and no more cries arose, there was silence; then
the voice of someone cried out loudly for him, so that all
the hairs on their heads stood up in sudden fear. For god
called him again and again, "Oedipus, Oedipus, why are we
waiting? Your journey is long delayed." When he realized
that god was calling him, he asked for Theseus, the lord
of this land, to come, and when he drew near he said, "O
friend, give me the pledge of your right hand for these
children; you, children, give a pledge to him. Promise never
to betray them willingly and to accomplish for them whatever
you judge appropriate."

Theseus, as is proper for a noble man, without lament
swore to accomplish these things for his friend. When he
had done these things, Oedipus felt around for his children
with his blind hands, and said, "Children, you must be brave
in your hearts and leave this place, nor desire to see what
is unlawful nor hear what should not be heard. Go as quickly as possible. Let only lord Theseus be present to bear
witness to what is happening." All of us heard him speak
thus, and we too groaned deeply with the maidens. When we
had gone, in a short time we turned and saw that Oedipus was
no longer there, but only the king with his hand thrown up to

shield his eyes, as if something dreadful and not to be seen
had appeared. But then not long afterwards we saw him salute
both the earth and the home of the gods, Olympus, in the
same prayer. By what sort of fate Oedipus perished, no one
among mortals except Theseus can say. No fiery thunderbolt
consumed him nor any blast from the sea stirred up at that
time, but either a messenger from the gods, or else the
depths of the lower world were split open for him without
pain and with kindness. For the man did not pass away with
lamentation nor by sickness nor in pain, but in a wondrous
fashion, beyond the usual fate of man. ...

Heracles

     The popularity of Heracles places him in a separate
category from other heroes, for he was known all over the
Greek world, worshipped with many different rites and remembered with many different legends. The presence of
diverse cults of Heracles, some of which honored him as a
hero, others as a god, confused Herodotus, who in his
Histories attempted to resolve the confusion, with the results shown in the first selection. Next, the Hellenistic
mythographers Apollodorus and Diodorus give the account of
his death, immolation and heroization. Finally, from the
Roman period, Pausanias describes the cult of Heracles in
the Greek city of Sikyon, and Athenaeus reports a ceremony
in his honor at Athens. See S. Woodford, "Cults of Heracles
in Attica," in *Studies Presented to G.M.A. Hanfmann* (ed.
D.G. Mitten *et al.*, Mainz, 1971), pp. 211-225.

(Herodotus, *The Histories* II. 43-45.)

     In the case of Heracles I hear this story, that he was
one of the twelve gods. But concerning the other Heracles,
whom the Greeks know, I heard nothing in Egypt. And that
the Egyptians did not take the name of Heracles from the
Greeks, but rather the Greeks from the Egyptians, and in
particular those Greeks who gave the name to the son of
Amphitryon, though there have been many other proofs, they
favor this one in particular, that the parents of Heracles,
Amphitryon and Alkmene, were both in origin Egyptians. They
do not recognize the name of Poseidon and the Dioskouroi,
nor do they number these gods among their gods. If they had

taken the name of any *daimon*, they would have remembered
these, if indeed at that time they were making sea voyages
and some of the Greeks were seafarers, as I suppose and believe. So the Egyptians would have known the names of these
gods rather than that of Heracles. But nevertheless Heracles
is an ancient god among the Egyptians. As they themselves
say, the change from eight to twelve gods was made seventeen
thousand years before the reign of Amasis, and among these
gods they include Heracles.

I wanted to get clear information on these matters to
the extent possible, so I sailed to Tyre in Phoenicia, because I understood that there was a holy temple to Heracles
there. I saw it; it was richly furnished with a variety of
other offerings, but in particular there were two *stelai* in
it; one was of pure gold, another of emerald, which shone
brightly in the night. In my conversations with the priests
I asked how long ago the temple was built. I discovered
that their story did not correspond with that of the Greeks.
They said that the construction of their temple coincided
with the foundation of Tyre, and Tyre was founded twenty
three hundred years ago. I saw in Tyre another temple of
Heracles called the Thasian. Then I went to Thasos and
found there a temple to Heracles constructed by the
Phoenicians who settled there while on a voyage to seek
Europe. They did these things five generations before the
birth of the son of Amphitryon, Heracles, in Greece. What
I have now investigated clearly shows that Heracles is an
ancient god, and those Greeks seem to me to have acted most
correctly who established and practice two cults of Heracles;
the one they worship as an immortal and call him Olympian,
to the other they bring offerings as to a hero.

The Greeks tell many thoughtless tales, but particularly
silly is the story told about Heracles that when he came to
Egypt the Egyptians crowned him and led him in procession to
sacrifice him to Zeus. For a time he followed quietly, but
when they began the sacrifice at the altar he defended himself and killed them all. The Greeks who tell this tale seem

to me to be totally ignorant of Egyptian nature and customs.
It is thought impious for them to sacrifice domestic animals,
except sheep and calves and bulls, if they are unblemished,
and geese; how could they sacrifice human beings? Furthermore, if Heracles were alone and a mere man, as they say,
how then could he have destroyed a countless crowd? I am
willing to go only this far in the matter, and may I have
the good will from the gods and heroes!

(Apollodorus, *Library* II. 7.7, a mythological compendium of
the second century B.C.)

When Heracles had put into the headland of Euboea,
Kenaion, he built an altar to Zeus Kenaios. Wishing to offer sacrifice, he dispatched an herald to [his home in]
Trachis to bring back fine clothing. From this man Deianeira
[his wife] learned about Iole [his concubine], and feared
that he might prefer her. She believed that the blood shed
by Nessos was a love potion and saturated the entire tunic
with it. Heracles put it on and sacrificed. But as soon
as the tunic became warm, the hydra's poison [in Nessos'
gift] began to consume his flesh. He snatched Likos by the
feet and cast him from the headland. He tried to tear off
the tunic clinging to his body, but his flesh was torn away
as well. Belabored by such misfortunes he was carried on
board ship for Trachis. When Deianeira realized what happened, she hung herself. Heracles then commanded Hyllos,
his eldest son by Deianeira, to marry Iole, when he became
a man, and he himself went to Mt. Oita, in the territory of
the Trachinians. There he built a pyre, mounted it, and
ordered that it be ignited. No one was willing to do this,
except Poikis, who was passing by looking for his flocks.
To this man he gave his bow. While the pyre was still burning, so the story goes, a cloud passed under Heracles and
lifted him up to heaven with a peal of thunder. Thereafter
he obtained immortality and having been reconciled with Hera
he married her daughter Hebe.

(Diodorus Siculus, *Library of History* IV. 38-39, of the
first century B.C.)

When the companions of Iolaos came to gather up
Heracles' bones, they could find no bones at all, and concluded that Heracles had been moved from among men to the
company of the gods in accordance with the oracle.

These men performed the rituals for the dead as for
a hero; they heaped up a funeral mound and returned to
Trachis. According to their example Menoitios, son of
Aktor and friend of Heracles, sacrificed a boar and a bull
and a ram to him as a hero and commanded that in Opous each
year he should receive the sacrifice and honors of a hero.
The Thebans did pretty much the same thing, but the Athenians
first of the others honored Heracles with sacrifices as a
god and held up to all other men their own piety towards
the god. Thereby they induced first all the Greeks and then
all men in the inhabited world to worship Heracles as a god.

(Pausanias, *Description of Greece* II. 10.1)

In the gymnasium not far from the market place is
located a Heracles in stone, the work of Skopas. There is
also another shrine of Heracles, at the precinct called the
Paidize [Play-ground]. In the middle of it is the shrine,
and in it is an ancient wooden image, a work of Laphaes of
Phlious. Their custom is to sacrifice here in this way:
they say that Phaistos came to Sikyon and discovered them
offering to Heracles rites appropriate to a hero, but he
insisted that instead they sacrifice to him in the manner
appropriate to a god. Thus even today the Sikyonians sacrifice lambs to him and burn the thighs upon an altar; some
of the meat they eat in the manner of the gods' ritual,
other portions they burn and bury as is done for heroes.
The first of the two days in the festival which they celebrate in Heracles' honor is called the *Olympia*,[7] the second
is *Heracleia*.

(Athenaeus, *Deipnosophists* XI. 494f.)

When the eighteen-year-old boys are about to have their long hair cut off, says Pamphilus, they offer to Heracles a large cup which they have filled with wine. They call this *oinisteria*, and after offering a libation, they give it to their companions who have congregated for this purpose.[8]

C.   Men Who Became Heroes and Gods

The dignity and worship accorded a hero or a god were
not confined to legendary characters. The following cases
exemplify the situation of actual historical characters who
attained some sort of divine status, usually after their
death, though some, such as Alexander the Great, were a bit
more eager. On the process of deification, see L. Cerfaux
and J. Tondriau, *Le Culte des Souverains dans la Civilisation
Gréco-Romaine* (Paris, 1956) and J.W. Gardner, *Leadership
and the Cult of Personality* (London, 1974). We begin with
the general description of the process offered by the Christian writer Theodoretus.

(Theodoretus, *Graecarum Affectionum Curatio* III. 24-28.)

Afterwards they deified those who had done anything

well, or had demonstrated bravery in battle, or begun some

kind of agriculture, or provided a wine for anybody, and

even constructed temples for them. Indeed Sanchoniathon

said that even Kronos was a human being. ... The Greeks

also made Heracles a god because he was noble and brave.

And after his death they described Asclepius as a god, since

he discovered the art of medicine. For the same reason the

Egyptians thought Apis worthy of divine address. However

the Greeks say that Heracles cremated himself due to the

successful plot of Deianeira, and thus ended his life. But

in the case of Asclepius, a man, who relieved many men of

all sorts of diseases through his medical skill, was struck

by a thunderbolt from Zeus and died. These facts, as well

as others, are found in the fourth book of Diodorus' Librar-

ies. Although the Greeks have learned the truth, they still

persist in addressing Heracles and Asclepius as gods.

Sophocles-Dexion

(*Etymologicum Magnum*, s.v. "Dexion".)

Sophocles was named "Dexion" by the Athenians post-

humously. They say that the Athenians, in their desire to

do honor to Sophocles after his death, built a hero's shrine

to him and called him Dexion, "he that receives," from his
reception of Asclepius. For he took the god into his own
house, and constructed an altar for him. For this reason
he was called Dexion.

Lysander

(Plutarch, *Life of Lysander*, 18.)

Lysander set up in Delphi from the booty a bronze
statue of himself and of each of his admirals and golden
statues of the Dioskouroi, which disappeared before the
battle of Leuctra [371 B.C.]. In the treasury of Brasidas
and the Acanthians a trireme was placed made of gold and
ivory two cubits long, which Cyrus sent to Lysander in honor
of his victory. Alexandrides of Delphi writes that a deposit
of Lysander lay there, one talent of silver, and fifty-two
minae and eleven staters in addition, which conflicts with
the general agreement concerning his poverty. At that time
Lysander seemed to be more powerful than any Greek before,
and seemed also to cultivate a pride more extensive than his
power. He was the first Greek, as Duris tells us, to whom
the cities erected altars as to a god and made sacrifices,
and he was the first to whom songs of praise were sung.
One of these has been handed down and begins
    We will sing the general of great Greece
    Who comes from wide-spaced Sparta
    O, Io, Paean.

Alexander the Great

The following passages describe some of the stages in
Alexander's request to the Greek cities to be worshipped as
a god. From Arrian's biography come a brief mention of
Greek ambassadors who in 324 B.C. approached him as a god,
and the slightly later incident in which his companion
Hephaistion was honored after his death with a hero-shrine
in Alexandria. Later in his career, Alexander apparently
requested divine honors for himself, and the selections from
Aelian and Hyperides indicate the types of reaction that the
request elicited. For special studies of this episode, see
C.A. Robinson, "Alexander's Deification," *American Journal
of Philology* 64 (1943) 286-301; J.P.V.D. Balsdon, "The

'Divinity' of Alexander the Great," *Historia* 1 (1950) 383-388; Cerfaux and Tondriau, *Le Culte des Souverains*, pp. 125-144.

(Arrian, *Anabasis of Alexander* VII. 23.2.)

Embassies came from Greece and ambassadors came forward with their heads wreathed, and crowned him with golden crowns, as if they came on a sacred embassy to honor a god.

(Arrian, *Anabasis of Alexander* VII. 23.6.)

There came also from the oracle of Zeus at Ammon the envoys whom he had dispatched to inquire what honors it was lawful to pay to Hephaistion. They said that the oracle permitted sacrifice to be paid to him as to a hero. Alexander rejoiced in the oracle and henceforth had him honored as a hero.

To Kleomenes, an evil man who had worked much harm in Egypt, he sent a letter, and I don't find fault with the letter to the extent that it shows affection for Hephaistion even after death and a desire to remember him, but I do find fault with it in other respects. The letter ordered that a hero-shrine be built for Hephaistion in Alexandria in Egypt, both in the city itself and on the island of Pharos, where the lighthouse is located; the shrines were to be very large and be conspicuously costly. Kleomenes was to see to it that the island be named after Hephaistion, and that the name Hephaistion be inscribed on all the tokens used by the merchants in their exchanges with each other.

(Aelian, *Varia Historia* II. 19.)

When Alexander conquered Darius and acquired power over the Persians, he thought a great deal of himself and, buoyed up by the good fortune surrounding him, he proclaimed himself a god, and commanded that the Greeks pass decrees that he was a god. For what he did not have by nature he sought from men, and he profited. Some voted one way, some another, but the Spartans decreed the following: "Since Alexander wishes

to be a god, let him be a god." In a Laconian answer and
in a fashion typical of themselves they pointed out the
stupidity of Alexander.

(Hyperides, *Against Demosthenes*, 31.)

When you [Demosthenes] thought the council would dis-
like those who had the gold, you became warlike and upset
the city in order that you might knock out the inquiry. But
when the council postponed its conclusions, saying that it
had not yet come to the end of the matter, then you agreed
that Alexander might be the son of Zeus and of Poseidon, if
he wished.

D. The Cult of Asclepius

Asclepius the physician, son of Apollo, was already known at the time of the Homeric poems, in which he appears as the human father of the Greek physicians at Troy. Pindar (in the Third Pythian Ode) called him a hero, and in the fifth century, when medical knowledge was becoming more systematic and effective, the cult of Asclepius became more wide-spread. Besides the old shrines in Trikka and Epidauros, new cult centers were established in Athens, Kos and elsewhere, and Asclepius was often referred to as a god. His shrines served as a sort of hospital - the sick came, prayed, consulted the priests, spent the night (in the rite of incubation), saw the god in a dream and received advice or were cured, and in the morning went away. Those who were cured often left testimonies to the god's power; and this fact emphasizes Asclepius' appeal to the individual - he was a god who produced results in the devotee's own life, and he was approached by that devotee as an individual, and not as a member of city or family. The selections given here illustrate some details of personal devotion to Asclepius in the classical age, and includes some later material which refers back to the classical period. At the end of the fourth century, a collection of testimonies was made at Epidauros, cf. E.J. and L. Edelstein, *Asclepius, A collection and interpretation of the testimonia* (Baltimore, 1945), pp. 221-237 and R.M. Grant, *Hellenistic Religions* (Indianapolis, 1953), pp. 53-59.

The Myth of Asclepius

In this rather complicated passage, the Roman author Pausanias gives various versions of the story of how Asclepius was born, and how he came to be associated with Epidauros.

(Pausanias, *Description of Greece* II. 26.3-10.)

This is the story of how the land came to be especially sacred to Asclepius: the Epidaurians say that Phlegyas came into the Peloponnese, ostensibly to see the country, but really as a spy, to find out the number of its inhabitants and whether the people were very warlike. Phlegyas was the most belligerent person alive at that time, and each time he encountered a community he would attack and carry off crops and drive off livestock.

69

When he came into the Peloponnese, he was followed by
his daughter, who had not let her father know that she kept
secret from him the fact that she was pregnant by Apollo.
In the land of the Epidaurians, she gave birth and exposed
the child on the mountain which today is named Tithion [the
Nipple], at that time called Myrtium. As the child lay
abandoned one of the she-goats being pastured on the mountain
gave him milk, and the goatherd's dog guarded him.

Aresthanas - for that was the goatherd's name - when
he discovered that one of the goats was missing and that
the dog had not returned to the flock either, made a diligent
search and, when he found the baby, was very eager to rescue
it. As he approached, he saw a flash of lightning coming
from the child, and taking it as the divine sign that it was,
he turned away in reverence. In a short time the news spread
over all the earth and sea that he found at his discretion
cures for the sick whenever he wanted, and even that he was
raising the dead.

In addition to this another version is also told: according to it Koronis, while she was pregnant with Asclepius,
had illicit intercourse with Ischys the son of Elatos, and
was killed by Artemis to defend Apollo's honor. The pyre
had already been kindled when Hermes is supposed to have
snatched the baby from the flame.

The third version, which makes Asclepius the son of
Arsinoe the daughter of Leukippos, seems to be the least
likely of the tales. For when Apollophanes the Arcadian
went to Delphi to inquire of the god whether Asclepius was
the son of Arsinoe and a citizen of Messene, he received
this answer from the Pythian priestess of Apollo:

O Asclepius, great joy to all mortals,
Whom Phlegyas' daughter conceived by me and bore,
Desirable Koronis, in rocky Epidauros.

This oracle makes it perfectly clear that Asclepius was not
the son of Arsinoe, but that Hesiod or one of the interpola-
tors of his works fabricated the tale to please the Messenians.

Further evidence that the god was born in Epidauros
is the realization that the most famous sanctuaries of
Asclepius have originated from Epidauros. For example,
the Athenians, saying that they included Asclepius in their
initiation rite, name that day "Epidauria" and claim that
Asclepius has been considered a god by them since that time.
In addition Archias the son of Aristaichmos, who had sprained
himself while hunting on Mount Pindasos in Asia Minor, introduced the god to Pergamum after he had been healed at
Epidauria.

In our own day the sanctuary of Asclepius by the sea
at Smyrna was founded from the one at Pergamum. As for the
Asclepius called Iatros [Physician] at Balagrae in Cyrene,
he too is from Epidaurus. And from the sanctuary at Cyrene
was founded the Asclepieum at Lebene on Crete. One point
of difference between the rites at Cyrene and at Epidauros
is that the Cyrenaeans sacrifice goats, a practice that is
not sanctioned by the Epidaurians.

Among the evidence that convinces me that Asclepius
was considered a god from the beginning rather than gaining
the honor in the course of time are the words in Homer
spoken about Machaon by Agamemnon:

Talthybios, summon hither Machaon,
The mortal son of Asclepius.[9]

As if he means that the man is the son of a god.

Epiphanies

Asclepius exercised his divine power by appearing in
dreams and by responding directly to needs and prayers.
The first passage here reports a general statement about
such epiphanies by Celsus, a pagan apologist of the Christian period. The second passage is ascribed to the famous
fifth-century physician Hippocrates, and describes his own
dream-vision of the god.

(Origen, *Against Celsus* III. 24.)

Celsus asks us to believe of Asclepius that a great many
people, both Greeks and foreigners, acknowledge that they
have often seen, and still continue to see, not the image,

but the god himself performing cures and good deeds and
foretelling the future.

(Hippocrates, *Letters*, 15.)

It seemed that I saw Asclepius himself, and he appeared
very close. ... Asclepius appeared, not as his statues portray him, mild and gentle, but with animated gesture, fear-
some to behold. Snakes were following him, enormous speci-
mens of serpents, speeding along in broad coils, hissing
horribly, as in the desert or in forest dells. Companions
came behind him with very tightly bound boxes of drugs.
Then the god stretched out his hand to me; I took it joyfully
and besought him to join me and not to neglect my ministra-
tions. But he said, "At present you have no need of me,
but this goddess [i.e., Truth], whom immortals and mortals
share, will be your guide...." And the divinity departed.

In the following passage, Aelian tells how the fourth-
century Athenian writer of comedies Theopompos was cured of
tuberculosis by Asclepius.

(Aelian, frag. 99 in the edition of R. Hercher, *Leipzig*,
1864-1866.)

Asclepius healed Theopompos the Athenian, who was being
worn out and drained from tuberculosis, and he urged him on
to produce comedies again, since he had made him whole and
safe and sound. This is proven by the relief of Theopompos
in Parian marble. (The inscription identifies him by his
father's name, for he was the son of Tisamenos.) The appearance of the affliction is very visible. The bed itself
is also of marble. On it, by the artist's operation, lies
the image of him in his sickness. And the god stands nearby
and reaches out his healing hand to him. There is also a
young boy; he is also smiling.

A Night in the Temple of Asclepius

From Aristophanes' comedy *Ploutos* ["Wealth"] comes the following description of the process of incubation. It is a classic account, even if slightly distorted by Aristophanes' jokes. In the play the poor Athenian Chremylos sets out to cure Ploutos of blindness, so he can distribute his prosperity more justly, and he sends his slave Karion to attend Ploutos. The place for the cure, of course, was the temple of Asclepius, which in Athens was on the south slope of the Acropolis. Cf. pp. 78-80 below.

(Aristophanes, *Ploutos*, 654-695, 707-747.)

Karion: As soon as we arrived at the god with the man - pitiful in his blindness then, but now as happy and prosperous as anybody else - we took him first to the sea, and washed him.

Wife of Chremylos: Lucky old man, to bathe in the cold sea!

Karion: Then we went to the god's precinct. When cakes and offerings had been consecrated on the altar, and a cake given to the fire, we laid Ploutos down, as we were supposed to. Each of us arranged a make-shift bed.

Wife of Chremylos: Were others there too to ask healing from the god?

Karion: One was Neokleides, who is blind, but outdoes the sighted when he's stealing. There were also a lot of others with all kinds of ailments. The attendant [*propolos*] of the god extinguished the lamps and told us to go to sleep and to keep quiet if anyone heard a noise; we all lay down in good order. I wasn't able to fall asleep, but a pot of soup distracted me - it was sitting a short distance from an old woman's head and I was obsessed by a desire to sneak up on it. So I glanced up and saw the priest snatching away the cakes and figs from the holy table; after this he made the rounds of all the altars, to see if any cakes had been left behind. Those that were, he "consecrated" into a sack. I, thinking this was the pious thing to do, started up after that pot of soup.

Wife: Miserable wretch! Weren't you afraid of the god?

Karion: By the gods, afraid that he would get to the pot
first, with his garlands...his priest, after all, had taught
me how. The old woman, when she heard my noise, reached out
her hand; I hissed and took the hand in my mouth, as if I
were one of the sacred *pareias*-snakes. She immediately drew
back the hand, wrapped herself up and lay back quietly,
farting for fear worse than a cat. I gulped down a lot of
the soup, and when I was full, I stopped....After this I
got scared and wrapped myself up right away; the god went
around examining all the afflictions in perfect order. Then
an acolyte set a little stone mortar beside him, and a pestle
and a box.

Wife: Was the box made out of stone?

Karion: By Zeus, of course it wasn't.

Wife: How did you see, you damned wretch, if you say you
were all wrapped up?

Karion: Through my cloak. It had plenty of holes, by Zeus.
First of all he set to grinding a medicinal ointment for
Neokleides, tossing in three cloves of garlic from Tenos.
He ground them in the mortar and mixed in acid and squill.
Then he dissolved this in Sphettian vinegar, turned back the
man's eyelids (to make it sting more) and smeared it on.
He let out a yell and scream, jumped up and fled. The god
laughed and said, "Now sit there with your ointment, so I
can stop your filibustering in the assembly meetings."

Wife: So he's a patriot, the god - and a clever one too.

Karion: After this he sat down beside Ploutos; first he
felt his head, then he took a clean cloth and wiped around
his eyes. Panakeia dropped a red cloth over his head and
his whole face. Then the god gave a low whistle, and a pair
of snakes of enormous size darted out of the temple.

Wife: O dear gods!

Karion: These slid silently under the red cloth and licked
his eyelids - so it seemed to me, at least. And, my lady,
before you could have drunk off ten cups of wine, Ploutos
stood up, and saw! I clapped my hands for joy and woke up
the master. Right away the god made himself disappear, and

the snakes vanished into the temple. The people lying next
to him, as you'd expect, congratulated Ploutos and stayed
awake all night till day dawned. I kept praising the god
over and over because he had made Ploutos see right off,
but made Neokleides more blind.

The Formal Worship of Asclepius

These inscriptions list certain sacrificial and ceremonial regulations for the sanctuaries of Asclepius.

(*IG* IV². 1.40 and 41; *SIG*³ 998; from Epidauros, about 400
B.C.)

To Apollo sacrifice a bull, and to the gods who share
his temple a bull. On the altar of Apollo sacrifice these
and a hen to Leto and another to Artemis; for the god as
his portion a *medimnos* of barley, a half-*medimnos* of wheat,
a twelfth-*medimnos* of wine and the leg of the first bull.
The *hieromnemones* are to take away the other leg. Of the
second bull one leg is to be given to the cantors, and the
other leg and the intestines to the guards.

To Asclepius sacrifice a bull; to the gods who share
his temple a bull and to the goddesses a cow. On the altar
of Asclepius sacrifice these things and a cock. They are
to dedicate to Asclepius as his portion a *medimnos* of barley,
a half-*medimnos* of wheat, and a twelfth-*medimnos* of wine.
They are to lay a leg of the first bull on the altar for
the god, and the *hieromnemones* are to take away the other.
Of the second bull one is to be given to the cantors, the
other ...

(*IG* II². 4962; *SIG*³ 1040; *LGS* II. 18; from Piraeus, 4th c.
B.C.)

The Gods! Make the preliminary sacrifices in this manner: to Meleas three wheat-cakes; to Apollo three wheat-
cakes; to Hermes three wheat-cakes; to Iaso three wheat-cakes;
to Panakeia three wheat-cakes; to the dogs three wheat-cakes;
to the huntsmen three wheat-cakes.

(*LSAM* 24 (A), lines 25-38; from Erythrai in Euboia, 380-
360 B.C.)

    ...Whenever the city performs a sacrifice to Asclepius,
the city's sacrifice is made first on behalf of all; at a
festival no private person is to make the first sacrifice,
but during the rest of the year one may make the first sacrifice according to the aforesaid regulations. Those who sleep
in the temple, after they have incubated, when they render
sacrifice to Asclepius and Apollo, or else after they render
sacrifice after a prayer, when they place the sacred portion
[on the altar?] are first to sing this paian around the altar
of Apollo three times: "Hail Paian, O hail Paian, hail
Paian; O hail Paian, hail Paian, O hail Paian, O Lord Apollo,
spare the youths. ..."

Shrines of Asclepius

    In the first two passages, Pausanias describes two
sanctuaries of Asclepius, the great and famous one at
Epidauros and a smaller, local one at Sikyon, as they were
in the second century A.D.

Epidauros.   (Pausanias, *Description of Greece* II. 27.1-3.)

    The sacred grove of Asclepius is marked by boundary
stones in every direction. No one dies, nor do women give
birth, inside the precinct, according to the same custom
that prevails at Delos. Whether one of the Epidaurians
themselves or a foreigner does the sacrificing, they consume
the sacrificial victims completely inside the sanctuary boundaries. I know that the same thing is done at Titane. The
statue of Asclepius is half as large as the one of Zeus
Olympios at Athens, and is made of ivory and gold. An
inscription states that Thrasymedes of Paros the son of
Arignotos was the sculptor. He is seated on a throne holding a staff; he holds the other hand over the head of the
snake, and a dog is represented lying beside him. On the
throne are portrayed the deeds of the Argives, what
Bellerophon did to the Chimaira, and Perseus with the
Medusa's severed head. Beyond the temple is the place where

the supplicants of the god lie down to sleep. Near it
stands a round building of marble called the Tholos, worth
seeing. In it is a painting of Eros by Pausias: Eros has
thrown away his bow and arrows and is holding up a lyre in
their place. Also painted there is Methe [Drunkenness]
drinking from a crystal vessel, this too the work of Pausias;
in the painting you can actually see the vessel of crystal
and face of the woman through it. *Stelai* used to stand
inside the precinct, but in my day there are only six left.
On these are inscribed the names of men and women who have
been healed by Asclepius, as well as the ailment from which
each suffered and how each was cured; they are written in
the Doric dialect.

Sikyon.   (Pausanias, *Description of Greece* II. 10.2-3.)

From here the road passes on to the sanctuary of
Asclepius. As you go into the precinct there is a double
building on the left. In the front part lies Hypnos [Sleep],
though nothing remains except his head. The inner chamber
is devoted to Apollo Karneios, and only the priests are
permitted to enter it. In the colonnade lies a bone of a
sea monster of great size, and beyond it is a statue of
Oneiros [Dream], as well as Hypnos putting a lion to sleep,
which bears the epithet Epidotes [Bountiful]. As you go
into the temple of Asclepius there is on one side of the
entrance a seated statue of Pan, on the other one of Artemis.
Inside is the god, portrayed beardless, made of gold and
ivory, the work of Kalamis; he holds a scepter in one hand
and in the other a cone of the domesticated pine. They say
that the god, in the form of a snake, was brought here from
Epidauros by a yoke of mules, and that a Sikyonian woman,
Nikagora the mother of Agasikles and wife of Echetimos, was
responsible for bringing him. There are small statues, also,
suspended from the roof; the woman on the snake is supposed
to be Aristodama, the mother of Aratos, who is himself considered a son of Asclepius.

Athens

During a lull in the Peloponnesian War, the Athenians officially introduced the cult of Asclepius into Athens while the Eleusinia were being celebrated in the fall of 420 B.C. The God's sacred snake was brought from Epidauros, and in the following years a temple was erected on the south slope of the Acropolis. See R. Martin and B. Metzger, "Recherches d'Architecture et de Topographie a l'Asklepieion d'Athènes," *Bulletin de Correspondance Hellenique* 73 (1949) 316-350. The first inscription gives a concise and fragmentary account of the stages in the establishment of the sanctuary. The second inscription is part of a record of the annual temple inventories, for the years 341/340 and 340/339 B.C., and is useful in helping imagine the kinds of dedications that filled Asclepius' sanctuaries. Finally, an undated passage from Aelian tells by indirection several facts about the administration of the temple.

(*IG* II^2. 4960; *SIG*^{3} 88.)

The god came up during the Great Mysteries and was escorted into the Eleusinion; and from his home he summoned the snake in a chariot, and Telemachos went out to meet him. Hygieia came along, and thus was founded the whole sanctuary in the year when Astyphilos the son of Kydantides was archon [420/419 B.C.]. In the archonship of Archias [419/4]8 B.C.] the Heralds laid claim to the property and [prevent]ed some work. [The details of several years are missing.] In the archonship of Teisandros [414/413 B.C.] the wooden gateway was constructed and the rest of the sacred furnishings were installed. In the archonship of Kleokritos [413/412 B.C.] the planting was done and he completed the decoration of the whole precinct at his own expense.

(*IG* II^2. 1533, lines 1-18.)

Gold ring, unweighed; Xenokrates dedicated it, in a case.
Silver crown which Dion dedicated, missing.
Diopeithes on a plaque, 50 drachmas.
Kallimachos on a plaque on the wall, 40 drachmas.
Mnesarete, 10 drachmas, 3 drachmas missing; she said that
    Diokles of Myrrhinous should pay it; an additional
    drachma is lacking on the part of Telesias.

Kallisto on the lintel, 2 drachmas.

Aischylides on a ribbon, 1 drachma, 3 obols; another on a
    plaque, 1 drachma; a small face on the wall in the
    chapel.

Demonstrate (dedicated) a bronze wine jar, Hedyle a bronze
    wine jar, Nikias a marble conch-shell.

Enporion on a plaque, 12 drachmas.

Onasis on a ribbon, 12 drachmas; 4 lacking; this lack
    Polyxenos paid off on behalf of himself.

A wooden thurible, gilded, a cubit long.

Minnion, 5 drachmas; the priest, Eunikides of Halai, said
    these are old.

Diodote, 10 drachmas.

Also, a gilded limb; a cloak; a wooden chair.

- The following were dedicated in the year Diokles was
    priest and Theophrastos was archon [340/339 B.C.] -

Miscellaneous silver, weight 4 drachmas.

Pasilea, in a case by (10) the wall, 20 drachmas.

Diphilos, on a plaque on the wall, a silver face, 10 drachmas.

Python on a plaque by the plaque of Antigona, 40 drachmas.

Hegemon of Athmonon, on a ribbon, 60 drachmas.

Klymene, on a plaque, 74 drachmas, 3 obols.

Nikomachos on a plaque, 10 drachmas.

Kallias son of Kallipos of Rhamnous, a silver libation bowl,
    in a case, unweighed; the weight is inscribed, 250
    drachmas.

A libation-bowl (which) Aristophon of Azenia dedicated; un-
    weighed; the weight is inscribed, 100 drachmas.

A libation bowl which Philon dedicated, unweighed, in a case.

Telesarchos of Cholargos, a silver drinking-cup, unweighed;
    the weight is inscribed, 62 drachmas, 3 obols.

(15) Where the little Nikai [figures of Victory] are:
    a small silver cup in a case which Theano dedicated,
    unweighed; which Phile dedicated, the weight is in-
    scribed, 50 drachmas.

Oinanthe, on a ribbon, 2 drachmas.

Meletos (dedicated) a silver heart and a little snake on a
    plaque.
Bronzes: Philon of Phaleron, a cauldron; Pamphile, a little
    tripod; Timoxenos, a drinking cup.
Jasper gems, 5 drachmas.
Crystal ring.
Crystal seals, 5 drachmas.
Grey clock.

[In subsequent years, noteworthy dedication included golden
eyes on a plaque, ritual offering-vessels, gazelle knucklebones, body-scrapers, a key, rings, seals, jugs, crown, a
pair of shoes, a beaker, a flute, more eyes, a pillow.]

(Aelian, *The Nature of Animals* VII. 13.)

    Into the temple of Asclepius came a robber of holy
things; he waited for the middle of the night and looked out
for the period of deepest sleep of those who were sleeping
in the temple. Then he stole many of the offerings secretly
(or so he thought). There was a good guard on duty at the
time, a dog, better than the temple guards at keeping alert.
This dog followed in pursuit of the man and barked continu-
ously, striving with all his power to announce what had
happened. At first the thief and his henchmen in the unholy
deed threw stones at him; finally they threw bread and cakes.
Cleverly (or so he thought) he had taken these along to be
dog bait. Since the dog kept barking even when the thief
entered the house where he was staying and again when he
came out, it was known where the dog was. The records and
the spaces where the offerings were lodged indicated what
was missing. The Athenians judged that this was the man,
and having tortured him they discovered everything. The
thief was punished in accordance with the penalties of the
law, but the dog was honored by public meals and care, as
a faithful guard and inferior to no one of the temple stewards
in his alertness.

E. Local Heroes: The Salaminioi

The following two inscriptions are illustrative of
the technical operation of a local cult. Both inscriptions
talk of a quarrel between two rival groups for control of
the sanctuary, and the resolution of the dispute through
arbitration; in addition rules are set down governing procedures and practices at the sanctuary. It is clear that
the first attempt, in 363/2 B.C., did not handle all the
problems, for a century later, in c. 263 B.C., a second
resolution is needed. For details, see the article by
W.S. Ferguson, "The Salaminioi of Heptaphylai and Sounion,"
in *Hesperia* 7 (1938) pp. 1-75.

1. [363/2 B.C.]

Gods! In the archonship of Charikleides in Athens
[363/2 B.C.] the arbitrators Stephanos of Myrrhinous,
Kleagoras of Acharnae, Aristogeiton of Myrrhinous,
Euthykritos of Lamptrae, Kephisodotus of Aithalidai settled
the quarrels between the Salaminioi of Heptaphylai and the
Salaminioi from Sounion on these terms. Both parties agreed
that the arbitrators had decided wisely. The priesthoods
shall be jointly held by both for all time, i.e. those of
Athena Skiras, Heracles at Porthmos, Eurysakes, Aglauros
and Pandrosos and Kourotrophos. When one of the priests
or priestesses dies, a successor shall be chosen by lot
from both groups meeting in common. The one selected shall
serve on the same terms as those who held the priesthood
before. The land of the shrine of Heracles at Porthmos
and the other land [or, the land at the Hale] and the *agora*
at Koile shall be divided equally and each shall take its
part and mark it with boundary stones. They will sacrifice
to the gods and heroes in the following manner. Whatever
victims the city provides from the public treasury or from
the *oskophoroi* and *deipnophoroi*, these both shall sacrifice
in common and each take half of the meat raw. Whatever the
Salaminioi sacrifice from rentals, these they shall sacrifice
from their own funds as was the ancestral custom, each party
contributing half towards the whole sacrifice.

To the priests and priestesses the following gifts are
to be paid as listed: to the priest of Heracles as *hierosyna*
30 drachmas, for *pelanos* 3 drachmas, half to be contributed
by each group. From the victims which he sacrifices for the
community let him take of flayed animals the skin and the
leg, of burnt victims the leg. From an ox nine pieces of
meat and the skin. To the priests of Eurysakes as *hierosyna*
6 drachmas. For *pelanos* for both cults 7 drachmas, in place
of the bone and skin of the Eurysakeion 13 drachmas; let
each party contribute half. For the hero at the Hale let
him take from the sacrifices the skin and leg. To the
priests and priestesses in the shrines where each officiates
let a portion come from each party. Let them distribute
the wheat loaves in the shrine of Skiras as follows: selecting out from the whole number those customarily set
apart according to ancestral custom. To the herald a loaf,
to the priestess of Athena a loaf, to the priest of Heracles
a loaf, to the priestess of Aglauros and Pandrosos a loaf,
to the *kalathephoros* of Kourotrophos also a loaf, to the
millers a loaf. As for the rest let them each take a half.
Let them select in turn by lot from each an *archon* who shall
in turn select the *oschophoros* and *deipnophoros* with the
priestesses and herald according to the ancestral customs.
Let both sides inscribe these regulations on a common *stele*
and place it in the temple of Athena Skiras.

The same man is to be priest of Eurysakes and of the
Hero at the Hale. If anything needs repair in the shrines
let both parties repair them, each contributing half. During
the archonship of Charikleides the men from the Heptaphylai
provided the *archon*. All the records shall be common to
both. Let the man who has the contract till the land until
the rental period elapses, and let him pay half the rental
fee to each party. Let each party in turn perform the sacrifices which precede the contest and each take half of the
flesh and skins. The priestly office of herald is to belong
to Thrasykles according to ancient custom. All other charges,
both private and public, up to the month Boedromion in the
archonship of Charikleides are to be dropped.

vacat

In the archonship of Diphilos son of Diopeithes of
Sounion for the Salaminioi. The following members of the
Salaminioi took the oath: Diopeithes son of Phasyrkides,
Philoneos son of Ameinonikos, Chalkideus son of Andromenes,
Chariades son of Charikles, Theophanes son of Zophanes,
Hegias son of Hegesias, Ameinias son of Philinos. In the
archonship for the Salaminioi of Antisthenes son of Antigenes
of Acharnai. These men for the Heptaphylai swore the oath:
Thrasykles son of Thrason, of Boutadai, Stratophon son of
Straton, of Agrylai, Melittios son of Exekestides, of
Boutadai, Aristarchos son of Demokles, of Acharnai, Arkeon
son of Eumelides, of Acharnai, Chairestratos son of Pankleides,
of Epikephisia, Demon son of Demaretos, of Agrylai.

Archeleos proposed. In order that the Salaminioi may
ever sacrifice to the gods and heroes according to the
ancestral custom and that the terms on which the arbitrators
arbitrated the dispute may become effective and to which
the persons chosen took the oath, the Salaminioi decree that
the *archon* Aristarchus inscribe all the sacrifices and the
fees of the priests on the stele on which the terms for
settlement are inscribed, so that as *archon* succeeds *archon*
for both parties, they may know what amount of money each
party must contribute for all the sacrifices from the rent
of the land and be it decreed that he set up the *stele* in
the Eurysakeion.

Mounichion. At Porthmos: to Kourotrophos a goat, 10
drachmas; to Ioleus a sheep burnt whole, 15 drachmas; to
Alkmene a sheep, 12 drachmas; to Maia a sheep, 12 drachmas;
to Heracles an ox, 70 drachmas; to the Hero at the Hale a
sheep, 15 drachmas; to the Hero at Antisara a suckling pig,
3 drachmas and 3 obols; to the Hero at Pyrgilion a suckling
pig, 3 drachmas and 3 obols; to Ion the sacrifice of a sheep
in alternate years. Wood for the sacrifices and for those
sacrifices which the state gives by law, 10 drachmas. On
the 18th of the month: to Eurysakes a pig, 40 drachmas;
wood for the sacrifice and incidentals, 3 drachmas.

Hekatombaion. At the Panathenaia: to Athena a pig, 40
drachmas; the wood for the sacrifices and incidentals, 3
drachmas.

Metageitnion. On the 7th of the month: to Apollo Patroos
a pig, 40 drachmas; to Leto a suckling pig, 3 drachmas and
3 obols; to Artemis a suckling pig, 3 drachmas and 3 obols;
to Athena Agelaa a suckling pig, 3 drachmas and 3 obols.
Wood for the sacrifices and incidentals, 3 drachmas and
3 obols.

Boedromion. To Poseidon Hippodromios a pig, 40 drachmas;
to the hero Phaiax a suckling pig, 3 drachmas and 3 obols;
to the hero Teucer a suckling pig, 3 drachmas and 3 obols;
to the hero Nauserios a suckling pig, 3 drachmas and 3
obols; wood for the sacrifice and incidentals, 3 drachmas.

Pyanepsion. On the 6th of the month: to Theseus a pig,
40 drachmas; incidentals, 3 drachmas. At the Apatouria:
to Zeus Phratrios a pig, 40 drachmas; wood for the sacrifices
and incidentals, 3 drachmas.

Maimakterion. To Athena Skiras a pregnant sheep, 12 drachmas;
to Skiros a sheep, 15 drachmas. Wood for the altar, 3
drachmas.

The total which all parties must pay for the sacrifices
is 530 drachmas and 3 obols.

These sacrifices they are to make in common from the
rental of the land at the shrine of Heracles at Sounion,
each party contributing for all the sacrifices. If anyone
proposes, or any *archon* puts a motion forward to nullify any
of these provisions or to direct the money elsewhere, he
shall be accountable to the whole *genos* and the priests likewise and be liable to a private action undertaken by any of
the Salaminioi who wishes.

2. [C. 263 B.C.]

Good Fortune. In the archonship of Phanomachos, in
Mounichion, at the festival of Heracles. The *gene* were
reconciled to each other, those of Sounion and those of
Heptaphylai, by those mediators selected by them, Antigenes

of Semachidae and Kalliteles of Sounion, on the following
terms: in respect to the precinct of Heracles the part
including the altars and what extends beyond the railing
to the first olive trees is sacred. The rest of the precinct is to be bounded on the north by the first stone wall,
on the east by the markers which divide the fields, on the
west by the *embateres*, both the one which lies by the sea
and the one above; this precinct shall be open to both
gene. The Salaminioi from Sounion shall construct a
threshing floor at their own expense in the common precinct
which is to be as large as their own, and this threshing
floor shall belong to the Salaminioi of Heptaphylai. The
house which impinges upon the precinct shall be part of the
property of the Salaminioi of Heptaphylai as the gates which
lead on both sides from the sea and the boundary stones
which divide the land and which stretch out in a straight
line. The second house, the one to the east, shall belong
as of old to the Salaminioi of Sounion as the gates which
lead from the sea and the boundary markers stretching out
straight. The gardens and half the well shall belong to
each *genos*. The Hale and the *agora* in Koile shall be common
to both *gene*; of the fields the ones lying to the east shall
as of old belong to the Salaminioi from Sounion as the
markers lie, while those to the west belong to the Salaminioi
from Heptaphylai as of old as the markers lie, and the
sacred field.

CHAPTER III. PUBLIC RELIGION

A. Ethics: Justice and the Gods

The passages from Homer which are quoted in Chapter I above do not show a very developed sense of religious ethics inasmuch as the gods do not generally concern themselves with the behavior of men toward other men. In the *Odyssey* Zeus and Athena do occasionally express a kind of moral disapproval over the actions of Clytemestra or of the suitors, but it is in Hesiod that we find a formal statement of the view that Zeus is concerned with Justice (*Dike*), punishes the wrong-doer and rewards the righteous. On early concepts of *Dike*, see. W.K.C. Guthrie, *The Greeks and their Gods* (Boston, 1951), pp. 123-127; H. Lloyd-Jones, *The Justice of Zeus* (Berkeley, 1971), pp. 35-43. Hesiod is here addressing the nobles who administer justice, preparatory to a discussion of the virtues of hard work. Hesiod lived, probably, in the later eighth century B.C.

(Hesiod, *Works and Days*, 220-262.)

Justice makes a clamor when it is being dragged where bribe-eating men do their business and make decisions with crooked judgments. She follows along weeping for the city and the people's abodes, wrapped in mist, bringing trouble to the men who drive her out and do not administer her aright. But those who dispense right judgments to strangers and neighbors and who do not transgress that which is just have a blossoming city, and a people flourishing in it; peace is on their land, raising children, and Zeus the far-seeing never imposes baneful war upon them. Famine never dwells among upright men, nor does Ruin; instead they tend their cultivated fields with festivities. The earth brings them long life, the oaks on the hills bear acorns at the top and honeybees in the trunk. Their wool-bearing sheep are heavy with fleece. The women bear children in their parents' image, and they continue to blossom with good things. They do not sail on ships, but rather the fertile soil bears its fruit. It is different for those who are given to violence and recalcitrant deeds - Zeus the far-seeing son of

Kronos imposes justice on them. Often the whole city is
involved along with the bad man who commits offense and
devises wickedness - upon them the son of Kronos hurls great
war from heaven - famine and pestilence with it, and the
people perish. Women do not bear, houses decline at the
devising of Olympian Zeus. At one time or another he destroys their army, or deprives them of their fortifications
or their ships on the sea.

O you princes, consider this Justice - the immortals
are constantly present among men; they perceive those who
wear others out and have no respect for the god's regard.
On the abundant earth are three times ten thousand immortals,
Zeus' wardens of mortal men, wrapped in mist and roaming
all over the earth, who guard judgments and recalcitrant
deeds. And there is Justice the virgin, begotten of Zeus,
renowned and respected of the gods who dwell on Olympus,
and whenever anyone causes obstruction with crooked accusa-
tions she sits by her father Zeus son of Kronos and chants
the intentions of unjust men, so that the people pay for
the wickedness of the princes, who with evil intent mis-
direct judgments with crooked decisions.

Solon, writing in Athens in the early sixth century
B.C., is concerned with the social setting in which Zeus
enforces justice. He confronts the problem, evident in his
city, of the wicked man who prospers. The conclusion he
reaches is that a man's guilt extends throughout his family;
he may escape punishment, but his descendants will pay.
Solon's Zeus and his interest in human morality is discussed
by W. Jaeger, *Paideia* I (Oxford, 1939), pp. 134-149;
H. Lloyd-Jones, *The Justice of Zeus* (Berkeley, 1971), pp. 43-
45.

(Solon, 1, lines 1-32.)

Radiant daughters of Mnemosyne [Memory] and Olympian
Zeus, ye Muses of Pieria, hear my Prayer. Grant me to have
prosperity from the blessed gods and a good reputation before all men: to be sweet to my friends, regarded with respect, and bitter to my enemies, regarded with fear. I desire
to have money, but am unwilling to obtain it unjustly - for

always Justice follows afterward. When the gods give wealth,
a man finds it steadfast from deepest root to highest peak,
but when men go after it with violence, it comes all dis-
ordered: induced by unjust doings, it follows along against
its will. Ruin is mixed up in it immediately, and it begins,
like a fire, with a little - a trifle at first, it ends in
catastrophe. The deeds of violence do not last men long.
Zeus, however, regards the end of all things; as when a
spring gale suddenly scatters the clouds, stirs up the depths
of the boundless billowing sea, ravages the fair worked
fields on the grain-bearing earth, and arrives at high heaven,
the seat of the gods, and makes the air clear again; the sun
shines on the fair, fertile earth, and not a cloud is to be
seen. Such is the retribution of Zeus. He does not, like
a mortal, become angry at each thing; but the man of sinful
mind does not get away unnoticed in perpetuity. Inevitably
he is found out in the end. One pays immediately, another
pays later; some escape, and their due from the gods misses
them themselves. Still, it does arrive: the innocent pay
for their deeds, their children or their posterity.

    Aeschylus' *Oresteia* is a cycle of three plays exploring
blood-revenge and its relationship to a more civic-oriented
system of justice under the protection of society's gods.
The following short passage from the first play, *Agamemnon*,
draws its contrast between the claims of position (noble
birth, wealth and prestige) and those of right behavior.
Justice neglected brings ruin even to the noblest of families; Justice revered is a glorious possession even in humble
surroundings. For discussion of the moral and religious
attitudes of Aeschylus, see F. Solmsen, *Hesiod and Aeschylus*
(Ithaca, 1949), pp. 112-123; A. Podlecki, *The Political
Background of Aeschylean Tragedy* (Ann Arbor, 1966), pp. 63-
78.

(Aeschylus, *Agamemnon*, 750-781.)

    The old saying has long been told among mortals, that
when a man's wealth grows to greatness it produces offspring,
and does not die childless; from good fortune blooms forth
in turn insatiable grief. I have my own opinion, different
from others: to me it is the impious deed that breeds progeny

befitting its own descent; just, upright households produce
in due course the blessing of beautiful children.

Old Violence inclines sooner or later to breed, when
the day fixed for fruition arrives, renewed violence in the
evil acts of mortals, and it breeds the incontestable, in-
·vincible *daimon* that unholy affront to homes, Ruin, black
in its parents' image.

But Justice shines in smoke-filled houses, it respects
the righteous life. With eyes averted it departs from halls
gold-flecked with filthy hands; it approaches reverent homes;
it does not honor the value of wealth struck with counterfeit
praise; and it brings everything to its culmination.

The claims of two types of laws, the time-honored
rituals of the gods, and the *ad hoc* decrees of civic authority, conflict in Sophocles' *Antigone*, written and produced
near the middle of the fifth century B.C. King Kreon has
forbidden the burial of Polyneikes, a son of Oedipus who
had attacked his own city of Thebes. Polyneikes' sister
Antigone defies Kreon's edict and buries the corpse; in the
following speech she justifies her actions, arguing that
following the traditional religious practices is more just
than obeying a transitory, man-made law.

(Sophocles, *Antigone*, 449-470.)

Kreon: And how did you dare to violate these laws?
Antigone: It does not seem to me that Zeus proclaimed them,
nor did Justice, who dwells with the gods below, proclaim
such laws; I did not think *your* decrees could so prevail
that a mere mortal would outstrip unwritten, unshaken usages
of the gods. The usages live, not just today and yesterday,
but forever - no one knows even when they first came to
light. I was not about to risk paying the penalty of violating these usages, not out of fear of any man's opinion:
I will die: I knew it, how could I not, even if you had not
proclaimed it. If I shall die before my time, I count that
as gain. Where a person lives, as I do, in the midst of many
evils, how can death bring anything but gain? To me, to meet
this fate is negligible pain; but if I allowed my mother's
dead son to lie a corpse unburied, at that I would feel grief.

But I am not grieved by what I have done, and if it seems
to you that I am being foolish, perhaps the foolishness is
in the eye of a fool. ...

   The importance of an inner sense of morality, rather
than a merely external code of behavior is given classic
expression in Socrates' brief prayer preserved in Plato's
Phaedrus. Plato's own researches into the nature of justice
are set forth in the *Republic*, where however the reference
to the gods is superceded by a more generally humanistic
concept.

(Plato, *Phaedrus*, 279b-c.)

Socrates: "O dear Pan and all ye other gods in this place,
grant me to become inwardly fair, and as for everything I
possess externally, may it be concordant with my inner disposition. May I consider the wise man wealthy, and may I
have as much gold as only the moderate man can take and
bear."

B. Delphic Piety

The oracular shrine at Delphi assumed an important
role in the life of Greece as early as the seventh century
B.C., and continued to prosper until the period of Roman
domination. Its prestige was unmatched, and city-states,
kings and private individuals made requests of the oracle,
and proved their devotion by dedicating elaborate gifts.
On the history of the oracle, see H.W. Parke and D.E.W.
Wormell, *The Delphic Oracle* (Oxford, 1956); W.G. Forrest,
"Colonization and the rise of Delphi," *Historia* 6 (1957),
160-175. On the archaeological excavations, see the detailed
accounts in *Fouilles de Delphes* (Paris, 1906-   ). Briefer
treatments are by A. Kalogeropoulou in *The Greek Experience*
(ed. Evi Melas, New York, 1974), pp. 59-74; R.A. Tomlinson,
Greek Sanctuaries (New York, 1976).

Croesus

One of Delphi's most enthusiastic supporters in the
sixth century B.C. was Croesus, king of Lydia in Asia Minor.
This account of his testing of the oracles and of the elaborate dedications he made at Delphi is by Herodotus, who
used the monuments at Delphi as primary documentary sources
in the research for his history of the Persian Wars and
their background.

(Herodotus, *The Histories* I. 46-54.)

Croesus began to consider if it would be possible to

contain the growing might of the Persians before they be-

came too powerful. With this idea in mind he set out to

test the oracles of Greece and Libya, sending messengers to

Delphi, to Abai in Phokis, and to Dodona, to the oracles of

Amphiaraos and Trophonios, and to Branchidai at Miletus:

to these Greek oracles Croesus sent his inquiries, as well

as to the oracle of Ammon in Libya. He wanted to test the

perceptions of the oracles; if they were found to perceive

truly, he intended to send a second inquiry, whether to

undertake a campaign against the Persians. (47) He gave

instructions to the messengers and sent them on their trial

of the oracles: on the 100th day after setting out from

Sardis [Croesus' capital], they were to inquire of the oracles

what Croesus, son of Alyattes, king of the Lydians, was doing;

then they were to have each oracle's response written down
and bring it back to him. Now the responses of the others
are not recorded by anyone at all, but at Delphi as soon
as the Lydians entered the sanctuary to inquire of the god,
while they were still asking what they had been commanded,
the Pythia gave this verse response:

> I count the grains of the sand, and I measure out the
>   sea's vastness,
> I understand the mute, and I hear the man who does
>   not speak.
> Now an aroma comes to my senses, of sturdy-shelled
>   tortoise,
> Cooking and boiling in cauldron of bronze, in a stew
>   of young lamb's flesh,
> Bronze underneath spreads out, and above is laid a
>   bronze cover.

(48)   The Lydians had the Pythia's response written, and
then returned to Sardis. When the other deputations brought
their oracles back, Croesus read them, but none of them came
close. When however he heard what came from Delphi, he
welcomed the response and uttered a prayer, recognizing the
Delphic oracle as the only one because it had revealed to
him what he had been doing: for when he sent out the embassies to the oracles he waited for the appointed day and then
devised this plan, thinking up things which it would be next
to impossible to invent or desire - by himself he chopped
up a tortoise and a lamb and boiled them in a bronze cauldron,
putting on a bronze cover. (49) Such was the response from
Delphi. As for the answer of the oracle of Amphiaraos, I can
not say what its response was to the Lydians after they had
performed the customary rites there (for this is not recorded
either), other than that he also recognized that it too pos-
sessed a faultless oracle.

   (50) After this he made petition to the god at Delphi
with magnificent sacrifices: he sacrificed all the proper
animals, then piled up a great pyre with gilded and silvered
couches, golden libation bowls and purple robes and cloaks,

and set fire to it, hoping by this to increase the god's
favor toward him. He also ordered all the Lydians to sacrifice everything they could afford. When the sacrifice was
finished, he melted down an immense quantity of gold and
cast 117 ingots, six palms long, three palms wide and one
palm high; of these four were of pure gold, weighing 2 1/2
talents each, and the rest were of white gold, amounting to
two talents. He also had made a pure gold statue of a lion,
weighing ten talents. When the temple at Delphi burned down,
this lion fell from the ingots [on which it had been placed].
It now stands in the Corinthian treasury - it weighs 6 1/2
talents, for 3 1/2 talents melted away in the fire. (51)
In addition Croesus also sent: two large wine bowls, one
gold and one silver: the gold one used to stand on the
right of the temple entrance, and the silver one on the
left. These were also moved during the fire; the gold is
in the treasury of Klazomenai (it weighs 8 1/2 talents and
12 minas) and the silver at the corner of the fore-temple;
it contains 600 amphorai - the Delphians fill it with wine
at the festival of the Theophania. The Delphians say it is
the work of Theodoros of Samos, and I agree that it is an
uncommonly fine work. He also sent four silver jars, which
stand in the Corinthian treasury, and he dedicated two
water basins, a gold and a silver (a false inscription says
the gold one is a dedication of the Lacedaemonians, but it
is also Croesus', and one of the Delphians added the inscription to flatter the Lacedaemonians. The child with water
flowing through his hand was made by the Lacedaemonians, but
neither of the water basins is.) Croesus also sent other
dedications without inscriptions, including circular round
basins and a three-cubit high gold statue of a woman which
the Delphians call "Croesus' baker-woman." Besides this
Croesus also dedicated the necklace and belt of his own
wife... .

(54.2) The Delphians granted to Croesus and the Lydians
the right of prior consultation, exemption from taxes, the
right to a front row seat at festivals, and the right in
perpetuity for any of them to become a citizen of Delphi.

The Morality of the Oracle

The prestige of the oracle at Delphi was reflected in
a moral tradition summarized in the precepts "Nothing in
Excess" and "Know Thyself." Delphi's moral authority is
asserted in the following selections - first, Socrates yields
to it the establishment of religious usages; then Plutarch
summarizes the brief maxims posted near the entrance to
Apollo's temple; finally an inscription lists the precepts
of the seven sages, which were erected on a column in front
of the temple at Delphi. On Delphi's role as moral arbiter,
see M.P. Nilsson, *Greek Piety* (London, 1947), pp. 41-52.

(Plato, *Republic* IV. 427b-c.)

"We are finished with our part of the law-making," I
[Socrates] said, "but the greatest, finest, most important
legislation remains for Apollo of Delphi to do." "What is
it?" he said. "Establishment of temples, sacrifices, and
other rites of gods, *daimones* and heroes; burial of the
dead and the various duties to those in the Beyond which are
necessary to propitiate them. We know nothing of such matters, and if we are sensible in founding our city we will
not follow the instructions of any interpreter of divine
love other than the traditional one, for he is a god who is
the traditional interpreter of such things to all men, sitting on the *omphalos* [navel] to deliver the interpretation."

(Plutarch, *On Garrulity*, 511a.)

The brevity of the ancients is admired: in the temple
of Pythian Apollo the Amphictyons have inscribed not the
Iliad or the *Odyssey*, nor the hymns of Pindar, but "Know
thyself," "Nothing in excess" and "Pledge, and do harm."

(*SIG*[3] 1268.)

Column I.
Aid friends. Control anger. Shun unjust acts. Acknowledge
sacred things. Control pleasure. Consider luck. Honor
forethought. Do not use an oath. Love friendship. Hold
on to learning. Pursue good repute. Praise virtue. Do
just acts. Return favor. Be well disposed to friends.

Avoid enemies. Cultivate kinsmen. Keep from evil. Be
common [? i.e., accessible, affable?]. Guard your property.
Oblige a friend. Hate violence. Be soft-spoken. Pity
suppliants. Educate sons.

Column II.

Accomplish your limit. Be kind to all. Rule your wife.
Do well by yourself. Be affable. Answer at the right
moment. Work with a good reputation. When you err, re-
pent. Control your eye. Guard friendship. Consider the
time. Act promptly. Dispense justice. Practice concord.
Despise no one. Keep secret things hidden. Respect the
prevailing power. Trust time. Do not make pleasant small-
talk. Worship the divine. Accept opportunity. Dissolve
enmity. Do not boast in your strength. Accept old age.
Use what is advantageous. Practice speaking words of good
omen. Be ashamed of a lie. Shun enmity. ...

Consulting the Oracle

The following passage from Euripides' play *Ion* con-
sists of the song of the temple attendant who while sweeping
the front steps points out some of the sights and then out-
lines, in soliloquy and in a conversation with some newly
arrived visitors, the process of consulting the oracle. For
the procedures followed in making a request of the oracle,
see H.W. Parke and D.E.W. Wormell, *The Delphic Oracle*
(Oxford, 1956), pp. 17–45.

(Euripides, *Ion*, 83–108, 219–228.)

Ion: Those are the brilliant four-horse chariots; Helius
already casts his light upon the earth, and before the
ethereal flame the stars flee into the sacred night.

The untrod peaks of Parnassus, lightened, receive the
rim of day's wheel for mortal men. The smoke of dry incense
floats up to the roofs of Phoebus.

The Delphian woman sits on the most holy tripod, singing
to the Greeks whatever sounds Apollo murmurs.

But do you go, O Delphian attendants of Apollo, to the
silvery swirls of Castalia; bathe in the pure waters and
proceed to the temples, guard your mouths in well-omened

silence - it is good so - and reveal well-meaning speeches
to those who intend to consult the oracle. My own tasks
are those I have performed since childhood, with branches
of laurel and sacred fillets to make Phoebus' entrance
clean, and the floor moist with drops of water; and to put
to flight with my arrows the flocks of birds which foul the
holy dedications.

Chorus of slave women; to Ion: You there, beside the
temple: is it lawful for us to tread upon the recesses of
the shrine, with pure foot...

Ion: It is not, strangers.

Chorus: Might we then ask you for some information?

Ion: What is that you want?

Chorus: Does the temple of Phoebus really contain the
navel of the earth?

Ion: Yes - wrapped in fillets, with Gorgons all around.

Chorus: ... just as the story says!

Ion: If you have sacrificed a wheat-cake before the temple
and want to make some inquiry of Phoebus, proceed to the
altar; but you must slaughter a sheep to enter the temple's
inner recess.

Oracular Responses from Delphi

      This selection of oracles from the seventh through the
fourth centuries B.C. illustrates the range of the oracle's
interest and authority. They include (A) Croesus' request
for political and military advice, (B) a spontaneous rejection of an embassy on grounds of moral impurity, (C) a
miraculous cure, (D) a pair of warnings to the Athenians
to flee before the Persian invaders in 480 B.C., (E & F)
admonitions to simple piety, (G) Socrates' advice on how to
consult the oracle, (H) requests to settle inter-city
rivalries, (I) advice on the establishment of a new colony,
(J) an ambiguous oracle culminating in just punishment,
(K) a response about proper sacrifices after an omen appeared in the sky, (L) a request from Philip, the father
of Alexander the Great, about a domestic matter, (M) an
oracle demanding reparation from the killer of a poet, and
(N) an inscription from Athens providing for an elaborate
procedure to assure an impartial answer from the god.

A. (Herodotus, *The Histories* I. 53.1.) Croesus commanded
the Lydians who were going to take his gifts to the shrines
[of Delphi and Amphiaraos] to ask the oracles whether he
should conduct a military campaign against the Persians and
should add some friendly army to his own as an ally. ...The
responses of both oracles agreed in advising Croesus that,
if he were to campaign against the Persians, he would destroy
a mighty empire; they also advised him to find the strongest
of the Greeks and make them his allies.

B. (Aelian, *Varia Historia* III. 43.) [During a revolution
at Sybaris a harp-player was killed when he sought sanctuary
at an altar. Later] the Sybarites sent an embassy to Delphi,
and the Pythia answered,

> Go from my tripods away, for all over thy hands still
> > is dripping
> Murder vast and unchecked, and it holds thee back from
> > my threshold.
> Never to thee will I prophesy, thou who hast killed at
> > the altar of Hera
> One holy slave of the Muses; thou hast not avoided
> > gods' vengeance.
> Those who do evil must pay the full measure of justice:
> > no mercy
> And no delay may be granted, not even to great Zeus's
> > offspring.
> But fast to their own heads, and in the midst of their
> > children,
> It keeps on clinging, and grief upon grief comes upon
> > all their households.

C. (Plutarch, *Bravery of Women*, 245c-d.) They say that
Telesilla, who was of an important family, was sick in her
body, and sent to the god to ask about health. The response
was that she should serve the Muses. Obedient to the god
she dedicated herself to musical performance and composition;
she straightway recovered from her affliction, and was admired
for her skill.

D. (Herodotus, *The Histories* VII. 140.) The Athenians had
sent envoys to Delphi and were prepared to consult the
oracle. When they had performed the traditional rites
around the shrine, entered the temple chamber and taken
their seats, the Pythia, whose name was Aristonike, gave
this response:

> Why do you sit here, you wretched ones? Go, flee
>   away to the farthest
> Ends of the earth, leave the wheel-shaped city
>   surrounding its lofty
> Citadel. Neither the head will remain intact, nor
>   the body;
> Neither the nethermost feet, nor the hands will be
>   left, neither any
> Part in between: it will all disappear, be cast down
>   into ruin;
> Fire and the Syrian chariots of Ares the fierce will
>   destroy it.
> He will demolish as well many other strong forts, not
>   yours only.
> And he will put many temples of gods to the ravishing
>   war-fire.
> Temples which now still stand, but stand all dripping
>   and sweating,
> Shaking and quaking with fear, while down from the
>   loftiest roof-tops
> Black blood pours as an omen, presaging the onset of
>   evil.
> Go now from this holy chamber, and let your mind dwell
>   on these evils.

When the Athenian envoys heard this, they took it as disastrous news. As they were giving in to despair at the
predicted catastrophe, Timon the son of Androboulos, one of
the most respected of the Delphians, advised them to take
olive branches and to go back a second time as suppliants
to consult the oracle. The Athenians were persuaded by
this and said, "O Lord, give to us some more favorable

response concerning our fatherland, and respect these boughs
which we bear. Otherwise, we will not depart from the
sanctuary, but will remain until we gain our end."

In answer the prophetess gave this second response:

Pallas cannot now completely prevail with Zeus on
    Olympus

Pleading her suit with plenty of craftily compacted
    speeches;

But I will speak this word once again, hard as steel
    adamantine:

Though everything will be captured between the
    boundaries of Kekrops

And the recesses enclosed by the most holy mountain
    Kithairon,

One refuge only does Zeus grant Athena, the Trito-born
    goddess,

That is a wall of wood, which will benefit thee and
    thy children.

Now must thou not stay quiet, awaiting the onslaught
    of horses:

Do not delay till the infantry comes from afar - no,
    withdraw now

Turning thy back in flight: there will still be a day
    to confront him.

Salamis, thou, divine island, wilt bring death to the
    souls of the mothers,

Whether in season of scattering seed or of gathering
    harvest.

E. (Theopompus, in Porphyry, *On Abstinence* II. 16; frag.
344 in F. Jacoby, *FGrH* 115.) Theopompus reported that a rich
man from Magnesia in Asia Minor arrived at Delphi. He was
very wealthy, the owner of many herds of cattle... It was
his habit every year to make many magnificent sacrifices on
account of his prosperity, piety and desire to please the
gods. Being so religiously inclined he came to Delphi leading
a procession of a hundred cattle for sacrifice to the god,

and after a glorious display of honor to the god he passed
into the consultation chamber in order to question the
oracle. In his confidence that of all men he worshipped
the gods best, he asked the Pythia to declare who worshipped
the deity best and most devotedly and who made the most
pleasing sacrifices - he supposed that first place would be
given to him. But the priestess answered that Klearchos,
a resident of Methydrion in Arcadia, worshipped the gods
best of all. He was utterly amazed at this and eager to
meet this man and learn how he performed his sacrifices.
So he immediately went to Methydrion, noticed with disdain
that it was a small and insignificant place and thought that
not even the whole town, much less any of its private citizens, could honor the gods more magnificently and finely
than he. Nevertheless he found the man and asked him to
tell how he honored the gods. Klearchos said that he performed the sacrifices earnestly at the appropriate times,
on the new moon of each month crowning and cleaning Hermes
and Hecate and the other images which his ancestors had
left and that he honored them with incense, barley-cakes
and wheat-cakes. Each year he took part in the public
sacrifices, omitting none of the festivals. At these festivals he worshipped the gods not by slaughtering and butchering
victims, but by sacrificing whatever he happened to have,
preferably some of the available seasonal fruits which he
received from the earth, and rendering first-fruits to the
gods; some he would offer fresh, others as burnt offerings.

F. (Plutarch, *Letter to Apollonius*, 109a-b.) Pindar the
poet says that Agamedes and Trophonios built the temple in
Delphi, and when it was finished they asked Apollo for their
reward; he promised to pay them in seven days; he advised
them to enjoy themselves in the meantime. They did what he
had commanded, and on the seventh night they lay down to
sleep, and died.
    The story is told that when envoys were sent by the
Boeotians to the god's oracle, the poet Pindar enjoined them

to inquire what the best thing for men is. The prophetess
replied that he knew that perfectly well himself, at least
if he really was the author of the poem about Trophonios
and Agamedes; if he wanted to learn by experience, it would
become clear to him in a short time. When he heard this,
he inferred that he was near death, and after a little
while he died.

G. (Xenophon, *Anabasis* III. 1.5.) Socrates advised Xenophon
to go to Delphi and consult with the god about his journey.
So Xenophon went and asked Apollo to which god he should
sacrifice and pray in order best to make the trip which he
intended and to do it in health and safety. Apollo in
response named the gods to whom he ought to sacrifice. When
he came back, he told the oracle to Socrates, who criticized
him because he had not first asked whether it would be better to make the journey or to stay at home, rather than
deciding to go and then asking how best to make the journey;
"Since, however," he said, "you have already asked, you must
do everything that the god has commanded."

H. (Diodorus, *Library of History* XV. 18.1-2.) In Asia
Minor... the Persian admiral Tachos founded a city on a
cliff near the sea, which is called Leuke and has a sacred
shrine of Apollo. A little later [383 B.C.] he died, and
the people of Klazomenai and of Kymai came into conflict
over this city. At first the cities tried to decide the
issue by war, but someone suggested that they ask the god
which of the cities ought to be in control of Leuke. The
Pythia decided that it was the one which first offered
sacrifice in Leuke: they were to start out, each from their
own city, at sunrise on that day to which both parties would
agree.

I. (Scholiast on Clement of Alexandria, *Protrepticus* II.
11.) Karanos of Argos, the son of Poianthes, intended to
send a colony to Macedonia; so he went to Delphi, and Apollo
gave him this oracle:

Noble Karanos, consider and take well to heart now
    my message.
Leaving your Argos and Hellas, the home of fair,
    beautiful women,
Go all the way to the source of the river that's
    called Haliakmon.
There when you first see goats grazing, then that
    is the time it is fated:
Dwell there in happiness, you and all of your future
    descendants.

J. (Lycurgus, *Against Leocrates*, 93.) Who of the old does
not remember, or who of the young has not heard of,
Kallistratos, whom the city condemned to death. He went
into exile and heard from the god at Delphi that if he went
to Athens he would gain the benefit of the law. So he went
back and took refuge at the altar of the Twelve Gods; nevertheless he was put to death by the city. This was right,
for in the case of criminals the benefit of the law is to
get punishment.

K. (Demosthenes, *Against Macartatos*, 66.) The Athenian
people inquires about the sign which has occurred in the
sky, and what the Athenians should do, or to which god they
should sacrifice or pray, in order for the best result to
come from the sign. Reply: Concerning the sign which has
occurred in the sky, it is advantageous for the Athenians
to sacrifice with good omens to Zeus Hypatos [Most High],
Athena Hypate [Most High], Heracles, Apollo Soter [Savior],
Lato and Artemis, to fill the streets with the aroma of sacrifices, to arrange choirs and bowls of mixed wine and to wear
garlands, in the traditional manner, in honor of all the
Olympian gods and goddesses, holding up right arms and left,
and to bring the traditional offerings. To the founding hero
whose name you bear, offer the traditional sacrifices and
native gifts. If any persons die on the appointed day, any
passers-by are to perform the proper rites for them.

L. (Plutarch, *Life of Alexander*, 2-3.) A while after his
marriage, Philip had a dream in which he saw himself placing
a seal on his wife's womb; the figure on the seal was a
lion... After this vision Philip sent Chairon of Megalopolis
to Delphi, where he is said to have received an oracle from
the god commanding him to sacrifice to Ammon and to revere
that god most, adding that he would lose one of his eyes,
the one with which he had spied through the chink in the
door and seen the god in the form of a serpent lying with
his wife.

M. (Plutarch, *The Divine Vengeance*, 560e.) The man who
killed the poet Archilochus in battle was Kallondas, nick-
named Korax [the Crow]. At first he was thrown out by the
Pythia, because he had killed the holy man of the Muses
["Thou who hast struck down the Muses' attendant, get out
of my temple!"]. Then using various prayers and entreaties
to justify himself, he was ordered to go to the dwelling of
Tettix (at Tainaros) and supplicate the soul of Archilochus.

N. (*SIG*[3] I. 204, lines 31-51; *IG* II[2] 204, from 352/1 B.C.)
[The Athenian people are unsure whether they may cultivate
the sacred plot of the goddesses Demeter and Kore; ...the
alternatives are to be engraved on tin plates and the appropriate official] is to wrap each plate in wool and put
them in a bronze jar in the presence of the people. The
presiding officers [*prytaneis*] are to prepare these things,
and the treasurers of the goddess [Athena] are immediately
to bring a gold jar and a silver jar into the midst of the
people. The *epistates* is to shake up the bronze jar and
draw out each tin plate in turn, and put the first one into
the gold jar and the other into the silver jar, then to tie
them up. The *epistates* is to mark it with the public seal,
and any other Athenian who wishes may put his own seal on
besides. Then the treasurers are to carry the jars to the
Acropolis. Next the people is to choose three men, one from
the council and two from the whole citizen body, to go to

Delphi and ask the god which of the written plans the
Athenians should follow in regard to the sacred land, that
in the gold jar or that in the silver. When they come back
from consulting the god, they are to deliver the jars and
both the prophecy and the writing on both tin plates are
to be read to the people: whichever writing the god indicates is more advantageous to the Athenian people, so shall
it be done...

C.   Sacrifices

The Ceremony

The central religious act of the Greeks was the sacrifice of fruit, grain or (most spectacularly) an animal.   Two
passages from Homer's *Odyssey* illustrate the details of
animal sacrifice accompanied by prayer.   The first describes
a public festival occasion at which Nestor, king of Pylos,
celebrates a solemn sacrifice to Poseidon.   The second is
more private; it takes place in the hut of Eumaios, the
swine-herd of Odysseus, and is not much more than the
ritualized butchering of a pig for supper.

(Homer, *Odyssey* III. 439-463.)

Stratios and noble Echephron led an ox by the horns,
and Aretos came from the chamber bringing them lustral water
in a flower-decked cauldron; in the other hand he held barley-
meal in a basket.   Thrasymedes stood by with a sharp axe in
his hand to strike the ox dead.   Perseus held a bowl [to
receive the blood].   Old Nestor, the horseman, began to pour
down the lustral water and sprinkle the barley-meal.   He
made many prayers to Athena, setting aside as first-fruits
hairs from the victim's head and tossing them in the fire.
When they had prayed and sprinkled out the barley, bold
Thrasymedes, Nestor's son, moved up and struck: the axe
cut the neck tendons and stunned the ox.   The women let out
a shrill cry, Nestor's daughters, daughters-in-law and wife,
Klymenos' eldest daughter Eurydike.   The men raised it from
the ground, and Peisistratos cut its throat.   Its dark blood
flowed out, its life left its bones.   Straightway they
quartered it, and cut off all the thigh-pieces, covered them
with fat, folded them double, and placed pieces of raw flesh
on them.   The old man burnt them on split wood, and poured
sparkling wine on it.   The young men, beside him, held forked
spits in their hands.   When both the thighs had burned up
and they had tasted the intestines, they cut the rest into
smaller pieces and skewered them on spits, then took the
sharp spits in their hands and roasted them.

(Homer, *Odyssey* XIV. 418-436.)

[The swineherd] cut the wood with his bronze axe, and
the others brought in a fat five-year-old boar and made it
stand by the hearth. The swineherd did not forget the immortals, for he had a good spirit. Setting aside as first-
fruits hairs from the head of the white-toothed boar he
tossed them in the fire and prayed to all the gods for
Odysseus to return to his home. He raised himself up and
struck with a piece of oak which he had cut, and the life
left the boar. The others cut its throat and singed its
hair. Straightway they quartered it and the swineherd laid
on pieces of raw flesh, starting with all the limbs and
ending with the fatty tissue. They tossed these in the fire
and sprinkled it with barley-meal. They cut the rest into
smaller pieces and skewered them on spits. They roasted
them carefully and removed them, and piled them on wooden
platters. The swineherd stood up to distribute it, for he
had a sense of fairness. He divided it all up in seven
portions - one for the Nymphs and Hermes, the son of Maia,
which he set aside with a prayer,[10] and the rest he distributed to each person.

The Rationale

As the preceding passages from the *Odyssey* show, it was
customary for the human participants in a sacrifice to eat
the best parts of the victim. Hesiod, in the *Theogony*, gives
an aetiological explanation of this custom. Cf. J. Rudhardt,
"Les mythes Grecs relatifs a l'instauration du Sacrifice,"
Museum Helveticum 27 (1970) 1-15; J.P. Vernant, "Pensée
Sociale et Religieuse de la Grèce Ancienne," *Annuaire de
l'Ecole Pratique des Hautes Études* (Paris), v[e] Sec., Sc.
Relig. 81, 3 (1973-74) 259-276.

(Hesiod, *Theogony*, 535-557.)

Once when the gods and mortal men were disputing at
Mekone, Prometheus divided up a large ox with careful thought
and set it before them, intending to deceive Zeus. To the
men he served flesh and intestines rich in fat inside a skin,
covered with the ox's stomach. To Zeus in turn he served the

white bones of the ox arranged with tricky craft, and he
covered it with white fat.

Then the father of men and gods said to him, "Prometheus,
son of Iapetos, most renowned of all sovereigns, esteemed
one, what a discrepancy there is in the portions you have
distributed." So spoke Zeus in mockery, for he knew about
resourceful schemes.

Wily Prometheus spoke to him in answer, with a little
smile as he remembered his crafty trick: "Zeus, most glorious, most great of the ever-living gods, choose whichever
of these your heart urges you to take."

He said this in his craftiness, but Zeus who knew about
resourceful schemes was aware of the trick. He espied
trouble for mortal men and he intended to bring it about:
so with both hands he selected the white fat - anger surrounded him, and wrath went through his heart, when he saw
the white bones of the ox, the crafty trick. Ever since,
the human race on the earth burns white bones to the immortals on smoking altars.

In spite of Hesiod's explanation, it seemed to many
Greeks that sacrifices were often nothing more than excuses
for a big banquet. In the following selection Knemon, the
grouch-hero of one of Menander's comedies (written in the
fourth century) complains about the increasing elaboration
and irreverence of sacrifices.

(Menander, *Dyskolos*, 447-453.)

What sacrifices these scoundrels make! They bring their
picnic boxes, their wine-jars, not for the gods, but themselves. The incense and barley-cake is holy enough. The
god gets all that, put there on the fire; and they put on
the tail bone and the bile, because they are inedible, for
the gods - then they gulp down all the rest.

Sacrificial Procedure

Each month the Elean attendants at the sanctuary of Zeus
at Olympia conducted sacrifices at a solemn procession to a
long series of altars in and around the sacred precinct.

Pausanias' guide-book to Olympia details the order of the
sacrifices, and concludes with the following account of the
procedure. It illustrates incidentally the personnel in
attendance at the ceremony.

(Pausanias, *Description of Greece* V. 15.10-12.)

    Once each month the Eleans sacrifice on all the altars
listed. They sacrifice in an ancient manner, burning incense
on the altars along with wheat kneaded with honey, then lay
on olive twigs and pour a libation of wine - except at the
altars to the Nymphs, to the Ladies [*Despoinai*], and to all
the gods in common, where it is not proper to offer wine.
The sacrifices are under the supervision of the *theokolos*
who holds that office for the month, the soothsayers, the
libation-bearers, the *exegetes* [interpreter], the flute-
player and the wood-man. They speak traditional words at
the libations in the *prytaneion* and sing hymns, but it is
not fitting for me to introduce them into my account. They
pour libations not only to the Greek gods but also to the
god in Libya [Ammon], to Hera Ammonia and to Parammon.
(Parammon is an epithet of Hermes.) ... The Eleans also pour
libations to the heroes and the wives of heroes who are paid
honor either in the district of Elis or in Aetolia. The
hymns they sing in the *prytaneion* are in the Doric dialect,
but they do not say who composed them.

Sacrifice and Augury

    In addition to the verbal communications of the oracles,
the gods were also thought to speak to men by means of the
entrails of sacrificial victims. The following episode from
Xenophon's account of a military expedition at the end of
the fifth century shows him consulting the sacrificial victims for help in a personal decision, whether to assume sole
command of the army.

(Xenophon, *Anabasis* VI. 1.17-24.)

    In choosing a commander ... they turned to Xenophon.
The captains came to him and said that this was the army's
judgment and each of them showed good will and tried to

persuade him to take the command. Xenophon himself was
inclined to desire the command, because he thought that he
would gain more honor among his friends and a greater reputation when he came home. It might also happen that he
would be the cause of some good to the army. These reflec-
tions urged him to take sole command. But on the other hand
he noted that for every man the outcome of the future is
unclear and for this reason there was danger that he might
lose the good reputation he had already acquired, and so
he was in doubt.

Since he could not decide, he thought it best to consult the gods. He brought two victims to the altar and
offered sacrifice to King Zeus as was prescribed for him by
the oracle at Delphi, and because he thought that from that
god came the dream which he had when he took the initial
step towards a share of the command. He remembered that
when he was setting out from Ephesus to join Cyrus an eagle
screamed on his right; however, it was sitting down, which
the soothsayer who was escorting him said was a bird for
the great rather than for the ordinary person, and its appearance symbolized glory, but also hard work, for other
birds attack the eagle when it is sitting. The bird also
did not prophecy profit, for the eagle captures its food
while flying. So Xenophon offered sacrifice and the god
signified clearly that he should not seek the command, not
accept it if he were selected. So the matter ended.

Sometimes the gods refused to accept the sacrifices
offered to them. In this passage Sophocles has the prophet
Teiresias report on the bad omens he has observed both in
the patterns of flying birds and in the inauspicious occur-
rences at sacrifices; both indicate the gods' displeasure
with King Kreon, who has forbidden the burial of his nephew
Polyneikes, in violation of Greek funeral custom.

(Sophocles, *Antigone*, 998-1011.)

Teiresias: You will know the trouble, when you hear the
signs my art interprets. I was sitting at the old place of
augury, where I observe the gathering of every sort of bird;

I heard the cryptic voice of the birds, set to clamoring
unintelligibly, goaded by some evil; I realized that they
were tearing at each other with murderous claws; there was
meaning in the flapping of wings.

With sudden fear I made trial of the burnt-offerings
on the kindled altars - from the sacrifices none of
Hephaestus' fire shown forth; instead the thigh portions
became soggy and sodden, smoldering and sputtering. The
gall bladder burst and sputtered bile, and the dripping
thigh-pieces lay bared of their wrapping of fat.

The Swearing of Oaths

To swear an oath with proper solemnity and efficacy,
it was necessary to call the gods to witness and implicate
their divine prestige in the oath. In the *Iliad*, Agamemnon
returns the girl Briseis to Achilles with an apology and
an oath that he has not violated her. Homer appropriately
surrounds the oath-taking with a scene of sacrifice - this
sacrifice differs from most in that the victim is not eaten,
but devoted entirely to the god, as Pausanias points out
in his account of the athletes' oath to Zeus at Olympia.

(Homer, *Iliad* XIX. 252-268.)

Agamemnon drew a knife which he always wore in his
sword's scabbard; setting aside as first-fruits hairs from
a wild boar and raising his hands to Zeus, he prayed; and
all the Argives stood silently by him in order, listening
to the king. Making his prayer he looked toward broad
heaven and said, "May now Zeus know first, most high and
most perfect of the gods, and Earth and Sun and the Furies
who under the earth punish men who swear false oaths: I
have not laid a hand upon the girl Briseis, neither to sleep
with her nor for any other reason. She has remained, untouched, in my tent. If any of this is falsely sworn, may
the gods give me all the many pains which they give to a
person who commits sin against them when he swears."

So he spoke, and slit the throat of the boar with the
pitiless bronze. Talthybios spun it around and hurled it
into the great expanse of the sea.

(Pausanias, *Description of Greece* V. 24.9-11.)

   The statue of Zeus in the council-house [at Olympia]
is made, more than any of his other statues, to strike wrong-
doers with terror. It is called Zeus of the Oaths, and
holds a thunderbolt in each hand. It is customary for the
contestants, their fathers and brothers, and even their
trainers, to swear on the sacrificial flesh of a wild boar
that there will be no cheating on their part in the Olympic
games. The contestants swear in addition that for ten con-
secutive months they have perfectly followed all the training
rules.

   Those who examine the boys and the colts which compete
also take an oath to make their examination fairly and without bribes, and to keep secret the reasons for approval or
rejection. I did not think to ask what it is the custom to
do with the boar on which the athletes take their oath,
since among the ancients custom ordained in regard to sacrifices that the victim on which an oath was made was not to
be eaten by any man. Homer shows this, for the boar on which
Agamemnon swore that Briseis had not shared his bed was thrown
by the herald into the sea.

A Calendar of Sacrifices from Marathon

   Individual localities had their annual and biennial
cycle of rites, as attested by this inscription, a list of
the official sacrifices held by the Athenian deme of Marathon
and the cost of each. The inscription, published and discussed briefly by R.B. Richardson, "A sacrificial calendar
from the Epakria," *American Journal of Archaology* 10 (1895)
209-226, is dated to the early fourth century.[11]

(*IG* II[2] 1358, col. ii, lines 1-53.)

   [The deme-leader of the Ma]rathonians makes the following sacrifices [in the first quarter of the year: ...within]
ten days. To the Hero, [a pig, 3 drachmas; to the Heroine,]
a pig, 3 drachmas. A table[12] for the Hero [and the Heroine,
1 drachmas.] In the month Boedromion, before the Mysteries
[- - -] an ox, 90 drachmas, a sheep, 12 drachmas; to
Kourotrophos [. . .].

In the second quarter: in the month Posideon [- - -]
an ox, 150 drachmas; a sheep, 12 drachmas; to the Heroine,
[a sheep, 11 drachmas, priestly portion,] 7 drachmas. To
Ge [Earth] "in the Fields," a pregnant cow, 70 [drachmas,
priestly portion - - -]. (line 10) To Telete,[13] *spylia*,[14]
40 drachmas.

In the third quarter: in the month Gamelion: To
Daira,[15] a pregnant ewe, 16 drachmas, priestly portion, 1
drachma. To Ge "at the Oracle," a sheep, 11 drachmas. To
Zeus Hypatos [Most High], [- - - drachmas]. To Ioleus, a
sheep, 12 drachmas. To Kourotrophos, a pig, [3 drachmas,
a ta]ble, 1 drachma, priestly portion, 2 drachmas, 1 1/2
obols. To the hero Pheraios, [a sheep, 12 drachmas,]; to
the Heroine, a sheep, 11 drachmas, priestly portion, 3
drachmas. In the month Elaphebolion, on the 10th: [To Ge
"at the] Oracle," a completely black goat, 15 drachmas,
priestly [portion, 1 drachma].

In the fourth quarter, in the month Mounichion, to
Ar[- - -] (line 20) Nechos, an ox, 90 drachmas, a sheep,
12 drachmas; to the Heroine, a sheep, 11 drachmas, priestly
[portion], 7 drachmas. To Neanias, an ox, 90 drachmas, a
sheep, 12 drachmas, a pig, [3 drachmas], to the Heroine,
a sheep, 11 drachmas, priestly portion, 7 drachmas, 1 1/2
obols.

The deme-leader of the Marathonians makes the following
sacrifices. To the Hero "in [?]rasileia," a sheep, 12
drachmas, a table, 1 drachma; to the Heroine, a sheep, 11
drachmas. To the Hero "by the Hellotion,"[16] a sheep, 12
drachmas, a table, 1 drachma; to the Heroine, a sheep, 6
drachmas. In the month Thargelion: to Achaia,[17] a ram,
12 drachmas, a ewe, 11 drachmas, priestly portion, 3 drachmas.
To the Moirai [Fates], a pig, 3 drachmas, priestly portion,
1 1/2 obols.

(line 30) In the month Skirophorion, before the Skira.[18]
To Hyttenios, fruits in season, a sheep, 12 drachmas. To
Kourotrophos, a pig, 3 drachmas, priestly portion, 2 drachmas,
1 obol. To the Tritopateres,[19] a sheep, priestly portion,
2 drachmas. To the Akamantes, a sheep, 12 drachmas, priestly
portion, 2 drachmas.

The following in alternate years: first set - In Hekatombaion, to Athena Hellotis, an ox, 90 drachmas, three sheep, 33 drachmas, a pig, 3 drachmas, priestly portion, 6[+] drachmas. To Kourotrophos, a sheep, 11 drachmas, a pig, 3 drachmas, priestly portion, 1[+] drachmas. [- - -] boughs of laurel, 7 drachmas.

The following sacrifices are offered in alternate years beginning in the archonship in the Tetrapolis[20] of Euboulos: (line 40) second set - In Hekatombaion, to Athena Hellotis, a sheep, 11 drachmas; to Kourotrophos, a pig, 3 drachmas, priestly portion, 1 drachma, 1 1/2 obols. In Metageitnion, to the Eleusinian goddess, an ox, 90 drachmas; to Kore, a ram, 12 drachmas, three pigs, 9 drachmas, priestly portion, 6 drachmas, 4 1/2 obols, 1/6 *medimnos* of barley, 4 obols, a *chous* of wine [- - -]; to Kourotrophos, a sheep, 11 drachmas, priestly portion, 1 drachma; to Zeus Anthaleus ["Flowering"], a sheep, 12 drachmas, priestly portion, 2 drachmas. In Anthesterion, to the Eleusinian goddess, a pregnant sow, (line 50) 20 drachmas, priestly portion, 1 drachma, 1 obol. To Chloe "beside Medylos' place," a pregnant sow, 20 drachmas, priestly portion, 1 drachma, 1/6 *medimnos* of barley, 4 obols, *chous* of wine, [- - -]. In Skirophorion, before the Skira, to Galios, a ram, 12 drachmas, priestly portion, 2 drachmas, from the well[?], 6 drachmas; to the Tritopateres, a table, 1 drachma.

D. Festivals

A Festival of Apollo at Delos

The *panegyris* was a major festival held regularly in
honor of a god. The "Homeric" hymn to Apollo describes such
a festival at the god's shrine on the island of Delos. This
annual festival was an occasion for Greeks from many of the
Ionian cities (Athens, many of the Aegean islands and the
west coast of Asia Minor) to gather and celebrate their
common ancestry.[21]

(*Homeric Hymn to Apollo*, 146-164.)

Phoebus, thy heart taketh greatest delight in Delos,

where the Ionians in their long tunics assemble, with their

children and their modest wives. In remembrance they de-

light thee with boxing, with song and with dance, when they

hold their assembly. One who comes upon them then, when

the Ionians are gathered, might say they are immortal, ever

ageless, for he would see their grace, and his heart would

rejoice at the sight of the men and the fair-girded women,

their swift ships and manifold possessions. Added to this

is the great, amazing, imperishable glory of the Delian

maidens, the servants of the far-shooting god, who first

hymn Apollo, then Leto and Artemis the shooter of arrows;

then they sing a hymn in remembrance of men and women of

old, and they enchant the tribes of men. They know how to

imitate the voices and sounds of all men, and each might say

it were he himself singing, so concordant is their fair song.

The Panathenaic Festival

The greatest festival of the Athenian religious calendar
was the Panathenaia; it was celebrated each year on the 28th
of the month Hekatombaion (July/August), the birthday of
Athena. Every fourth year the festival was celebrated in
a more elaborate way, as the Greater Panathenaia. The first
two selections describe the officials responsible for the
administration of the sacrifices, the great procession (which
is also depicted on the frieze of the Parthenon), and the
athletic and musical competitions. The last two documents

are decrees, one passed in 335/4 B.C. (part of the reorgani-
zation of the festival by Lycurgus) regulating the purchase
of sacrificial victims and the other, from the first half
of the fourth century, with a fragmentary listing of the
prizes for the contests. The festival is discussed in
general by J.A. Davison, "Notes on the Panathenaea," *Journal
of Hellenic Studies* 78 (1958) 23-42; *ibid.* 82 (1962) 141-
142; H.A. Thompson, "The Panathenaic Festival," *Archaeolo-
gischer Anzeiger* 1961, 224-231; H.W. Parke, *Festivals of
the Athenians* (London and Ithaca, 1977), pp. 35-50.

(Aristotle, *Constitution of the Athenians*, 54.6-7.)

The people also elect by lot ten *hieropoioi* [commis-
sioners for sacred rites] charged with the expiatory sacrifices, who perform the sacrifices required by oracles and
who, when it is necessary to do so, watch for good omens
along with the soothsayers during sacrifices. It also
elects by lot ten others who serve for a year and are
charged with performing certain sacrifices and administer-
ing all the four-yearly festivals except the Panathenaia:
these four-year festivals are (1) the one at Delos (there
is also a five-year festival there), (2) the Brauronia,
(3) the Heracleia, (4) the Eleusinia. The fifth is the
Panathenaia, and it is not held in the same year as any of
these others. Recently (since the year when Kephisophon
was archon [329 B.C.]) the Hephaistia has been added to the
list.

(Aristotle, *Constitution of the Athenians*, 60.)

It also elects by lot ten men as *athlothetai*, [commis-
sioners of the games], one from each tribe. After a hearing
into their qualifications, they serve for four years, they
administer the procession of the Panathenaia, the musical
competition, the athletic contests and the horse race, have
the *peplos* made, in cooperation with the council they have
the oil-jars made, and they award the olive oil to the com-
petitors. This oil is gathered from the sacred olive trees.
The *archon* is to control the levies on the owners of the
fields on which the trees are located, three half-*kotylai*
from each tree. ... When the *archon* has collected the oil

accruing in his year of responsibility, he hands it over
to the treasurers on the acropolis, and he is not allowed
to move on and take his place [as a former *archon*] in the
Areopagos until he has handed the whole amount over to the
treasurers. The treasurers store it on the acropolis until
the Panathenaia; at that time they dole it out to the
athlothetai and they in turn award it to the winners of the
contests. The prizes are: silver and gold for the music
competition, shields for the winner in physical fitness,
olive oil for the athletic contests and horserace.

(*IG* II^2 334; *SIG*^{3} 271; *LGS* 29.)

...In order that the procession may be equipped and
marshalled in the best possible way each year for Athena
on behalf of the Athenian people, and that all the other
necessary arrangements may be made for the festival as it
is being properly celebrated on every occasion for the
goddess by the *hieropoioi*, it is voted by the people, in
accordance with the resolution of the council: when the
hieropoioi make the sacrifices, they are to distribute the
portions of meat from two of them, that to Athena Hygieia
and that in the old temple, performed in the traditional
way, in the following proportions: five shares to the
prytaneis, three to the nine *archons*, one to the treasurers
of the goddess, one to the *hieropoioi*, three to the board
of generals and division-commanders, and the usual shares
to the Athenians who participated in the procession and the
maidens who act as *kanephoroi*; the meat from the other sacrifices they are to distribute to the Athenians. From the
41 minas which represent the rent of the sacred land, the
hieropoioi, along with the cattle-buyers, are to buy the
sacrificial cattle; when they have conducted the procession,
they are to sacrifice all these cattle to the goddess on
the great altar of Athena, except for one which they are
to choose ahead of time from the finest of the cattle and
sacrifice on the altar of Nike; all the rest of the cattle
bought with the 41 minas they are to sacrifice to Athena

Polias and Athena Nike and distribute the meat to the
Athenian people in the Kerameikos in the same fashion as
in the other distributions of meat. They are to assign
the portions to each deme [residential district] in proportion to the number of participants in the procession from
each deme. Fifty drachmas are appropriated for the expenses
of the procession, for the immolation and for the outfitting
of the great altar and the other items which must be provided for the festival, and for the all-night celebration.
The *hieropoioi* who administer the annual Panathenaia are
to perform the night celebration in the finest manner possible and to conduct the procession at sunrise; they are to
punish with the penalties of the laws anyone who does not
obey their instructions. The Athenian people are to select
certain men from the whole body of Athenians who shall ...

(*IG* II^2 2311; *SIG*^{3} 1055.)

[For the rhapsodes: first prize,] a c[rown and -- drachmas)];
    second, [-- drachmas; third -- drachmas]
For the singers to the lyre: first prize, a crown of gold
    leaf worth 1000 drachmas and 500 silver drachmas;
    second, [7?]00 drachmas; third, [6?]00 drachmas; fourth,
    [4?]00 drachmas; fifth, 300 drachmas.
For the flute-players, male: first, 300 drachmas the worth
    of his crown, and 10 drachmas cash; second, 100 drachmas.
For the lyre-players, male: first 500 drachmas the worth
    of his crown, and 300 drachmas cash; second, [?]00
    drachmas; third, 100 drachmas.
For the flute-players: first, [?]00 drachmas the worth of
    his crown; second, -- .
For the winner of the boys' footrace, a jar of wine worth
    [50] drachmas; second, 10.
For the winner of the boys' pentathlon: 30 jars of oil;
    second, 6.
For the winner of the boys' wrestling: 30 jars of oil;
    second, 6.

For the winner of the boys' boxing: 30 jars of oil;
    second, 6.
For the winner of the boys' pancration: 30; second, 8.
For the winner of the youths' footrace, 60 jars of oil;
    second, 12.
For the winner of the youths' pentathlon: 40 jars of oil;
    second, 8.
For the winner of the youths' wrestling: 40 jars of oil;
    second, [8].
For the winner of the youths' boxing: [40 jars of] oil;
    [second, 8].
[For the winner of the youths' pancration: 40 jars of oil;
    second, 8]
F...... [men's events are missing from the stone]
For the race of pairs of foals: 140 jars of oil; second,
    40.
For the race of luxury pairs of horses, 140 jars of oil;
    second, 40.
Military events:
    For the winner on the mounted horse, 16 jars of oil;
        second, 4.
    For the winner on pairs of horses, 30 jars of oil;
        second, 6.
    For the winner on a processional pair, 4 jars of oil;
        second, 1.
    For the javelin-throw from horseback, 5 jars of oil;
        second, 1.
Prizes for team events:
    Boys' Pyrrhic dance, an ox worth 100 drachmas.
    Youths' Pyrrhic dance, an ox worth 100 drachmas.
    Mens' Pyrrhic dance, an ox worth 100 drachmas.
    To the tribe which wins the physical fitness contest,
        an ox worth 100 drachmas.
    To the tribe which wins --, an ox worth 100 drachmas.
    To the winner of the torch-race, a water-jar worth 30
        drachmas.
Prizes of the ships' crews:
    To the winning tribe, 300 drachmas.

E. Sanctuaries and their Administration

The Greeks built their shrines, temples and altars at
holy places sanctified by ancient custom, by an evocative
natural feature such as a spring or dramatic fissure in the
earth, by the grave of a hero, or by the epiphany of some
god. The area set aside for the god was called his *temenos*,
literally the portion "cut off" for him from the surrounding
land. On the architectural embellishment of these sanctuaries see B. Bergquist, *The Archaic Greek Temenos* (Lund,
1967); a survey of how the sanctuaries were consecrated,
administered and utilized may be found in R.A. Tomlinson,
Greek Sanctuaries (New York, 1976); cf. also P.E. Corbett,
"Greek temples and Greek worshippers, the literary and
archaeological evidence," *Bulletin of the Institute of
Classical Studies* (University of London) 17 (1970) 149-158.

The Founding of the Cult of Pan in Athens

In 490 B.C., faced by invasion by a great Persian army,
the Athenians sent the runner Philippides to Sparta to request military aid. Like Hesiod's meeting with the Muses
(below, pp. 154-155), Philippides' encounter with the rustic
god Pan took place in a remote and lonely mountain. After
their victory over the Persians at Marathon, the Athenians
responded to Pan's request by establishing a cult in the
city and by dedicating to him a cave at the site of the
battle: cf. E. Vanderpool, "News Letter from Greece,"
American Journal of Archaeology 62 (1958) 321-322; A.
Orlandos, *Ergon tis Archaiologikis Etairias* 1958, 15-22.

(Herodotus, *The Histories* VI. 105.)

While they were still in the city, the generals dispatched Philippides as a herald to Sparta. He was an Athenian man, a trained runner in very good condition. The god
Pan, as Philippides himself said in his report to the Athenians, fell in with him on Mount Parthenion above Tegea: Pan
called Philippides' name and commanded him to inquire of
the Athenians why they paid no attention to him, even though
he was well-disposed toward the Athenians, had on many occasions already proven to be good to them, and would continue
to be so. The Athenians, after their affairs had been well
settled, showed their faith in these events by establishing

123

a shrine of Pan below the Acropolis; as a result of his
revelation, they worship him with annual sacrifices and a
torch-race.

Sanctuary Regulations

These four inscriptions emphasize how the consecrated
land of a precinct is set off, how certain activities are
considered inappropriate within it. It is interesting to
note that all four documents are decrees of the citizen
body or its council, illustrating the close natural concern
of the city-state for its cults.

(*LGS* 95; from Amorgos, late 5th century.)

Resolved by the council and the people, on the motion
of Orthsileus: No one is to light a fire in the sanctuary
of Hera at the corner of the new building [*oikos*] and the
temple, nor at the Lykeion. If anyone does light one, he
is to pay a fine of ten drachmas, sanctified to Hera.

(*IG* XII. 7.2; *SIG*³ 981; *LGS* 96; from Amorgos, on the same
stone as the preceding, but inscribed a century or so later.)

Resolved by the council and the people, on the motion
of Agenor, when Meliton was presiding officer: No stranger
is permitted to put in at the sanctuary of Hera; the temple
attendant [*neokoros*] is to take care to keep them out. If
he does not keep them out, he is to pay a fine of ten
drachmas, sanctified to Hera, for each day. The superintend-
ents [*neopoioi*] are to take care to inscribe this decree in
front of the doors.

(*SIG*³ 986; from Chios, early fourth century.)

Resolved by the council, Tellis presiding: In the
sacred groves there is to be no pasturing or dumping of
manure. If any one does herd sheep, pigs or cattle, the
person who sees it should report it to the authorities
[*basileis*] in order to remain pure in the god's sight. The
fine for the shepherd, swineherd or cowherd shall be 1/12
stater for each animal. If any one is caught dumping manure,

he shall pay five staters to become pure in the god's sight.
If the person who sees it does not report it he shall pay
five staters, sanctified to the god...

(IG II^2 1362; SIG^3 984; LGS 34; from a shrine of Apollo
"Erisatheus" near Athens, end of the 4th century.)

Gods! The priest of Apollo Erisatheus announces, on
behalf of himself, the members of the deme and the Athenian
people, that it is forbidden to cut wood in the sanctuary
of Apollo, or to carry wood or branches, whether with leaves,
without leaves or dry, out of the sanctuary. If any one is
caught cutting or carrying any of the forbidden things out
of the sanctuary, if it is a slave who is caught he shall
be given fifty lashes and the priest shall turn him over to
the king-*archon* and the council along with the name of his
master, according to the decree of the council and the
Athenian people. If he is a free man, the priest together
with the deme-leader shall fine him fifty drachmas and turn
his name over to the king-*archon* and the council, according
to the decree of the council and the Athenian people.

The Lease of a Shrine

This interesting document preserves the text of the
contract by which the *orgeones* (a religious association
devoted to the cult of a specific god or hero) of the hero
Egretes rent out, in 306/305 B.C., the sanctuary of their
patron hero. The lessee, Diognetos, agrees to perform certain tasks of maintenance and to arrange for the annual
festival of the association. In addition to the few benefits specified in the text, Diognetos presumably had the
use of the land belonging to the sanctuary, and would be
entitled to its produce. The inscription is interesting
for the details of sanctuary equipment and of the cult life
of an association of *orgeones*, but also for its indication
of how the *orgeones* financed their religious activities, by
using the sacred land as an income-producing endowment.

(SIG^3 1097; LGS 43.)

Gods! The *orgeones* rent the sancuary of Egretes to
Diognetos, son of Arkesilos from the deme Melite, for ten
years, at the rate of 200 drachmas each year; he is to manage

the sanctuary and the buildings constructed in it as a
sanctuary; Diognetos shall whitewash the walls which need
it, and shall construct and arrange whatever else he wants.
At the expiration of the ten-year period, he shall take
away with him the woodwork, the roof-tiles and the doors
and posts; but he shall remove none of the other furnishings.
He shall tend the trees growing in the sanctuary; if any
dies, he shall replace it and hand on the same number.
Diognetos shall pay the rent money to the treasurer of the
orgeones in office each year, one half (that is, 100 drachmas)
on the first day of Elaphebolion. When the *orgeones* sacrifice to the hero in Boedromion, Diognetos is to have open
the structure where the shrine is, as well as the shed, the
kitchen, and the couches and tables for two dining rooms.
If Diognetos does not pay the rent at the times specified,
or does not fulfill the other specifications of the lease,
the lease is to be void and he is to be deprived of the
woodwork, the roof-tiles and the doors and posts, and the
orgeones are free to rent to whomever they wish. If any tax
is assessed, it is to be deducted from the fee to the
orgeones. Diognetos is to inscribe this lease on the stone
which stands in the sanctuary. The term of the lease begins
in the year when Koroibos is *archon*.

Assessments and Contributions to a Cult

This document provides for the financial needs of the
shrine at Lindos, on the island of Rhodes, of Enyalios.
This is a common cult-name of Ares, god of war, and this
decree (again, made by the citizen body of the city-state)
assesses certain contributions to the cult by the soldiers
in the armies of Lindos, and also by any individual Lindians
who go to war on their own, presumably as mercenaries. The
inscription incidentally gives interesting details of the
sacrifices and processions with which the god was worshipped.

(*SEG* IV. 171; *LSCG* 85; late fifth century B.C.)

Resolved by the council and the people; on the motion
of Agatharchos: Any soldier from Lindos who goes on public
or private campaign shall contribute the sixtieth part of

his wages to Enyalios; the general shall collect the amount
and convey it to the priest. The fees paid by others are
to be conveyed to the priest by the individuals themselves.
Each year the priest is to report to the council and convey
[the treasury] to the incoming priest. The *epistatai* are
to record the sums which the generals and the others on
campaign had. The *prytaneis* on duty in the month Artimition
are to make sacrifice to Enyalios; they shall sacrifice to
Enyalios a wild boar, a dog and a kid. The council is to
arrange the procession: the hoplites are to come after the
priests whom the council will appoint. A shelter shall be
built for Enyalios; when the money is donated by private
individuals at Lindos, the council shall collect it. If
the generals do not collect the money from the soldiers let
it be a sacrilege against the god and let him [i.e. the
general] be liable; likewise in the case of private individuals who go on campaign. Both the generals and the private
individuals shall come and deposit the money with the priest
within a month. The decree shall be recorded on stone and
deposited beside the altar of Enyalios.

Duties of a Priest

The oracular shrine of Amphiaraos was located on the
coast of Attica about 50 km. north of Athens, near the town
of Oropos. The oracle enjoyed considerable prestige, as
Herodotus knew (cf. p. 94 above), and this inscription lists
the sacred laws requiring that the priest spend some time
each month in the sanctuary, to be available for those who
wanted to sacrifice or spend the night ("incubate") there.

(*IG* VII. 235; *SIG*[3] 1004; *LGS* 65.)

Gods! From the onset of winter until the spring plowing
season the priest of Amphiaraos is to go into the sanctuary
when winter arrives and until the sowing season with no
greater interval than three days between visits, and he is
to be in residence there not less than ten days in each month.
He is to require the *neokoros* [temple attendant] to care for
the sanctuary in accordance with the law and also for those
who visit the sanctuary. If anyone commits a crime in the

sanctuary, whether stranger or member of the deme, the
priest has authority to fine him up to a maximum of five
drachmas, and he is to require security from the person so
fined. Should he pay the fine, he is to deposit it in the
treasury in the presence of the priest. If anyone suffers
some private injury in the sanctuary, whether stranger or
member of the deme, the priest is to give judgment up to a
maximum of three drachmas; as for larger sums, the judgments
provided in the laws for each victim are to be in effect here
also. Any summons arising from an offense in the sanctuary
must be issued on the same day. If the defendant does not
make restitution, a trial is to be held on the next day.

When a person comes to be healed by the god, he is to
donate a first-fruit offering of at least nine obols[22] of
silver, and deposit it in the treasury in the presence of
the *neokoros*. When he is present, the priest is to say the
prayers over the sacrifices and place the victim on the
altar; when he is not present the person making the sacrifice
is to do this. During the public sacrifice each person is
to say the prayers for himself, but the priest is to say
them over the public sacrifices, and he is to receive the
skin of all the victims sacrificed within the sanctuary.
Each person may offer whatever sacrifices he wishes. No
portions of meat are to be carried out of the precinct.
Sacrificers are to donate the shoulder-portion of each victim to the priest except during a festival; at that time he
is to receive the shoulder portion only from the public
victims. ...

Rules for incubation: the *neokoros* is to record the
name and city of the incubator when he deposits his money,
and to display it on a bulletin board for anyone to read.
In the sleeping-hall men and women are to lie separately,
the men to the east of the altar, the women to the west ...

The Purchase of a Priesthood

Few Greek cults had a professional priesthood. Instead
ordinary citizens served - in some cases they were elected,
in others appointed; in still other cults the priesthood and

its prestige and perquisites were sold. This inscription
lists the duties and privileges of the man who purchased
a certain priesthood on the island of Chios.

(*LSCG* 77.)

The man who purchases the priesthood shall exercise it
for life, provided he continues to live in the city. He is
to be exempt from all taxes and receive for himself the
first portions from the one who makes a sacrifice, of entrails, shanks, knees, tongue, two double portions of meat,
Hermes-cakes, the offerings of which anyone makes burnt-
sacrifices. And, in addition, an appropriate share of the
banquet. If the city holds a banquet, he is to receive 1/12
gold stater. If outsiders sacrifice, [he receives the same
share as in the case of a Chian, but] the sacrificer [adds
in addition ...]

F. Rural Cults and Customs

Reverence for the forces of nature permeated much of Greek religion. Every river had its deity, every tree and spring its nymph; along streets and cross-roads were small shrines of Hecate, Apollo and Hermes. The cycle of agriculture was observed in sowing festivals each autumn, and harvest festivals in spring, including processions with May boughs rich with fertility symbolism. For a discussion of the cults of the Greek countryside, see M.P. Nilsson, *Greek Folk Religion* (New York, 1940), ch. 2.

The World of Nature Spirits

Hesiod's collection of ritualistic prescriptions tells how to avoid giving offence to the immortals; it is clear testimony to faith in river gods, wood nymphs and other ubiquitous nature divinities. In the next passage the geographer Strabo describes the countryside of Elis in the western Peloponnese, full from end to end with shrines of the gods of nature.

(Hesiod, *Works and Days*, 724-741.)

After daybreak, never with unwashed hands pour sparkling wine as a libation to Zeus or to the other immortals. Do not urinate standing, turned to face the sun, but be mindful to do it after it sets, and toward its rising; do not urinate either on the road, or off the road as you travel, or uncovered; nights, you see, belong to the gods. The godly man who is prudent does it sitting, or else facing the wall of an enclosed courtyard.

At home, do not approach the earth and expose yourself when your genitals are stained with semen; avoid this. Do not beget children after returning from an inauspicious burial, but do it after a feast of the immortals. Never cross the fair water of ever-flowing rivers on foot before you have looked into the clear stream, washed your hands in the lovely bright water, and said a prayer. Whoever crosses without washing his hand is stained by evil: the gods despise him and give him grief in return.

131

(Strabo, *Geography* VIII. 343.)

The Alpheios River flows through Phrixa, Pisatis and
Triphylia, past Olympia itself and into the Sicilian Sea
between Pheia and Epitalion. Near its mouth is the sacred
grove of Artemis Alpheionia or Alpheiousa (both forms are
used), 80 stades from Olympia. A festival is also celebrated every year in Olympia in honor of this goddess, as
well as to Artemis under the names Elaphia and Daphnia.
This whole land is full of shrines of Artemis, Aphrodite
and the Nymphs, most of them in well-watered, flowering
groves. It is also thick with shrines of Hermes along the
roads, and of Poseidon on the shore.

Wayside Gods: Hecate, Apollo Agyieus, Herms

This series of short passages shows how commonly shrines
were located along streets and roads. At cross-roads in
the country Hecate was worshipped with small offerings of
food. In cities Apollo had his altars outside each house,
and Thucydides and Timaeus reflect the local importance of
the Herms, square pillars outfitted with human heads and
genitals. See M.P. Nilsson, *Geschichte der Griechischen
Religion*[2] I (Munich, 1955), p. 203.

(Plato, *Laws* XI. 914b.)

If a person leaves any of his possessions behind,
whether deliberately or accidentally, anyone who happens
on them is to let them lie, in the belief that the Wayside
Daimon guards such things which are consecrated to the goddess by the law.
(Ancient Scholiast on this passage.) By wayside *Daimon*
Plato means Artemis, or the Moon [Hecate], since both she
and Apollo Agyieus ["of the Streets"] fill the roads with
light, he, as the Sun, during the day, she during the night.
Hence they place them along the roads. They also call Hermes
the "Wayside Leader," to acknowledge how necessary his
guidance is in business affairs. For this reason they also
erect columns by the roadside to represent him.

(Aristophanes, *Ploutos*, 594-597.)

You can inquire of Hecate whether it is better to be
rich or poor. She says the wealthy send dinner out to her
every month, but the poor grab it up before it ever gets
deposited.

(Ancient Scholiast on this passage.) It was the custom for
the rich to dedicate bread and other things to Hecate, and
for the poor to take some of them. They sacrifice to Hecate
on the thirtieth. The poor live off the sacrifices.

(Helladius in Photius, *Library*, 535b, ed. J. Bekker.)

They used to worship the Loxias [i.e. the Apollo] which
each person places in front of his door; they build a round
altar beside it; passers-by stop and crown it with myrtle-
wreaths. They call this altar Loxias Agyieus.

(Ancient Scholiast on Aristophanes, *Ploutos*, 1153.)

"Pivot-god" [or "Hinge-god"] is an epithet of Hermes
in that he is placed beside doors to protect against other
thieves.

(Thucydides, *History* VI. 27.)

In the mean-time most of the stone images of Hermes in
Athens had their faces hacked off in a single night: these,
according to local custom, are squared off and many are at
the doors of private houses and in sanctuaries.

(Timaeus in Athenaeus, *Deipnosophists* X. 437b; frag. 158 in
FGrH 566.)

Dionysios the tyrant on the festival of the *Choes*
promised a golden wreath to the first man to drain the
pitcher dry. When Xenokrates the philosopher drained it
and received the golden wreath, he untwined it and placed
it on the Hermes located in the courtyard. It was his custom to do this each evening when he returned home with his
wreathes of flowers. For this he was admired.

Water Nymphs

The rites of propitiation to the nymph-spirits of
springs and of the sea are described in these selections.
Both Pausanias and Polemon are late authors, but they preserve ceremonies reflecting very ancient usages.

(Pausanias, *Description of Greece* III. 23.8.)

As you go on from Epidauros Limera about two stades,
on the right is the "Water of Ino," about as large as a
small lake, but going deeper into the earth. They throw
barley-cakes into this water on the festival of Ino. If
the water keeps them submerged, it is auspicious for the ·
person who threw them in; but if it returns them to the
surface, it is judged a bad omen.

(Pausanias, *Description of Greece* VIII. 38.4.)

On Mount Lykaion is the spring of Hagno. It is like
the River Danube in that it produces the same amount of
water in winter and in summer. If a drought lasts a long
time and seeds in the earth and the trees are beginning to
dry up, on such occasions the priest of Zeus Lykaios addresses a prayer to the water, makes the customary sacrifices
and lets an oak-branch down onto the surface of the spring,
but not deeply into it. When the water has been stirred a
steam-like mist rises; in a short while the mist gathers
other clouds to itself and causes rain to fall on the land
of the Arcadians.

(Athenaeus, *Deipnosophists* XI. 462b-c.)

Polemon in his book about Morychos says that in Syracuse,
at the very tip of the island, there is a hearth outside the
city-wall next to the sanctuary of Olympian Ge [Earth]. He
says that sailors, when they set out to sea, take a cup from
this hearth and convey it until they can no longer see the
shield on the temple of Athena. At that point they let down
into the sea an earthenware cup, after they have put into it
flowers, honeycomb, lumps of frankincense and with them certain other fragrant herbs.

Harvest Festivals

Feasting and thank-offerings followed naturally enough
on the gathering of the harvest. Aristotle emphasizes the
fertility imagery and the revelry of leisure time in such
traditional harvest festivals. The following selections
present testimonies for examples of such agricultural ceremonies as rustic singing contests, and the decoration and
carrying of the May-pole and similar shrubs. Cf. also the
phallic procession in honor of Dionysus, pp. 206-207 below.
See M.P. Nilsson, *Griechische Feste* (Leipzig, 1906), pp.
164-165, 199-200.

(Aristotle, *Nicomachean Ethics* VIII. 1160a, 19-20; 23-28.)

Some kinds of associations seem to be formed for the

purpose of enjoyment, such as those devoted to religious

revels [*thiasoi*] and to feasting [*eranoi*]; these exist for

the sake of sacrifice and fellowship: they hold their

sacrifices and meetings, portioning out honors to the gods,

and providing themselves with pleasurable refreshment. In

ancient times, for instance, sacrifices and meetings were

held as a kind of first-fruits following the gathering of

the crops, since they had the most leisure at those seasons.

The Thalysia at Syracuse. (Prolegomena to Theocritus,
Bucolicorum Graecorum ... *Reliquiae* II, p. 5, ed. H.L.
Ahrens, 1859.)

There was at one time civil unrest in Syracuse, and

many citizens died. When the citizens gathered to make

reconciliation they determined that Artemis had been re-

sponsible for the discord. So the farmers brought gifts

and sang a joyful hymn to the goddess. Later they set aside

a place and made these rustic songs into a customary event.

They say that as they sang they had draped over themselves

(1) a loaf of bread with the figures of wild beasts on it,

(2) a purse full of every type of seed, and (3) a goat-skin

with wine; they poured out libations for all those they met,

wore a garland and deer antlers, and carried a shepherd's

rabbit-prod in their hands. The one who wins receives the

bread of the defeated. The winner stays in the city of

Syracuse, but the defeated ones go into the hinterland to

gather their own food. They also sing certain other songs
of a playful, funny nature, first saying in reverent tones,
    Receive good fortune, receive good health
    Which we bring from the goddess, by which she gave
        her command.

The Daphnephoria at Thebes.   (Proclus in Photius, *Library*,
p. 321b, ed. J. Bekker.)

The so-called Parthenia [Maiden-festival] is character-
ized by choruses of maidens; it belongs to the same type as
the Daphnephoria [Carrying of the Laurel]; for instance in
Boeotia the priests bear laurel branches over an eight-year
period to the rites of Apollo, and they have a chorus of
maidens sing hymns to him. At the Daphnephoria they twine
laurel branches and fresh flowers around a pole of olive
wood. At the tip a bronze ball is attached, and they fit
other smaller balls on to it. Then they decorate the middle
of the pole with purple garlands which are smaller than the
ball at the tip, and they wrap the bottom of the pole in a
saffron cloth. The ball at the top signifies the sun, by
which they also mean Apollo; the lower one means the moon,
and the smaller ones attached mean the stars, and the garlands symbolize the course of the year, for they make 365
of them. A child who has both parents living leads the
procession [as "laurel-bearer"] and his closest relative
carries the decorated pole, which they call *kōpō*. The
laurel-bearer comes after it, holding the laurel, with his
hair unbound, wearing a golden crown, a bright long gown,
and Iphicrates-style shoes. The chorus comes after him,
holding out branches for the chants of supplication. The
procession is conducted all the way to the sanctuary of
Apollo, Ismenios and Chalazios.

The Pyanepsia at Athens.   (Pausanias in Eustathius, *Commentary
on the Iliad* XXII. 495.)

The *eiresione* is a branch of olive wrapped in wool, on
which various fruits of the earth are hung. A child who has
both his parents living carries it and places it before the

doors of the sanctuary of Apollo at the Pyanepsia. According to tradition Theseus, when he was sailing to Crete, landed at the island of Delos during a storm, and prayed to Apollo that he would deck him with olive branches and hold a sacrifice, if he killed the Minotaur and got back safe. And so he decked out this branch as a sign of supplication, cooked up pots of broth and gruel, and established an altar. The rite is called the "pyanepsia" [Cooking of the Beans]; beans used to be called *pyanoi*. They also used to conduct these rites in order to avert a famine. The children sang this song:

> The *eiresione* brings figs and rich bread,
> Honey in a pot and olive oil to mix in,
> And a cup of strong wine, so that she may
> Get drunk and go to sleep.

After the festival they put them outside the fields next to the doors. Krates says that once when Athens was suffering a drought they wrapped branches in wool and dedicated them to Apollo as a sign of supplication. Others report that a white wreath and a purple one were hung on the branch, that a supplication was offered to Apollo on the day on which Theseus' companions were rescued, and that they poured libations of sauces and a cup of mixed wine on that day, and sang the foregoing song.

CHAPTER IV. PRIVATE RELIGION

A. Family Religion

From a modern perspective, the cult practices "writ large" in the cults of the city-state are most easy to see and understand. To a citizen of an ancient city-state, however, there were other relatively more intimate areas of religious activity which would have come more immediately into focus. Each citizen could claim his citizenship, as a general rule, because he was a member of a group called a "phratry"; this was in actuality or legal fiction a kinship group based on common descent from an often legendary ancestor. Another constituent of the tribes which made up the state was the *genos*, a word cognate with the English words "gene," "generation" and "genesis," and meaning something like "clan"; each *genos* had its own sacrifices and other observances. Classical literature has many allusions to the way in which the religious and also the political life of the city-state was rooted in kinship groups; and the following brief passage shows how crucial Plato considered the family gods to be in his utopian society.

(Plato, *Laws* V. 729c.)

When a person honors and respects the family relationship and the whole community of his kindred gods [*homognioi theoi*] which shares the same descent and blood, he would, correspondingly, enjoy the favor of the familial gods [*genethlioi theoi*], who will be well disposed toward his own begetting of children.

The following selection from Aristotle shows how the gods of the clan and of the family were considered touchstones of true and legitimate descent within one of the families which made up the city-state.

(Aristotle, *Constitution of the Athenians*, 55.2.)

The nine archons undergo a scrutiny first in the Council of 500, and then again in a court-hearing; their secretary, like the other magistrates, undergoes it only in a court-hearing; but all, both those chosen by lot and those elected by a show of hands, submit to a scrutiny before they serve

139

their term. In former times anyone whom the Council rejected
was ineligible to serve, but now there is the right of appeal to a court hearing, and the outcome of its scrutiny
always prevails. During the scrutiny the first question
they ask is, "Who is your father, and from which deme, who
is your father's father, who is your mother, who is your
mother's father, and from which deme?" After this they ask
whether he has an Apollo Patroos ["of the Ancestors"] and
Zeus Herkeios ["of the Enclosure"], and where these shrines
are; then whether he has family tombs and where they are;
then whether he treats his parents well, and pays his taxes,
and has performed his military service.

Rites of the Phratry

The following inscription, of the early fourth century
B.C., was found at Dekeleia in Attica. It records the regulations of the phratry of the Demotionidai. It establishes
criteria for membership in the phratry and procedures for
screening applicants based on the legitimacy of their claims
to kinship. One indication of the importance of the phratry
as a kinship group is the pair of sacrifices mentioned in
the inscription: the *meion* was offered by fathers of sons
born during the preceding year; the *koureion* was offered
when a son reached military age and became a full member of
phratry and city. On the phratry (and this inscription in
particular) see A. Andrewes, "Philochoros on Phratries,"
Journal of Hellenic Studies 81 (1961) 1-15; W.K. Lacey, *The
Family in Classical Greece* (London and Ithaca, N.Y., 1968),
pp. 92-96. For a document of a *genos*-cult, see the
Salaminioi decrees, above pp. 81-85.

(*IG* II^2 1237; *SIG*^{3} 921; *LGS* 17.)

Theodoros the son of Euphantides, the priest of Zeus
Phratrios, carved and erected this inscription. The following parts of sacrificial victims are to be given to the
priest: from the *meion*, a thigh, a flank, an ear, and three
obols of silver; from the *koureion*, a thigh, a flank, an ear,
a pancake made from a *choinix* of flour, half a *chous* of wine,
a drachma of silver.

Resolved by the members of the phratry during the archonship at Athens of Phormion [396/5 B.C.], when Pantakles of
Ion was leader of the phratry: Hierokles moved: Concerning

all those who have not yet been voted on according to the
rules of the Demotionidai, the members of the phratry are
to vote immediately, submitting to Zeus Phratrios and carrying the ballots from the altar. If it is determined that
someone has been introduced without being a member of the
phratry, the priest and the leader of the phratry shall
erase his name from the roster, both the one at the place
of the Demotionidai and the copy. The person who introduced
the rejected candidate shall owe a hundred drachmas, sacred
to Zeus Phratrios. The priest and the leader of the phratry
shall check this sum of money, or else be liable for it
themselves. From now on the balloting shall take place in
the year following that in which the *koureion* is offered,
on the "Koureotis" [the third day of the festival] of the
Apaturia. They shall carry the ballots from the altar. If
one of those who is voted down wishes to appeal to the
Demotionidai, it shall be allowed. The "house" of the
Dekeleians[23] shall choose five men over thirty years of age
as advocates on their behalf; the leader of the phratry shall
administer the oath to them, and the priest shall plead the
cause of justice and not permit anyone who is not a member
to conduct the business of the phratry. Of those who appeal,
any whom the Demotionidai vote down shall owe a thousand
drachmas, sacred to Zeus Phratrios, and the priest of the
house of the Dekeleians shall check the money, or else be
liable for it himself. Any other member of the phratry
besides who wishes to may check it. These regulations were
passed in the archonship of Phormion. Now the leader of
the phratry is to put to the vote the decision about those
who must be voted on each year. If he fails to do this, he
shall owe five hundred drachmas, sacred to Zeus Phratrios;
and the priest and any one else who wishes shall check this
money for the community. From now on they shall celebrate
both types of sacrifices at the altar in Dekeleia, and if he
does not sacrifice at the altar, he shall owe fifty drachmas,
sacred to Zeus Phratrios, and the priest shall check the
money or else shall be liable for it himself, unless some

plague or war is occurring; if such a case prevents it, then
they shall celebrate both types of sacrifices wherever the
priest prescribes. He shall publish it five days before
the "Dorpia" [the first day of the Apaturia] on a whitened
board at least one span in width, at the place where the
Dekeleians congregate in the city. The priest shall inscribe this decree and the sacrificial regulations on a
stone tablet in front of the altar of the Dekeleians at
his own expense.

Nikodemos moved: The foregoing provisions about the
introduction of children and the voting are to continue in
effect; and three witnesses which are provided at the preliminary examination from the members of the examinees' own
thiasos shall witness the questions and swear by Zeus
Phratrios; and the witnesses shall witness and swear while
holding on to the altar; if in this *thiasos* there are not
enough men, they are to be provided from the other members
of the phratry. When the voting takes place, the leader of
the phratry shall not put the vote about the children to
all the members of the phratry until the members of the
thiasos of the candidate vote, taking the ballots secretly
from the altar. The leader of the phratry shall count these
ballots in the presence of the whole membership in the marketplace and shall announce the result. If the members of the
thiasos vote to admit him to membership, but the others vote
him down, the members of the *thiasos* shall owe a hundred
drachmas, sacred to Zeus Phratrios, except for those who were
opposed to him in the debate. If the members of the *thiasos*
vote him down, and he appeals to the whole membership, and
they all vote to admit him to membership, then he shall be
registered in the common roster. If the whole membership
also votes him down, he shall owe a hundred drachmas, sacred
to Zeus Phratrios. If the members of the *thiasos* vote him
down and he does not appeal to the whole membership, the
vote of the *thiasos* shall stand. The members of the *thiasos*
shall vote about the children from their own *thiasos* separately from the other members of the phratry. The priest

shall add this resolution to the inscription on the stone
tablet. Oath of the witnesses at the induction of the
children: "I bear witness that the child is the legitimate
son of the man who is introducing him, born of a wedded
wife. This is true by Zeus Phratrios. If this oath is
true, may all good come to me; if it is false, the opposite."

Menexenos moved: Resolved by the members of the
phratry: the above provisions concerning the introduction
of the children shall stand, but in order that the members
of the phratry may be sure of those who are about to be
inducted, in the year immediately following the *koureion*-
sacrifice, the name of the father, his deme, mother's father
and his deme shall be registered with the leader of the
phratry, and he is to publish it where the Dekeleians congregate, and the priest is to write it on a whitened board
in the shrine of Leto.

Rites of the Household

The domestic worship of the family is not as explicitly
documented in ancient literature as the more spectacular
ceremonies of the city-state; the reason for this is probably that it was so common as to be taken for granted. The
following brief passages do cast some light on the homely
rites offered to the divinities of hearth (Hestia), pro-
tecting enclosure wall (Zeus Herkeios) and family possessions (Zeus Ktesios).

(Diodorus, *Library of History* V. 68.1.)

It is said that Hestia [hearth] invented the establishment of houses, and because of this blessing she has been
among almost all peoples installed in every house, receiving
her share of worship and sacrifices.

(Scholiast on Plato, *Euthydemus*, 302d.)

The Athenians call their homes "enclosures [*herkē*] hence
they have a "Zeus Herkeios"; they install him in their houses
for protection.

(Athenaeus, *Deipnosophists* XI. 473b-c.)

Philemon says that a *kadiskos* is a kind of drinking-
cup. It is also a vase in which they set the figures of
Zeus Ktesios, as Autokleides says in his book of interpretations: "The figures of Zeus Ktesios should be installed
in this way: take a new two-handled, lidded *kadiskos* and
garland its handles with white wool, with a fillet [hanging]
from the right shoulder and brow [of the officiant?], and
into it anything you find, and pour in *ambrosia*. This
ambrosia is a mixture of pure water, olive oil and all kinds
of fruit; put them in."

(Scholiast on Aristophanes, *Ploutos*, 768.)

In the case of newly purchased slaves, when they first
enter the house, or in general of any persons about whom
they desire to have good auspices, for example, a person
newly married, it was their custom to shower sweetmeats at
the hearth as a symbol of good seasons. The "showers"
consisted of dates, sweet cakes, candied fruit, figs and
nuts which the other slaves would snatch up.

The following passage is from a speech delivered in a
private law-suit during the fourth century B.C.; the plain-
tiff claims a share of Kiron's estate, and seeks to prove
she was a part of the family on the grounds that she was
allowed to participate in the intimate rites celebrated in
honor of the familial gods.

(Isaeus, *Orations* VIII. 15-16.)

...We also have other evidence that we are offspring of
Kiron's daughter. He treated us as children of his own
daughter, in that he never performed a sacrifice of any kind
without us; instead whether the sacrifice was small or great,
we were always at his side joining in the sacrifice. Furthermore not only were we invited on such occasions, but he also
always took us to the country for the Dionysia, and we used
to sit at his side at the performances, and we celebrated all
the festivals at his house. When he sacrificed to Zeus

Ktesios, a rite to which he was especially devoted, he
never admitted slaves or free strangers; rather he performed
all the rites himself, and we shared in them and joined in
handling the victims, placing offerings on the altar, and
performing the rest; and he prayed that we would receive
health and prosperity, as was proper for a grandfather.

   The next selection describes a domestic celebration in
honor of Zeus Ktesios, with its offerings, family meal and
the comfortable presence of a good friend. It presents a
vivid picture of the rites to which the preceding selections
have alluded, but it was not written just to illustrate
Greek domestic cults: it forms part of a speech in which
the speaker accuses his stepmother of poisoning his father;
it would have been delivered before the Athenian homicide
court of the Areopagos near the end of the fifth century B.C.

(Antiphon, *Orations* I. 14-20.)

There is a room upstairs in our house which Philoneos
occupied when he spent any time in the city; he was a good
man, a gentleman and our father's friend. Philoneos had a
concubine, but he intended to put her away in a brothel.
Now my brother's mother made friends with her. (15) When
she learned that she was going to be wronged by Philoneos,
she sent for the concubine, and when she came, she told her
that she too had been wronged by our father: if she were
willing to cooperate she said that she was ready to win
Philoneos for the concubine, and our father for herself
[with a love-potion]. She added that her own task was to
find a way, and the concubine's was to assist. (16) So she
asked if she would be willing to help, and she promptly, as
I suppose, promised to do it. Later, it happened that
Philoneos had a shrine of Zeus Ktesios in Peiraeus; my father
was about to sail to Naxos, so it seemed best to Philoneos,
since my father was his friend, to go to Peiraeus along with
him, and at the same time to perform the sacrifices and
share a meal with him. Philoneos' concubine went along to
help with the sacrifice. (17) When they were in Peiraeus,
he made the sacrifices as was proper. When he was finished,
the woman considered whether to administer the (supposed)

potion to them before or after dinner. She decided it
would be better to do it after dinner, thus attending to
the suggestion of that Clytemnestra. (18) It would take a
long time to tell all the details, but I will try to explain
briefly how she administered the potion. After they had
dined, Philoneos, as was proper, sacrificed to Zeus Ktesios
and received his friend, while he in turn, on the point of
sailing and enjoying the hospitality of his friend, poured
libations and put incense on them. (19) Philoneos' concubine, as she was preparing the libation with which they
would say prayers which were not to be fulfilled, put in the
potion. She thought it would be smart to give more to
Philoneos, perhaps so that, by giving him more, she would
be more beloved by Philoneos - she did not yet know that
she had been deceived by my step-mother, until she was in
the midst of the evil. For our father she put in less.
(20) Then, when they had poured a few drops as a libation,
they took their own death in hand and drank their last
draught. Philoneos died right away, but our father became
sick, and died twenty days later.

B. Personal Piety

Prayers

The Homeric poems convey a sense of relatively easy intimacy between gods and men - at least the men of heroic stature who dominate the *Iliad* and the *Odyssey*. Sometimes the gods appear to men in the form of some human or animal (see p. 154 below), and often mortals make prayers to the gods which ask for help of a personal nature. In this as in so much else Homer provides a model for behavior, and the three prayers quoted here form a model for later expressions of personal devotion. In the first example, the elderly Chryses prays to Apollo to punish the Greeks (Danaans) with a plague, since their general Agamemnon has refused to give up his concubine, Chryses' daughter. In the second, Achilles prays to Zeus to protect his friend Patroclus, who is going out in Achilles' place to fight the Trojans. Finally, Penelope in frustration and grief prays to Athena for the return of her husband Odysseus.

(Homer, *Iliad* I. 33-43.)

The old man was afraid [at Agamemnon's speech] and went quietly along the shore of the loud-roaring sea; going a long way off the old man prayed to the lord Apollo, whom fair-haired Leto bore: "Hear me, O Lord of the silver bow, you who protect sacred Killa and rule Tenedos in your strength, O Smintheus, if ever I have built you a pleasing temple, or if ever I have burned for you the fat thighs of bulls and goats, grant me this wish: may the Danaans pay for my tears at the mercy of your arrows."

(Homer, *Iliad* XVI. 220-256.)

Achilles went to his tent and opened the lid of a beautifully wrought chest which Thetis of the silver feet [his mother] had put on his ship for him to take along, filling it with tunics, wind-proof cloaks and woolen fleeces. He had there a well-wrought cup; no other man ever drank wine from it, nor did he ever use it to pour a libation to any god except to Father Zeus. He took it from the chest. First he

purified it with sulfur, then he washed it in streams of
fresh water, washed his hands and ladled gleaming wine into
it. Then he prayed, standing in the middle of the enclosure.
He poured the wine-offering, and gazed up toward heaven; and
Zeus who revels in the thunder paid heed to him:

"O Zeus, Lord of Dodona, Pelasgian one, who dwellest
afar and carest for storm-blasted Dodona; where dwell about
thee as interpreters the Selloi, who wash not their feet and
sleep upon the ground: if ever when I have prayed thou hast
heard my word and honored me at the expense of the Achaian
host, even so now fulfill this request for me. I myself
shall remain here at the ships, but shall send my comrade,
with many Myrmidons, to fight; grant to him glory, O Zeus
of the broad gaze, embolden the heart in his breast, so that
Hector may realize whether our comrade know how to fight
alone, or whether the hands he wieldeth be invincible only
when I too go into the crush of battle. But when he hath
held off the crash of battle from the ships, then do thou
let him come back to the ships unharmed, with all his armor
and his attendants in combat."

He uttered this prayer, and Zeus of the counsels heard
him: one prayer the Father granted him; the other he refused; he granted him to thrust war and battle back from
the ships, but refused safe return from battle.

When Achilles had made his libation and prayer to Father
Zeus he returned to his tent and put the cup back in the
chest. Then he went outside and stood in front of the tent.
In his heart he still wished to look upon the terrible combat of Trojans and Achaians.

(Homer, *Odyssey* IV. 759-767.)

When she had washed, she put clean clothes on her body
and went to her upstairs room with her attendant women; then
she put the barley for sprinkling in a basket and prayed to
Athena:

"Hear me, child of Zeus of the Aegis, Atrytone, if ever
resourceful Odysseus burned for thee in his house rich thighs

of oxen or sheep, now remember this on my behalf, and protect
my dear son, and keep at bay the suitors in their evil haugh-
tiness."

So she spoke, uttering a cry, and the goddess heard her
prayer.

In the *Hippolytus*, Euripides presents a picture of a
young man exclusively devoted to Artemis, chaste goddess of
the hunt. His neglect of Aphrodite and her determination
to punish him are the main themes of the tragedy, but in
the following passage the playwright gives a vignette of
intense personal devotion to one particular god. See A.J.
Festugière, *Personal Religion Among the Greeks* (Berkeley,
1960), chap. 1.

(Euripides, *Hippolytus*, 63-87.)

Chorus: Mistress, Mistress most majestic, offspring of
Zeus, hail, hail O Artemis, daughter of Zeus and Leto, by
far most benevolent of mistresses, thou who dost dwell in
the heavens in thy noble father's court, the all-golden
house of Zeus. Greetings, O most beautiful of all in
Olympus. Hail, Artemis.
Hippolytus: I bring thee this woven crown, which I have
plucked in thy pure meadow. There no shepherd would dare
to feed his flocks, nor would an iron plough ever come there;
only the bees of spring pass through the untouched meadow.
Reverence doth cultivate it with pure water from the rivers.
For those who are untutored, but are wise by nature, to
them alone is it permitted to gather here; for the wicked,
however, it is wrong. Now, O beloved Mistress, receive from
a pious hand this crown for thy golden hair. This privilege
is mine alone among mortals, to be with thee and to converse
with thee. I hear thy voice, but do not see thy face. At
the end of life may I round the turning point as I have begun.

Dedications

An important and characteristic type of personal devotion is expressed in the dedications which individuals make
to a god or goddess to express thanksgiving for past favors,
hope for future favors, or a more generalized piety.

The Acropolis at Athens

The following examples all come from the Acropolis in
Athens. Many of them were carved on the bases of the female
statues called *korai* [girls], in honor of Athena, the patron
deity of Athens to whom the Acropolis was sacred. They
show men and women of many occupations expressing their
aspirations and their private devotion to Athena in this
public way. Cf. A.E. Raubitchek, *Dedications from the
Athenian Akropolis* (Cambridge, Mass., 1949), *passim*.

(*IG* I^2 408, on a statue base.)   Aischines the son of Chares
dedicated (this) as first-fruit to Athena.

(*IG* I^2 422, on a statue base.)   Kapanis dedicated (this) as
a tithe to Athena.

(*IG* I^2 436, on the handle of a vase.)   Polykles the fuller
dedicated (this) to Athena.

(*IG* I^2 444, on a shield decorated with a gorgon.)   Phrygia
the bread-seller dedicated me to Athena.

(*IG* I^2 467, on a *stele*.)   Chairion the son of Kleodikos
dedicated (this) to Athena during his term as treasurer.

(*IG* I^2 473, on the base of a water basin.)   Smikythe the
washer-woman dedicated (this) as a tithe.

(*IG* I^2 485, on a statue base.)   Nearchos the potter dedicated (this) to Athena as first-fruit of his work. Antenor
the son of Eumares made the statue.

(*IG* I^2 487, on a statue base.)   Archemeros the Chian made
(me). Iphidike dedicated me to Athena Poliouchos [Guardian
of the City].

(*IG* I^2 499, on a statue base.)   Lyson dedicated (this) to
Pallas Athena as first-fruit of his possessions and as a
delight for the goddess. Thebades the son of [- - -] made
this statue.

(*IG* I^2 503, on a statue base.)   Timarchos dedicated me to
the mighty-hearted daughter of Zeus, after he had prayed for
an oracle of measured understanding. Onatas made (the
statue).

(*IG* I^2 606, on a statue base.)   Kallias the son of Didymios
dedicated (this). His victories [in the pankration]:
Olympic; Pythian, twice; Isthmian, five times; Nemean, four
times; Great Panathenaea.

(*IG* I² 643, on a votive column.) Lady Athena Poliouche
[Guardian of the City], may this city have this as a monu-
ment of Smikros and his boys and their flourishing business.
(*IG* I² 625, on a statue base.) Having achieved his prayer
Menandros dedicated this first-fruit to thee, Mistress, re-
paying thy favor; he is the son of Demetrios, from the deme
Aigialeia; do thou, O daugher of Zeus, preserve this wealth
which thou hast given.
(*IG* I² 631, on a votive pillar.) Vouchsafe great wealth to
him, O daughter of Zeus, and make grateful return for these
(dedications). He who dedicated me to Hermes, Oinobios the
herald, did it in thanksgiving for his skill, because of
his memory.
(*IG* I² 650, on a votive column.) Maiden, on the Acropolis
Telesinos of Kettos dedicated the statue; mayest thou delight in it and grant him to dedicate another.
(*IG* I² 658, on a votive column.) Philon dedicated this
little tripod to Athena, having won by a surprise.
(*IG* I² 684, on a votive tablet.) Diophanes dedicated me
to Athena Poliouchos, as a tithe of his estate, in fulfill-
ment of his son's prayer.
(*IG* I² 706, on a statue base.) [-]lochos dedicated this
kore-statue as first-fruit of his catch: this one boon the
Lord of the Sea with his golden trident granted.

A Shrine at Phaleron

     Around 400 B.C. a shrine was erected at Athens' old
port of Phaleron to the river-god Kephisos by a woman, apparently in thanksgiving for the education of her son
Xeniades. The first inscription records the dedication;
it was accompanied by a sculptured relief. The second was
inscribed on an altar in the shrine and lists Hestia in
her usual first place, then the god of the shrine, the three
gods of Delphi, Ileithyia the goddess of birth, two other
water divinities (Acheloos and Kallirhoe) and a not yet
identified Rhapso, perhaps a patron of seamstresses. Cf.
LSCG, pp. 44-45.

(*IG* II² 4548.) Xenokrateia constructed and dedicated this
shrine of Kephisos to him and the gods who share his altar
as an offering for the blessing of children[24]; she is the

daughter of (one) Xeniades and the mother (of another), from
the deme of Cholleidai. Anyone who wishes to sacrifice may
do so on payment of the appropriate fees.
(*IG* II^2 4547.) To Hestia, Kephisos, Pythian Apollo, Leto,
Artemis Lochia, Ileithyia, Acheloos, Kallirhoe, the familial
[*genethliai*] Nymphs of Geraistos, Rhapso.

The Vari Cave

   In the foothills of Mount Hymettos southeast of Athens
a cave had been considered sacred to Pan and the Nymphs ever
since the sixth century. The cult was a private one, and
these documents illustrate the pious activity of Archedamos,
an alien from Thera who resided in Athens around 400 B.C.
He furnished the cave with representations of the Nymphs
and, among others, the following three inscriptions. For
a report on the excavations of the cave, see C.H. Weller
et al., "The Cave at Vari," *American Journal of Archaeology*
7 (1903) 263-349.

(*IG* I^2 784.) Archedamos of Thera planted this garden to the
Nymphs.
(*IG* I^2 785.) Archedamos of Thera also erected a dancing-
floor to the dancing Nymph.
(*IG* I^2 788.) Archedamos of Thera, the Nymph-raptured one,
outfitted the cave at the admonition of the Nymphs.

Xenophon's Shrine at Skillous

   This passage neatly summarizes the appearance of such
privately dedicated sanctuaries, and the ways they were used
in the early fourth century. (Xenophon, as an Athenian exiled
for pro-Spartan sentiments and activity, went to Skillous
shortly after 394 B.C. For another example of his personal
piety, see p. 110 above.) This particular sanctuary was a
large stretch of park-land, appropriate to Artemis as goddess of the hunt.

(Xenophon, *Anabasis* V. 3.7-13.)

   When Xenophon was in exile and living in Skillous, near
Olympia, where the Lacedaemonians had established him as a
colonist, Megabazus visited Olympia to see the games and return to him his deposit. Xenophon took the money and with
it purchased a plot of land for the goddess where the oracle

of Apollo directed. It happened by chance that a river
named Selinos flowed through the grounds; at Ephesus too a
Selinos river flows past the temple of Artemis. In both
streams were fish and mussels; in the plot of land at
Skillous may be found many wild animals to be hunted. Here
Xenophon constructed an altar and a temple from the sacred
money; from that time on he would take ten per cent of the
crops and with it offer sacrifice to the goddess. All the
citizens and the men and women in the neighborhood shared
in the festivities. The goddess provided for the worshippers barley meal, bread, wine and dried fruit, and a portion
of the sacrificial victims from the sacred land and a portion
of the animals captured in the hunt. The children of
Xenophon and of the other citizens used to hold a hunt during
the festival time, and all the men who wished would participate. They captured some animals in the sacred precinct
and some on Mount Pholoe, wild boars and roes and deer.

The place is located on the road from Sparta to Olympia
and is about twenty stades [about 2 1/2 miles] from the
temple of Zeus in Olympia. Within the sacred precinct there
is a meadow and hills covered with trees - suitable for
raising pigs, goats, cattle and horses, so that even the
beasts of burden belonging to those who attend the festival
may be well fed. Around the temple itself is a grove of
cultivated trees which produces dessert fruits in season.
The temple is like the temple at Ephesus, though small in
comparison with that large one; the image of the goddess is
carved from cypress wood and is like the image in Ephesus,
although that one is made of gold. By the temple stands a
stele with the following inscription:

> This place is sacred to Artemis. He who owns it and
> enjoys its produce must offer a tenth each year, and
> from the excess must keep the temple in good condition.
> If someone fails to do these things the goddess will
> take care of it.

Epiphanies

Appearances of a god to a mortal, either in disguise
or in divine form, are reported with some frequency. In
myth and in epic, gods often appear to their favorites, and
a short passage from the *Odyssey* offers a typical example:
Athena, disguised as the mortal Mentor, appears in order to
encourage Odysseus in his battle with the suitors. Her
final manifestation as a bird is characteristic. The next
two selections differ in that they report specific encounters
of real, historical individuals with a particular god. The
historicity of any of these may well be open to doubt, but
together they demonstrate that such epiphanies were an
authentic feature of Greek religious experience. Cf. also
the appearance of Pan to Philippides, p. 123 above.

(Homer, *Odyssey* XXII. 205-210, 236-240.)

Zeus's daughter Athena came close beside them, in the

form and voice of Mentor. Odysseus rejoiced to see her,

and said, "Mentor, drive calamity away and remember your

dear comrade who has always offered you good things - you

are my contemporary." So he spoke, realizing that it was

Athena, who encourages the host. ... Athena spoke, but did

not yet completely grant decisive victories, but instead

made trial of the strength and might of Odysseus and his

glorious son. She herself darted up and sat on a rafter of

the sooty hall, in the shape of a swallow.

The Muses Inspire Hesiod

In the prologue to his genealogical history of the gods,
Hesiod (late 8th century B.C.) tells how, tending sheep alone
on Mount Helicon, he had a vision of the nine Muses. The
goddesses in effect ordain him their priest, and commission
him as an epic poet. A hymn-like catalogue precedes the
first-person testimony; the whole passage seems full of
reverent devotion.

(Hesiod, *Theogony*, 1-34.)

Let us begin to sing of the Heliconian Muses who occupy

the great sacred mountain of Helicon and dance with dainty

feet around the violet spring and the altar of the mighty

son of Kronos [Zeus].

Bathing their delicate bodies at Permessos or Hippokrene or sacred Olmeion, they implant their dances - their beautiful, lovely dances - on the peaks of Helicon, and they move their feet mightily. Starting thence, wrapped in thick mist, they came by night, raising their beauteous voices, singing of Zeus of the Aegis, and Hera the Mistress of Argos who treadeth on slippers of gold, of grey-eyed Athena the daughter of Zeus of the Aegis, of Phoebus Apollo and Artemis who rejoiceth in arrows, of Earthshaker Poseidon who upholdeth the earth, of Themis the Modest and Aphrodite of the arched brows, of gold-crowned Hebe and fair Dione, of Leto and Iapetos and Kronos the crooked of counsel, of Dawn and the great Sun and the bright Moon, of Earth and great Ocean and dark Night, of the holy race of the other immortals, living forever.

Once they taught Hesiod their fair song, as he was pasturing his sheep below sacred Helicon. First the goddesses, the Olympian Muses, daughters of Zeus of the Aegis, addressed this word to me:

"Shepherds of the fields, poor excuses, disembodied bellies, we know how to make lies in profusion seem like the truth, and we know how, when we want, to utter what is true."

So spoke the articulate daughters of great Zeus; and they plucked a branch of spectacular flowering laurel and gave it to me as a staff. And they breathed a divine song into me, that I might sing what will be and what has been before. And they bade me chant the race of the blessed ones, living forever, but always to sing first and last of them.

The Dioskouroi Visit Phormion's House

The divine twins Kastor and Polydeukes, known as the Dioskouroi, were born in Amyklai, a township of Sparta, and in this passage they appear in disguise to a man living in Amyklai. Cyrene, a colony in northern Africa, had close relations with Sparta in the seventh and sixth centuries B.C. The herb silphion was its major product for export.

(Pausanias, *Description of Greece* III. 16.2-3.)

[In Amyklai is a house in which] the sons of Tyndareus
originally lived, but later Phormion, a Spartan citizen,
acquired it. The Dioskouroi arrived at his door disguised
as strangers, claiming that they had come from Cyrene. They
requested lodging with him, and asked for the room which
they had enjoyed most when they were living among men. He
encouraged them to lodge anywhere they pleased in the rest
of the house, but he declined to let them have that particular room, since his maiden daughter happened to be living
in it. On the next day the maiden and everything that belonged to the child had disappeared, but in the room were
found statues of the Dioskouroi, and a table with silphion
on it.

Superstition and the Excesses of Religiosity

In the fifth and fourth centuries private individuals
were consulting seers and soothsayers for advice, in a manner similar to that in which the oracles had long been consulted. The seers produced their own oracles, which responded to personal needs and problems; associated with the
name Orpheus, these seers were known as early as the sixth
century. But the evidence suggests that they became more
conspicuous in the last half of the fifth century. Oracle-
mongers appear in Aristophanes (e.g. *Birds*, 959-991) and
are alluded to in Thucydides (II. 54) as present in Athens
during the terrible days of the Peloponnesian War. These
two passages of Plato illustrate some of the directions
toward private devotion and the superstitious manifestations
which reflect a fear of eternal punishment. The first
sketches the techniques of these "Orphic" seers and oracle-
mongers; the second represents an attempt to thwart such
charlatans and dealers in "indulgences" by outlawing private
cults altogether in the ideal city visualized in the *Laws*.
For Plato generally, religious rites were primarily public
expressions of civic life; for him, personal religion was
contemplative rather than ceremonial. Cf. p. 165 below.

(Plato, *Republic* II. 364b-365a.)

The most amazing tales are told about the gods and
virtue, for instance that the gods have ordained troubles
and an evil life for many good men, and the opposite for the
opposite kind of men. So begging priests and soothsayers go

to the doors of the rich and convince them that they [the
soothsayers] possess, vouchsafed of the gods, the power to
use sacrifices and incantations along with enjoyable festivals to cure any wrong committed by an individual or his
forebears; and if he wants to make an enemy suffer, they
claim the power to harm, at slight expense, just and unjust
alike; and they claim that by means of certain spells and
charms they constrain the gods to serve them. They adduce
the poets as evidence for these tales. They present the
easiness of evil, such as:

> Trouble and evil a man may discover and choose in
> abundance
> Quite easily: For the way will be smooth, close at
> hand, very easy.
> But as for virtue, the gods have put sweat and much
> labor before it.[25]

- as well as a long uphill road. Others cite Homer for the
way gods are led on by men, since he said:

> ...By prayer even gods can be moved;
> Men can divert them by sacrifice, praying in meek
> supplication,
> Offering incense and pouring libations, whenever
> they trespass.[26]

And they produce a pile of books by Musaeus and Orpheus,
descendants (they say) of the Moon and of the Muses. They
follow these books in their sacrificial rites, convincing
cities as well as individuals that there really are deliver-
ances and purifications from unjust deeds through sacrifices
and enjoyable diversions, both for the living and the dead.
These latter they call initiations, which deliver us from
the evils of the beyond, while terrible things await those
who have not made the sacrifices.

   The kind of religiosity which Plato criticized is
illustrated by a character in a fourth-century comedy by
Menander.

(Menander, *Dyskolos*, 260-263.)

My mother is going to make a sacrifice to some god or
other - she does this every day, and she wanders around in
a circuit, sacrificing through the whole deme.

Among the "Character Sketches" composed by Theophrastus
at the end of the fourth century B.C. is this description
of the man who carries religious devotion and scruples to
ridiculous extremes. The word translated "superstitious"
means literally "afraid of spirits (*daimones*)," and although
Theophrastus sketches broadly, the devotional acts his
spirit-fearer performs are typical of classical Greek piety
and can be paralleled as early as Hesiod (see p. 131 above).
Cf. M.P. Nilsson, *Greek Folk Religion* (New York, 1961),
pp. 102-142.

(Theophrastus, *Character Sketches*, 16.)

Now superstition might seem to be timidity with respect
to divinity, and the superstitious man one who [when he sees
a bad omen[27]] washes his hands, sprinkles himself with holy
water from a shrine, and walks around all day with bay-leaf
in his mouth. If a cat runs across the road, he will not
go on until someone passes by or until he throws three stones
across the road. If he sees a snake in his house and it is
a *pareias*, he calls on Sabazios; if it is the sacred kind,
he installs a hero-shrine then and there. If he passes one
of the "anointing stones" at a cross-roads he pours olive
oil from his jar, falls on his knees and worships, and then
takes his leave. If a mouse gnaws into his bag of barley-
meal, he goes to the soothsayer to ask what he should do;
and if his response is that he should give it to the leather-
worker to fix, he pays no attention to the advice, but goes
off to make propitiatory sacrifices. He is constantly purifying the household on the assumption that it has come under
the spell of Hecate. If owls hoot while he is walking along,
he is upset and says "Mighty Athena" before going on. He is
not willing to step on a grave, or approach a corpse or a
woman in childbirth, on the grounds that it is better for him
to avoid the pollution. On the fourth and the seventh of
the month he orders the domestics to boil wine while he goes

out to buy myrtle-wreathes, incense, and sacrificial cakes,[28]
then he comes back inside and spends the whole day putting
garlands on the statues of Hermaphrodite. When he sees a
dream, he goes to the dream-interpreters, to the seers, or
to the specialists in bird augury, to ask them to which god
or goddess he ought to pray. Every month he goes to the
masters of the Orphic mysteries to be initiated, and he takes
along his wife (if his wife is too busy, he takes the nurse)
and his children. He is so diligent in sprinkling himself
with holy water that he looks as if he has been for a dip
in the sea. If he notices that one of the cross-road gods
is garlanded with garlic, he goes off and washes his head,
then calls the priestesses and bids them purify him with
squill.[29] If he sees a madman or an epileptic he shudders
and spits into his breast.

C. The Orphic Way of Life

The presence of Orphic initiations and an Orphic "way
of life" which included sexual purity, abstinence from meat,
and holy writings are attested in the fifth century by the
following brief passages. On Orphism generally see M.P.
Nilsson, "Early Orphism and kindred religious movements,"
Harvard Theological Review 28 (1935) 181-230; W.K.C. Guthrie,
Orpheus and Greek Religion (London, 1935) and *The Greeks
and their Gods* (Boston, 1950), pp. 307-332; I. Linforth,
The Arts of Orpheus (Berkeley, 1941).

(Euripides, *Hippolytus*, 948-954.)

Are *you* the one who, like some paragon, consort with
gods? Are *you* the chaste one, all undefiled by evil? I'll
never let your pretensions mislead me into thinking the gods
are all that ignorant. No - go ahead and exult; play the
salesman with a vegetarian diet; call Orpheus your lord;
play the Bacchant; worship the smoky writings of all your
texts!

(Aristophanes, *Frogs*, 1030-1036.)

Consider how helpful the more noble poets have been,
from the very beginning: Orpheus showed us initiations and
abstention from slaughter; Musaeus oracles and ways to cure
diseases; Hesiod agriculture and seasons for harvesting and
ploughing; and the divine Homer, wasn't the source of his
honor and fame exactly this, that he taught useful things,
how to fight a battle, be a brave man, outfit a warrior?

D. The Pythagorean Way of Life

A specialized form of personal devotion was that
adopted by the Pythagoreans, who conducted their lives with
monastic rigor in communities in several Greek cities of
southern Italy in the fifth and fourth centuries B.C. Much
of our information about Pythagoras and his disciples comes
from later sources (such as Diogenes Laertius), but Plato's
comment suggests that Diogenes gives a basically accurate
picture of their high sense of justice and brotherhood, their
dietary restrictions, and their devotional procedures. On
the sources for the Pythagoreans of the Classical age, see
K. von Fritz, *Pythagorean Politics in Southern Italy* (New
York, 1940); most recently, see P. Gorman, *Pythagoras, a
Life* (London, 1979).

(Plato, *Republic* X. 600b.)

Is there any tradition that while Homer was still alive
he became a guide to any who enjoyed his company and who
handed on to their successors some "Homeric way of life"?
Pythagoras, for instance, was particularly revered in this
way, and his successors even today name their way of life
"Pythagorean" and are quite conspicuous among men.

(Diogenes Laertius, *Lives of the Philosophers* VIII. 22-24,
33.)

It is said that Pythagoras exhorted his disciples to
say this each time they came back home: "Where did I tres-
pass? What did I accomplish? What was left undone that I
ought to have done?" He ordered them not to offer blood
sacrifices to the gods, but to direct their worship only to
a bloodless altar; nor to swear by the gods, for one should
strive to present himself as trustworthy; to respect their
elders, in the belief that what has precedence in time is
more worthy of respect (in the world, for example, sunrise
has precedence over sunset, in a life beginning has precedence over death, and in nature generation has precedence
over destruction); (23) to respect gods before *daimones*,
heroes before men, and parents before other men; to deal
with each other so as not to make friends into enemies, but

163

to turn enemies into friends; to consider nothing one's own; to support the law, and fight against lawlessness; not to kill or damage a cultivated plant, nor any animal which does not injure men; to be modest and reserved, given neither to levity nor to gloom; to avoid the excesses of the flesh; when traveling to make exertion and also take rest; to exercise the memory; not to say or do anything in anger; to respect all divination; (24) to sing songs to the lyre and to give proper thanks with hymns to gods and good men; to abstain from beans because they cause flatulence and so share in the breath of life (besides which the stomach is kept in better shape if they are not ingested); furthermore with abstinence dreams also become more benign and calm. ... (33) not to offer the same honors to gods and to heroes - to gods at any time, with holy silence, dressed in white, in a condition of purity; to heroes only after the middle of the day. Purity is gained through washing, bathing, sprinkling, through keeping clean from mourning, child-birth and every sort of pollution, and through abstaining from the meat of dead animals, mullets, gurnards, eggs, animals hatched from eggs, beans and the other things which are enjoined by the priests who celebrate the rites in the sanctuaries.

E. Platonic Mysticism

Plato represents a refined type of personal religiosity, directed toward a mystical contemplation of the abstract reality of the truly Beautiful. This passage from the *Symposium* is ascribed to Diotima, the wise woman of Mantinea. It offers a kind of "discipline," a sequence of steps for attaining the spiritual disposition necessary for knowledge and contemplative worship of the Beautiful. Diotima uses the vocabulary of the mysteries (see Chapter V) in her discussion, and she alludes at the end to the power of the Beautiful to transform a person's life and make it more virtuous. Plato's mysticism is discussed in P.E. More, *The Religion of Plato* (Princeton, 1921) and A.J. Festugière, *Personal Religion among the Greeks* (Berkeley, 1954), pp. 42-52.

(Plato, *Symposium*, 209e-212c.)

Diotima: These then, O Socrates, are the mysteries of love into which even you might be initiated. But in reference to the complete and highest mysteries, for the sake of which these others exist, even if one were to proceed correctly, I do not know whether you are capable of attaining them. But I will explain them to you, she said, and I will spare no efforts. Try to follow my presentation, if you can.

It is necessary, she said, for the man who would proceed correctly to this end to begin as a young man to pay heed to beautiful bodies, and first, if the guide directs him properly, he will fall in love with one beautiful person and there produce noble thoughts; then he will understand that beauty in any one body resembles beauty in another and, if it is necessary to pursue the beautiful in its observable form, it is great folly not to recognize that the beauty in all bodies is one and the same. When he has made this analysis he must become a lover of all bodies and relax his fixation on one individual, because he realizes that such a passion is beneath him and of little value. Next he must realize that beauty of soul is worth more than beauty of body, so that if someone is capable in soul but has only a small bloom of beauty, he will be happy to love and nurture it, and produce and seek those kinds of thought which will make the young

165

better in order that he may be compelled to perceive beauty
in daily pursuits and laws and realize that each and every
thing is like itself, so that he will understand that physical beauty is a small thing. After daily pursuits it is
necessary to lead him to the sciences, in order that he may
contemplate their beauty in turn so that he looks to beauty
in the widest sense rather than to an individual instance,
like a slave who loves the beauty of a boy or some man or
some daily pursuit and because of that slavery is base and
petty; rather he must be drawn to the great ocean of beauty
and think and bring forth many beautiful and magnificent
sentiments and thoughts through abundant love of wisdom,
until he becomes strengthened and increased and catches sight
of one special science which is connected with the beauty I
will describe. Try to pay as close attention as possible.

The man who has been educated to this point in respect
to matters of love and who has observed the examples of
beauty in an orderly and correct fashion, as he comes to the
end of his examination of love will see a wondrous thing -
beauty in itself. This is the goal, Socrates, of all his
former efforts. First of all it is eternal and neither comes
into being nor decays, it does not increase or decrease. It
is not in one instance beautiful and in another ugly, nor at
one moment beautiful and at another not so, nor in reference
to one thing beautiful, but in reference to another not so,
nor beautiful here but ugly there, or to some beautiful but
to others ugly. This beauty will not resemble the beauty
of a face or hands or any other part of the body, nor like
that of a thought or of a science, nor like beauty in something else, such as in a living thing or the earth or the
heavens or something else, but absolute, always existing with
itself; all other beautiful things partake of it in such a
fashion that while they come into being and decay, it becomes
neither less nor more nor suffers change.

When a man, starting from these things through a right
use of pederasty begins to see this beauty, he is close to
attaining his goal. This is the correct way to enter on

erotic matters, or to be lead there by another, beginning
from examples of beauty in this world to ascend always to
that beauty as if mounting a staircase, from one to two,
from two to all beautiful bodies, from the beauty of bodies
to moral beauty, from moral beauty to beauty of knowledge,
and from knowledge to that final knowledge, which is concerned with nothing else than knowledge of that perfect
beauty. At last the initiate knows what is the Beautiful.

O dear Socrates, said the woman from Mantineia, this
is the area above any other where a man should live his life
- in the contemplation of absolute beauty. If you have seen
it, it will not seem good to you by the definition of gold
or clothing or beautiful boys and young men whom you and
others like you are so ready to observe and by whom you are
carried away, so that if you could see your beloved and
always be with them you would pass by food and drink to be
with them and admire them. What then, said she, do we think
about the man who could see perfect beauty in its essence,
pure, unmixed, instead of fixing upon human flesh and colors
and other such human rubbish, but could contemplate divine
beauty alone and apart? Do you think, said she, that that
is a poor life for a man who has his attention fixed there
and contemplates it in the proper way and lives with it?
Do you not see, said she, that it will be possible for him
there, contemplating beauty by the appropriate means, to
bring forth not the appearances of virtue, because he is
not touching appearances, but true virtue, because he is
touching true virtue? When he has given birth to and nurtured true virtue he will become a friend of god and to the
extent possible for a man immortal himself.

CHAPTER V. MYSTERY CULTS

A. The Mysteries at Phlya

At Phlya, on the east coast of Attica, was a local cult
of the Earth-goddess tended by the clan of the Lykomedai.
It continued through the classical period and still was known
in the second century A.D. when Pausanias wrote, though by
then the old traditional rituals had been supplemented by
so-called Orphic hymns. The following selections represent
nearly everything that is known about the mystery cult at
Phlya, and they are included to illustrate a local fertility
cult which never gained great prestige but maintained ties
with other shrines of the Earth goddesses.

(Pausanias, *Description of Greece* I. 31.4.)

At Phlya and Myrrhinos are altars of Apollo Dionysodotos,
Artemis Selasphoros [Bringer of Radiance], Dionysos Anthios
[Of the Flowers], the Ismenian Nymphs, and Earth, whom they
call the Great Goddess. Another temple has altars of Demeter
Anesidora [Who Sends Up Gifts], Zeus Ktesios, Tithrone Athena,
Kore Protogona [First-Born] and the goddesses called Semnai
[Reverend].

(Hippolytus, *Refutation of All Heresies* V. 20.5.)

The rites [*orgia*] of the so-called Great Goddess at
Phlias are prior to the Eleusinian mysteries.

(Plutarch, *Life of Themistocles*, 1.4.)

It is clear that Themistocles belonged to the clan of
the Lykomedai: when the initiation-hall at Phlya, which was
the common property of the Lykomedai, had been burned by the
barbarians [in 480 B.C.], he repaired it himself and decorated it with paintings, as Simonides says.

(Pausanias, *Description of Greece* IX. 30.12.)

Whoever has done research on poetry knows that each of
the hymns of Orpheus is very short and that the total is not

a very large number. The Lykomedai know them and chant
them at their ceremonies.

(Pausanias, *Description of Greece* IV. 1.5, 7.)

The Athenians say that Phlyos himself was the son of
Earth. The hymn to Demeter which was written for the
Lykomedai by Musaeus, agrees with them. ... (7) Methapos
was an Athenian by race, an official and founder of all
sorts of rites [*orgia*]. He established the initiation-rite
of the Kabeiroi at Thebes, and in the chapel of the Lykomedai
he dedicated a statue with an inscription which lends con-
viction to my account: "I sanctified houses of Hermes and
paths of Sacred Demeter and Kore Protogona where they say
Messene established a festival competition for the Great
Goddesses, instructed by Kaukon the descendent of glorious
Phlyos' son. I wondered that Lykos, the man of Pandion set
the holy acts of Attica in precious Andania."[30]

B.   The Eleusinian Mysteries

The Homeric Hymn to Demeter

The most prestigious of the mystery cults was at
Eleusis, and it attracted Athenians and foreigners, kings
(even Roman emperors, in time), and slaves to be initiated.
Before Eleusis became a part of the Athenian city-state in
the sixth century B.C., it was the site of a local agricultural cult which probably resembled the cult of the Lykomedai
at Phlya. Certain secret rituals commemorated the annual
rebirth of the grain and other fruits of the earth, and
associated the annual vegetation cycle with the myth of the
rape of Persephone (or Kore, "the daughter") by Hades (also
called Aidoneus, "the unseen one" or Plouton, "the wealthy
one") and the subsequent sorrow of the girl's mother, the
goddess Demeter (or Deo). This sacred legend is preserved
in the so-called Homeric Hymn to Demeter, composed probably
in the first half of the sixth century. It is a sacred text
of great importance, and we have included a translation of
the whole hymn because it not only gives the official version
of the founding of the mystery cult at Eleusis by Demeter
herself, but also contains many allusions to the ritual and
customs of the sanctuary. There is extensive scholarship
on the shrine and its cult, but among important works in
English we may note M.P. Nilsson, *Greek Folk Religion* (New
York, 1961), pp. 42-64; G. Mylonas, *Eleusis and the Eleusinian Mysteries* (Princeton, 1961); N.J. Richardson, *The Homeric
Hymn to Demeter* (Oxford, 1974); F.R. Walton, "Athens, Eleusis
and the Homeric Hymn to Demeter," *Harvard Theological Review*
45 (1952) 105-114.

(*Homeric Hymn to Demeter.*)

I begin my song of the holy goddess, fair-haired Demeter,

and of her slim-ankled daughter whom Aidoneus snatched away;

and Zeus the loud-crashing, the wide-voiced one, granted it.

She was playing with the deep-bosomed daughters of Ocean,

away from Demeter of the golden weapon and glorious fruit,

and she was gathering flowers throughout the luxuriant meadow

- roses, saffron, violets, iris, hyacinth, and a narcissus

which was a trap planted for the blossoming maiden by Earth

in accord with Zeus's plans, a favor to Hades the receiver

of many guests; it was radiantly wonderful, inspiring awe in

all who saw it, whether immortal god or mortal man; a hundred

171

stems grew from its root; and the whole wide heaven above,
the whole earth, and the salt surge of the sea smiled for
joy at its fragrance. The girl was charmed by it, and
reached out both hands to pluck the pretty plaything -
suddenly, the earth split open wide along the plain and
from it the lord host of many, Kronos' son of many names,
darted out on his immortal horses. (19) He grabbed her,
resisting and screaming, and took her away in his golden
chariot. She lifted her voice in a cry, calling upon father
Zeus, the almighty and good. But no one, god or mortal,
heard her voice, not even the glorious-fruited olive-trees,
except the childish daughter of Perses, Hecate of the
glistening veil, who - from her cave - heard, and so did
Lord Helios the glorious son of Hyperion, as the maiden
calling upon father Zeus, though he was sitting, removed
from the other gods, in his much-besought temple, receiving
fine sacrifices from mortal men.

(30) Her, all unwilling, with the approval of Zeus,
he took away on his immortal horses, Kronos' son of many
names, brother of her father, designator of many, host of
many. As long as the goddess could see the earth and the
starry sky, the flowing, fish-filled sea and the rays of
the sun, she still had hope that her holy mother and the
race of the immortal gods would see her, and there was still
much hope in her heart in spite of her distress....The peaks
of the mountains and the depths of the sea echoed back the
immortal voice, and her blessed mother heard her. (40) Then
sharp grief seized the mother's heart; she tore the head-
dress upon her ambrosial hair, and threw her dark veil down
from both her shoulders; and like a bird she darted over land
and sea, searching. None of the gods or of mortal men would
give her a true report, nor would any of the birds come to
her as a true messenger.

(47) For nine days then lady Deo wandered the earth,
holding blazing torches in her hands; in her grief she touched
neither ambrosia nor the sweetness of nectar, nor did she
bathe her body with water. (51) But when the tenth day dawned

Hecate, bearing light in her hands, encountered her and
spoke to her this message: (54) "Lady Demeter, bringer of
seasons and glorious gifts, who of the gods of heaven or of
mortal men has taken Persephone and pained your own heart?
I heard her voice, but did not see who it was. I am telling
you everything promptly, and accurately."

(59) So spoke Hecate. The daughter of fair-haired
Rheia did not answer a word, but she immediately darted off
with her, holding blazing torches in her hands, and they
came to Helios, the viewer of gods and men. They stood before his horses and the divine goddess said, (64) "Helios,
as a god, respect me, as a goddess, if ever in word or
deed, I have warmed your heart. The maiden whom I bore -
sweetest blossom - beautiful - I heard her voice, sobbing,
as if she were being raped, but I did not see her. But you
survey from the bright heaven all the earth and the sea with
your rays; tell me accurately whether you have seen who of
gods or mortal men has forced her and taken her away, all
unwillingly, in my absence."

(74) So she spoke, and the son of Hyperion answered
her: "Lady Demeter, daughter of fair-haired Rheia, you will
know all: I have great respect for you and pity you in your
grief for your slim-ankled child: none of the immortals is
responsible except Zeus the cloud-gatherer, who has granted
to Hades his own brother that she be called his tender wife;
and he has taken her, screaming a loud cry, away on his
horses down into the misty darkness. (82) So, goddess, stop
your loud lament; you should not rashly hold on to this
boundless anger; Aidoneus, the designator of many, is after
all not an unsuitable son-in-law for you, since you have the
same mother and father; and his honor he gained when at the
beginning a division into three parts was made; and he dwells
with those over whom the lot made him king." When he had
said this he called to his horses, and at his command they
bore the swift chariot like broad-winged birds.

(90) Then grief still more horrible and oppressive came
upon her heart, and in her anger at Zeus, shrouded in clouds,
she deserted the gatherings of the gods and went far from

Olympus to the cities and farms of men and for a long time
disguised her appearance. No man, no woman who saw her
recognized her, until she arrived at the home of clever
Keleos, who was the king of fragrant Eleusis at the time.
(98) At the Spring Parthenion where the citizens draw water
in the shade of a towering olive tree she sat by the side of
the road in the guise of an old woman, one who is beyond the
age of childbearing and the gifts of Aphrodite who bears the
garland of love, one who might be a nurse of royal children
or governess of important households. The daughters of
Keleos of Eleusis saw her as they came to draw water and
carry it in bronze vessels to their father's house. There
were four of them, like goddesses in youthful bloom -
Kallidike, Klesidike, lovely Demo and Kallithoe, the eldest
of them all. They did not recognize her, for gods are hard
for mortals to see. (112) They approached her and said,
"Old woman, who are you? Why have you kept away from the
city and not approached the settlement? There in the dusky
houses there are women as old as you and younger, who would
treat you kindly in word and deed."

(118) So they spoke, and the goddess mistress said in
answer, "Dear children, daughters of womanly mothers, be of
good cheer, and I will tell you, for it is right to tell you
the truth. The name my lady mother gave to me is Doso. I
have just come across the sea from Crete, forced by pirate
men who abducted me against my will. They brought their
swift ship to shore at Thorikos, and a crowd of women came
on board from the land and they all prepared their dinner by
the ship's stern-cables. But my heart had no desire for a
pleasant supper; instead I got up secretly and escaped those
arrogant overlords across the dark countryside, so that they
might not enjoy any profit from selling me. I wandered
about until I arrived here; but I do not know what land it
is nor which people dwell here. May all the gods who dwell
on Olympus grant you vigorous husbands and all the progeny
they want; but pity me, maidens; dear children, help me come
propitiously to some home of a man and woman where I may

provide the services of an aged woman for them: I could
hold their infant child in my arms and nurse it well, I
could keep house, make the master's bed in the inmost chamber, and instruct the women in their tasks."

(145) So said the goddess, and the maiden Kallidike,
most beautiful of Keleos' daughters, answered her, "Mother,
we humans endure the gifts of the gods, even under grievous
compulsion, for they are much mightier. I will explain it
all to you clearly, and tell you the men who hold the power
of authority here, and who stand out in the government and
direct the defense of the city with their counsels and
decisions. There are Triptolemos the clever, Dioklos,
Polyxeinos, Eumolpos the blameless, Dolichos, and our father
the manly one. Their wives manage everything in their households, and not one of them would dishonor you at first sight
by making you depart from their houses. They will receive
you, for you are godlike. If you wish, wait here while we
go to our father's house and tell Metaneira our deep-belted
mother all these things, and see whether she bids you come
to our house and not search for another's. A favorite son,
born to her late, is being nursed in the strongly built
palace; she prayed much for him, and rejoiced in him. If
you would nurse him and he would reach adolescence, any
woman would envy the sight of you, for she [Metaneira] would
give you so great a reward for nursing him."

(169) So she spoke, and she nodded her head, and then
they filled their shining jugs with water and carried them
proudly. Soon they reached their father's great house, and
quickly told their mother what they had seen and heard. She
told them to go quickly and bid her come, at a vast wage.
As deer or heifers frolic across the meadow eating to their
heart's content, so they darted along the road down the
gulley, holding up the folds of their lovely gowns, and their
hair streamed along their shoulders like saffron blossoms.
They reached the spot near the road where they had left the
glorious goddess, and they led her to their father's house.
She, grieved at heart, walked behind them with her head
veiled, and the dark robe trailed along around the slender
feet of the goddess.

(184) Soon they reached the house of Zeus-descended
Keleos, and went through the portico to the place where
their lady mother was sitting beside a column of the carefully made chamber, holding her new baby in her lap. The
girls ran to her, but Demeter trod upon the threshold, and
her head reached the roof-beam, and she filled the doorway
with a divine radiance. At this awe, reverence and pale
fear seized the woman. She rose from her chair and urged
her to be seated, but Demeter the bringer of seasons and
glorious gifts did not wish to be seated on the gleaming
chair, but silently cast down her beautiful eyes and waited
until Iambe understood and set a jointed stool out for her,
and threw a shining white fleece upon it. She sat down,
holding her veil in front with her hands. For a long time
she sat there on the stool sorrowfully, without speaking;
and made no contact with anyone in word or gesture. Without
smiling, without touching food or drink she sat, consumed
with yearning for her daughter, until Iambe understood and
made plenty of jokes and jests and made the holy Lady smile
with kindly heart, and ever afterward she continues to delight her spirit. Then Metaneira filled a cup of sweet wine
and offered it to her, but she refused it, for she said it
was not right for her to drink red wine. Instead, she asked
her to give her barley groats and water mixed with crusted
pennyroyal to drink. She made the compound, the *kykeon*, as
she commanded, and offered it to the goddess. Deo the greatly
revered accepted it for the sake of the ceremony.... (212)
Fair-belted Metaneira begin with these words, "Be of good
cheer, woman; I do not expect that you are sprung from base
stock, but from good; dignity and grace are manifest in your
eyes, like those of kings, stewards of the right. But we
humans endure the gifts of the gods, even under grievous compulsion, for a yoke lies upon our neck. But now that you
have come here, all that is mine shall be yours. Nurse this
child for me, whom the immortals have given me, late-born and
unexpected, but much prayed for. If you would nurse him and
he would reach adolescence, any woman would envy the sight of
you, for I would give you so great a reward for nursing him."

(224) Then Demeter of the fair crown said to her, "May
you also be of good cheer, woman, and may the gods grant you
all good things; I willingly accept the child, as you bid
me. I will nurse him, and I do not expect that he will be
injured by nurse's incompetence, supernatural attacks nor
magical cuttings, for I know an antidote more mighty than
the woodcutter, and I know a fine preventative against
malignant attacks.

(231) When she had said this she received him with her
immortal hands in her fragrant lap, and the mother's heart
rejoiced. So she nursed the glorious son of clever Keleos,
Demophon, whom fair-belted Metaneira bore, and he grew like
a god, eating no food, being suckled on no milk, for Demeter
would [feed and] anoint him with *ambrosia*, like the progeny
of a god, and she breathed sweetly on him and held him in
her lap. At night she would hide him like a fire-brand
within the might of the flame, without his parents' knowledge. It made them wonder greatly how he was so precocious,
and why his appearance was like the gods'. She would have
made him ageless and deathless, if it had not been that fair-
belted Metaneira foolishly kept watch one night and watched
her from her fragrant bed-chamber. She screamed and struck
both her thighs in fear for her child and in a frenzy of
mindlessness. Wailing, she said, "My child Demophon, the
stranger woman is hiding you in the blazing fire, and is
making grief and bitter sorrow for me."

(250) So she spoke, lamenting, and the divine goddess
heard her. Demeter of the beautiful crown was amazed at her;
with her immortal hands she put from her the dear child whom
[Metaneira] had borne, all unexpected, in the palace, and
threw him at her feet, drawing him out of the fire, terribly
angry at heart, and at the same time she said to fair-belted
Metaneira, "Humans are short-sighted, stupid, ignorant of
the share of good or evil which is coming to them. You by
your foolishness have hurt him beyond curing. Let my witness
be the oath of the gods sworn by the intractable water of
Styx, that I would have made your son deathless and ageless

all his days, and given him imperishable honor. But now it
is not possible to ward off death and destruction. Still
he will have imperishable honor forever, since he stood on
my knees and slept in my arms; in due season, as the years
pass around, the children of the Eleusinians will conduct
in his honor war (games) and the terrible battle-cry with
each other for ever and ever. I am Demeter, the Venerable,
ready as the greatest boon and joy for immortals and mortals.
So now, let the whole people build me a great temple, and
an altar beneath it, below the city and the towering wall,
above Kallirhoe on the ridge which juts forth. I myself
will establish rites so that henceforth you may celebrate
them purely and propitiate my mind."

(275) With these words the goddess altered size and
form and sloughed off old age; beauty wafted about her. A
lovely fresh smell radiated from her lovely gown and the
radiance from the skin of the immortal goddess shone afar.
Her blonde hair flowed down over her shoulders, and the
sturdy house was filled with light like a flash of lightning.
She went out through the palace. As for the other, her knees
gave way, and for a long time she was speechless. She did
not even remember the child, her favorite, to pick him up
from the floor. His sisters heard his piteous crying, and
they leapt down from their well-covered beds. Then one of
them took the child in her hands and put him in her lap,
one kindled a fire, and another hurried on gentle feet to
rouse her mother out of the fragrant chamber. Crowding
around they washed him, covering him with love as he squirmed;
his heart was not comforted, however, for less skillful nurses
and nurse maids were holding him now.

(292) All night long the women, quaking with fear, pro-
pitiated the glorious goddess. As soon as dawn appeared
they gave a full report to wide-ruling Keleos, as Demeter of
the beautiful garlands commanded. He summoned the people
from their many boundaries and ordered them to build an elaborate temple to fair-haired Demeter and an altar on the ridge
which juts forth. They obeyed him straightway, and hearkened

to him as he spoke, and started to build as he commanded.
And it grew at the dispensation of the divinity. When they
finished and ceased from their toil, each person went back
to his home. Blonde Demeter stayed there, seated far from
all the blessed gods, wasting with grief for her deep-belted
daughter.

(305) She made the most terrible, most oppressive year
for men upon the nourishing land, and the earth sent up no
seed, as fair-garlanded Demeter hid it. Cattle drew the
many curved plows in vain over the fields, and much white
barley seed fell useless on the earth. By now she would
have destroyed the entire race of men by grievous famine,
and deprived those who dwell on Olympus of the glorious honor
of offerings and sacrifices, if Zeus had not taken notice
and taken counsel with his mind. First he roused gold-winged
Iris to summon fair-haired Demeter, of the very desirable
beauty. So he spoke, and she obeyed Zeus wrapped in clouds,
the son of Kronos. She rushed down the middle and arrived
at the citadel of fragrant Eleusis. In the temple she found
Demeter dark-clad, and addressed her with winged words.
"Demeter, father Zeus who understands imperishable things
summons you to come among the race of the immortal gods.
So come, and let my message from Zeus not be fruitless."

(324) So she spoke in supplication, but Her heart was
not persuaded. Therefore the Father sent out the blessed,
ever-living gods one after another, and they went in turn
and implored her, and offered her many fine gifts and whatever honors she might choose among the immortal gods. None,
however, was able to persuade the heart and mind of the angry
goddess. She rejected their speeches firmly, and claimed
that she would never set foot upon fragrant Olympus, nor
allow any fruit to grow on the earth, until she saw with her
eyes the beautiful face of her daughter.

(334) When Zeus the loud-crashing, the wide-voiced one,
heard this he sent Hermes the slayer of Argos with his golden
wand to Erebos, to use smooth words on Hades and lead pure
Persephone out of the misty darkness into the light to join

the deities, in order that her mother might see her with her
eyes and turn from her anger. Hermes obeyed, and eagerly
rushed down under the recesses of the earth, leaving the
seat of Olympus. He found the Lord inside his house, seated
on couches with his modest and very unwilling wife, yearning
for her mother. ...

(346) The mighty slayer of Argos came near and said,
"Dark-haired Hades, ruler of the departed, Father Zeus has
ordered me to lead glorious Persephone out of Erebos to join
them, in order that her mother might see her with her eyes
and cease from her anger and terrible wrath, since she is
contriving a tremendous deed, to destroy the fragile race
of earth-born men, hiding the seed under the earth and ob-
literating the honors of the immortals. Her anger is terrible, she has no contact with the gods, but sits apart inside her fragrant temple, holding the rocky citadel of
Eleusis."

(357) So he spoke, and Aidoneus the lord of the underworld smiled with his brows, and did not disobey the injunc-
tions of Zeus the king. Promptly he gave the command to
diligent Persephone: "Go, Persephone, to your dark-clad
mother, and keep gentle the strength and heart in your
breast. Do not be despondent to excess beyond all others.
I shall not be an inappropriate husband for you among the
immortals; I am a brother of Father Zeus. Being there, you
will rule over all that lives and moves, enjoying the greatest
honors among the immortals. And there shall be punishment
forever on those who act unjustly and who do not propitiate
your might with sacrifices, performing the pious acts and
offering appropriate gifts."

(370) So he spoke, and Persephone the discreet was glad,
and swiftly leapt up for joy. But he gave her a honey-sweet
pomegranate seed to eat, having secretly passed it around
[himself?], so that she might not stay forever there by modest
dark-clad Demeter. Aidoneus, designator of many, harnessed
the immortal horses in front of the golden chariot, and she
stepped on the chariot; beside her the mighty slayer of Argos

took the reins and a whip in his hands and drove out of the
palace. The pair of horses flew willingly. They finished
the long journey quickly. Neither sea nor rivers nor grassy
glens nor mountain peaks held back the rush of the immortal
horses; they went above them, and cut through the high air.
He drove them where Demeter of the fair crown waited in front
of her fragrant temple, and he stopped them there. Seeing
them, she darted up like a maenad in the woods on a thick-
shaded mountain.

[(387) Demeter asked Persephone if she had eaten anything in the underworld. If not,] (395) "you will come up
and dwell with me and Zeus of the dark clouds, and be honored
by all the immortals. But if you have tasted anything, then
you shall go back down and dwell there for the third part
of the season, and for the other two, here with me and the
other immortals. Whenever the earth blossoms with all the
sweet-smelling flowers of spring, then you will come back
up from the misty darkness, a great wonder to gods and to
mortal men. But what trick did the powerful host of many
use to deceive you?"

(405) Persephone, the exceedingly beautiful, gave her
this response: "I will tell you, Mother, everything accurately. When the swift slayer of Argos came to me from
Father Zeus and the others in heaven with the message to
come out of Erebos, so that seeing me with your eyes you
might cease from your anger and terrible wrath, I leapt up
for joy. But he secretly insinuated a pomegranate seed,
honey-sweet food, and though I was unwilling, he compelled
me by force to taste it. How he snatched me away through
the clever plan of Zeus and carried me off, down into the
recesses of the earth, I will tell you and I will go through
it all as you ask. We were all there in the lovely meadow
- Leukippe, Phaino, Elektre, Ianthe, Melite, Iache, Rhodeia,
Kallirhoe, Melobosis, Tyche, Okyrhoe of the flowering face,
Chryseis, Ianeira, Akaste, Admete, Rhodope, Plouto, charming
Kalypso, Styx, Ouranie, lovely Galaxaure, Pallas the inciter
of battles, Artemis the shooter of arrows - playing and

picking the lovely flowers, a profusion of gentle saffron
blossoms, iris, hyacinth, rose birds and lilies, a marvel
to see, and narcissus, which the broad land grew like saffron. Full of joy, I was picking them, but the earth under
me moved, and the powerful Lord, the host of many, leapt out.
And he took me under the earth on his golden chariot, against
my will, and I screamed loudly with my voice. Grieved though
I am, I am telling you the whole truth."

(434) Then with minds in concord they spent the whole
day warming their hearts and minds, showering much love on
each other, and her mind found respite from its griefs, as
they gave and received joys from each other. And there came
near them Hecate of the glistening veil, and she also showered
much love on the daughter of holy Demeter, and ever since she
has been her attendant and Lady-in-waiting.

(441) Zeus the land-crashing, the wide-voiced one, sent
fair-haired Rheia as a messenger to them, to bring dark-
gowned Demeter among the race of the gods; he promised to
give her whatever honors she might choose among the immortal
gods. He granted that her daughter should spent the third
portion of the year in its cycle down in the misty darkness,
but the other two with her mother and the other immortals.

(448) So he spoke, and the goddess obeyed the biddings
of Zeus. Promptly she darted along the peaks of Olympus,
and came to the Rarian plain, the life-bringing udder of
plough-land formerly, but at that time not life-bringing at
all, as it stood all barren and leafless. The white barley
was concealed according to the plans of fair-ankled Demeter,
but at this time it was about to grow shaggy with waves of
grain as it became spring. In the field the rich furrows
were to be loaded with the grain, and they were to be bound
in sheaves. Here she first alighted from the boundless
aether, and they saw each other gladly, and rejoiced in
their hearts.

(459) Rheia of the glistening veil said to her, "Come
here, child. Zeus the loud-crashing, the wide-voiced one,
summons you to come among the race of the immortal gods, and

he has promised to give whatever honors you might choose
among the immortal gods. He has granted that your daughter
will spend the third portion of the year in its cycle down
in the misty darkness, but the other two with you and the
other immortals. So has he promised, and nodded his head
in affirmation. Go, now, my child, and obey; do not be
obdurately angry at Zeus of the dark clouds but give prompt
increase to the fruit, bringer of life to men."

(470) So she spoke, and Demeter of the fair crown
obeyed. Promptly she sent up fruit on the rich-soiled
fields, and the whole broad land was loaded with leaves and
flowers. She went to the royal stewards of the right and
to Triptolemos, Diokles the driver of horses, mighty Eumolpos
and Keleos the leader of the people. She showed the tendance
of the holy things and explicated the rites to them all, to
Triptolemos, to Polyxeinos and to Diokles - sacred rites,
which it is forbidden to transgress, to inquire into, or to
speak about, for great reverence of the gods constrains their
voice. Blessed of earth-bound men is he who has seen these
things, but he who dies without fulfilling the holy things,
and he who is without a share of them, has no claim ever on
such blessings, even when departed down to the moldy darkness.

(483) When the divine goddess had ordained all this,
she went to Olympus among the assembly of the other gods.
And there they dwell, sacred and reverent, with Zeus who
revels in thunder. Greatly blessed of earth-bound men is
he whom they propitiously love: to him they promptly send
to the hearth of his great house Ploutos [Wealth], who gives
abundance to mortal men.

(490) Now, ye that hold the people of fragrant Eleusis,
and sea-girt Paros and rocky Antron, Lady mistress Deo,
bringer of seasons and glorious gifts, thou thyself and
Persephone, the exceedingly beautiful, do ye bestow a heart-
warming livelihood in exchange for my song. Now I shall
recall thee, and also another song.

Cult Regulations

The Homeric Hymn provides the mythological framework
of the Mysteries. The inscriptions quoted here give information about their administration in the fifth century. The
first is dated about 460 B.C. Part A, not included because
it is too fragmentary to translate, concerns penalties for
impieties. Part B sets the timetable for the sacred truce
which accompanied the celebration of the Greater Mysteries
(which lasted from the 15th to the 23rd of the month
Boedromion) and the preparatory Lesser Mysteries (in the
month Anthesterion). The reference to other cities shows
that by the fifth century the Eleusinian cult's appeal
reached farther than Attica. Part C contains information
about cult personnel (especially the Heralds [*Kerykes*]
and *Eumolpidai*, the two noble families which had charge of
the sanctuary and its mysteries and the *hieropoioi*, sacred
agents), about financial arrangements, and about initiation
procedures.

(*IG* I² 6, B and C.)

B. (5) There is to be a truce for the initiates, the
epoptai, and the attendants and [possessions] of all the
foreigners and Athenians. The period of the truce is to
begin at the middle of the month Metageitnion and last
through Boedromion until the 20th of Pyanepsion. The truce
is to be in effect in all the cities which make use of the
sanctuary, and also for the Athenians there in the same
cities. For the Lesser Mysteries the truce is to last from
the middle of the month of Gamelion and through Anthesterion
until the 20th of Elaphebolion.

C. ...The sacred herald receives a half obol each day
from each initiate. The priestess of Demeter is to receive
at the Lesser Mysteries an obol from each initiate and at
the Greater Mysteries an obol from each initiate. All the
obols are for the Two Goddesses except for 1600 drachmas.
From this sum the priestess is to pay the expense as long
as it lasts. The Eumolpidai and Heralds are to receive from
each initiate all the parts from the sacrificial victims;
they are not to initiate any underage male or female initiate except for one who was initiated a[t the hearth(?)]; the
heralds are to initiate each of the initiates separately, and
the same is true of the Eumolpidai; if they do several, they

are to be liable for a thousand drachmas. Those of the
Heralds and Eumolpidai who are chosen by lot are to perform
the initiations.

It is allowed to the Athenians to control the expendi-
ture of the sacred funds, as long as they wish, as they do
the funds of Athena in the city. The *hieropoioi* are to be
custodians of the funds in the shrine inside the city.

The Eumolpidai are to hold the [certification (?)] of
the orphans, and the orphan children and the initiates are
each to make a preliminary sacrifice, the initiates sacrificing at Eleusis in the courtyard and inside the sanctuary,
and the others sacrificing in the Eleusinion in the city.

The priest stationed at the altar, th[e cleaner] of
the Two Goddesses, and th[e sacrosanct] priest is to receive
[as payment] from each of these [a half obol from] each
initiate, sacr[ed to the Two Goddesses.]

The Athenian state controlled Eleusis in the fifth
century, as shown in this document ordering the reorganiza-
tion of the sanctuary and providing for a regular payment
of grain to support the sanctuary. The date is in the
second half of the century, though experts disagree as to
the exact year (448, 422 and 418 have been suggested). The
cities mentioned are the subject-allies of Athens, members
of her empire.

(*IG* I^2 76.1-46.)

Resolved by the council and the people..., on the
proposal of the drafting committee: that the Athenians give
first-fruits of the grain to the Two Goddesses according to
ancestral custom and the oracle of Delphi - from every hundred *medimnoi* of barley, not less than 1/6 *medimnos*; from
every hundred *medimnoi* of wheat, not less than 1/12 *medimnos*.
If any produces more or less grain, he is to give first-fruits
in the same proportion. The deme-leaders in each deme are
to collect it and convey it to the *hieropoioi* from Eleusis
at Eleusis. They are to construct from the funds of the
Two Goddesses three silos according to ancestral custom at
Eleusis wherever seems convenient to the *hieropoioi* and the

builder. There they are to deposit the grain which they
receive from the deme-leaders. (14) The allies are also
to give first-fruits in the same way: the cities are to
select collection agents for the grain that the grain may
be collected in the best way. When it is collected, they
are to send it to Athens, and they are to take it and convey it to the *hieropoioi* from Eleusis at Eleusis. If they
do not receive it within five days after the proclamation
is made, the *hieropoioi* are to be liable, for a thousand
drachmas each, and they are to receive it from the deme-
leaders in the same way. The council is to choose heralds
and send them to the cities to announce the present vote of
the people, in the present case immediately and for the
future whenever the council decides; and the hierophant and
the torch-bearer are to order the Greeks to give first-fruits
of the grain to the mysteries according to ancestral custom
and the oracle of Delphi, and are to inscribe on a tablet
the amount of grain from the deme-leaders listed by each deme
and that from the cities listed by each city and they are
to place it in the Eleusinion at Eleusis and in the council-
chamber. (30) The council is also to make a proclamation
to all the other Greek cities in whatever way seems feasible
to it, telling them how the Athenians and the allies are
giving first-fruits and requesting, but not requiring, them,
if they wish, to give first-fruits according to ancestral
custom and the oracle of Delphi; and the *hieropoioi* are to
receive them from the cities in the same way, if any makes
a contribution. (36) The sacrifices: from the *pelanos*, as
the family of the Eumolpidai explicates; a triple sacrifice,
the first victim an ox with gilded horns, to each of the Two
Goddesses some of the barley and the wheat, and a perfect
victim each to Triptolemos, to the god [Plouton] and the
goddess [Persephone] and to Euboulos; and to Athena an ox
with gilded horns. The *hieropoioi* are to dedicate the rest
of the donated barley and wheat to the Two Goddesses, in
whatever form the people of the Athenians resolves, and they
are to inscribe on the dedications that they were dedicated

from the first-fruits of the grain, the offering of the
Greeks. (44) May there be many good things and an abundance
of grain of good quality to those who do this, whoever does
not act unjustly toward the Athenians, the city of the
Athenians, or the Two Goddesses. ...

The Meaning and Blessings of Initiation

The happiness of Eleusinian initiates is the basis for
the following selection from Aristophanes' *Frogs*. This is
a comedy, and in general full of raucous name-calling, slap-
stick and obscenity. Yet this choral passage, which is sung
by initiates in the underworld, celebrating their happiness
amid the gloom, is remarkably (if not completely) free of
vilification and comic trenchancy. The hymn is addressed
primarily to Iakchos, the divine personification of the
initiates' cry of enthusiasm (*iakche*).

(Aristophanes, *Frogs*, 324-336, 340-353, 369-413, 440-459.)

Chorus of initiates: O highly honored Iakchos, whose
dwelling-place is here, Iakchos, O Iakchos, come and dance
through this meadow to thy devout members of the *thiasos*,
shaking the fruit-laden crown of myrtle swelling around thy
head, and treading with bold foot the measure of the unin-
hibited, playful rite, with its full measure of the Graces,
the dance which is pure, holy to the sacred initiates. ...

Raise the blazing torches in your hands. Come among
us, Iakchos, O Iakchos, light-bringing star of the nocturnal
initiations. The meadow is ablaze with flame, the old man's
limbs are leaping, they shake off their griefs and the
lengthy spans of their aged years through the holy rites.
Do thou shine radiant with thy torch and lead us forth to
the flowering, marshy field where, blessed one, dances and
youthfulness bloom. ...

[To the doers of evil] I declare; and again I declare,
and again the third time I declare, stand aside from our
initiate choirs. But do ye waken your song and our night-
long revels which befit our festival.

Come now everyone bravely into the flowery breast of the
meadows, stamping and jeering and playing and mocking.
(There's been enough eating.)

But come that thou mayest raise thy voice in noble song
to exalt the Savior-goddess, who doth claim to save this
land for all seasons (even if Thorykion doesn't like it).

Come now, shout out another kind of hymn to the grain-
bearing Queen, the goddess Demeter, adorning it with sacred
song.

Demeter, Lady of pure rites, be present among us, and
save thine own choir. Grant me in security to play and
dance all the day.

And grant me to say many witty things, many serious
and, having played a jester worthy of thy festival, to wear
the victor's crown.

And now, with chants invoke hither the god of ripeness,
the fellow-pilgrim of our choral dance.

Much-honored Iakchos, who hast discovered the sweetest
part of the festival, accompany us toward the goddess and
reveal how thou dost accomplish thy long journey without
toil. Iakchos, who lovest the dance, be thou my escort and
guide.

For thou (for a laugh and economy's sake) hast ripped
my poor little sandal and these rags I wear, and hast found
a way for us to play and dance cheaply. Iakchos, who lovest
the dance, be thou my escort and guide.

Now have I caught sight of a young girl's - a beautiful
playmate's - nipple peeking out through a burst seam in her
dress. Iakchos, who lovest the dance, be thou my escort
and guide. ...

Proceed now along the holy circle of the goddess, along
the flowering grove, and play, ye who take part in the festival favored of the goddess. I with the maids and the women
shall go where they celebrate the goddess all night long,
and shall carry the holy blaze. Let us proceed to the
flowering, rose-filled meadows, playing in our special way,
with the most beautiful dancing, which the Fates, who bring
prosperity, do lead.

The sun and its holy blaze exist for us alone, who have
experienced initiation and have dealt in a respectul way with
strangers and private individuals.

By the end of the classical period, the Mysteries had
become famous throughout the Hellenic world. They were so
prestigious in the fourth century that the orator Isocrates,
speaking in extravagant praise of Athens' accomplishments,
uses the presence of the Mysteries in Attica as evidence
that Athens was the inventor of agriculture and all its
attendant blessings.

(Isocrates, *Panegyricus*, 28-29.)

That which in the first place our nature required was

provided by our city. Even if the story is mythical, never-

theless it is appropriate for it to be told now again. When

Demeter wandered about after the abduction of Kore she ar-

rived in this country; she was well disposed toward our

ancestors by reason of good deeds which may not be heard by

anyone except the initiates, and she gave those twin gifts,

the greatest which exist, the grains which caused us to

live a life no longer bestial and the initiation which gives

its participants pleasant hopes about the consummation of

life and eternity. (29) Our city showed its love not only

for the gods but also for our fellow men in that being in

possession of such good things it did not begrudge them to

others, but it gave to all of that which it had received.

And even today each year we reveal the rites; it has also,

in summary, taught the uses of grains, their cultivation

and the benefits which come from them.

The following passage shows how, in the last decade of
the fourth century, a foreign king was so eager to receive
initiation (for whatever reasons) as to force the Athenians
to accommodate him in spite of the calendar and ancestral
custom. The passage also shows the weakened political standing of Athens at the time, as well as a clear statement of
the schedule of the mysteries.

(Plutarch, *Life of Demetrius*, 26.)

At that time he was marching back to Athens, and he

wrote that he wished, as soon as he arrived, to be initiated

and to receive the whole set of ceremonies from the Lesser

to the *epoptika*. But this was not proper, and had never been

done before: the Lesser Mysteries were celebrated in the

month of Anthesterion, and the Greater in the month of
Boedromion, and they only conducted the *epoptika* after an
interval of at least a year. When his letter was read, only
Pythodoros the torch-bearer dared to oppose it, but he accomplished nothing. Instead, Stratokles moved, and it was
voted, to call Mounychion (the current month) Anthesterion
and consider it as such. Then they held the initiation
ceremonies at Agra for Demetrius. After this Mounychion
became Boedromion in place of Anthesterion, and he received
the rest of the initiation, including besides the *epopteia*.

The next four passages suggest the moral and spiritual
impact of the Eleusinian cult. First is a paraphrase from
Hermippos, an Athenian philosopher of the late fourth century, which gives the three moral and ritual admonitions
ascribed to Triptolemos, the legendary founder of the
Eleusinian cult. Next is Aristotle's analysis of the value
of the cult as a ceremony rather than a fixed body of doctrine. This is followed by two short quotations from fifth-
century authors singing of the rewards in the after-life
which initiates can expect.

(Porphyry, *On Abstinence* IV. 22.)

We understand that Triptolemos is the most ancient of
the Athenian lawgivers. Hermippos, in his second book on
lawgivers writes about him thus: "They say that Triptolemos
gave laws to the Athenians, and Xenokrates the philosopher
says that these three laws of his still survived at Eleusis
- 'Honor your parents; honor the gods with grain; do no harm
to animals.'"

(Aristotle, in Synesius, *Dio*, 10; frag. 15 in V. Rose,
Aristotelis ... Fragmenta, Leipzig, 1886.)

Initiates do not need to understand anything; rather,
they undergo an experience and a disposition - become, that
is, deserving.

(Sophocles, in Plutarch, *How to Study Poetry*, 21f; frag. 837 in A.C. Pearson, *The Fragments of Sophocles*, Cambridge, 1917.)

Thrice blessed of mortals are those who go to Hades after beholding these rites. To them alone is it given to live there; to others everything there is evil.

(Pindar, in Clement of Alexandria, *Stromateis* III. 3.17; frag. 121 in C.M. Bowra, *Pindari Carmina*, Oxford, 1935; frag. 137 in B. Snell and H. Maehler, *Pindarus*, Leipzig, 1975.)

Blessed is he who goes under the earth after seeing these things. He knows the consummation of life; he knows its Zeus-given beginnings.

Rites and Ceremonies

What went on in the Eleusinian mysteries, and what (if anything) was revealed as the climax of the initiation ceremony was never revealed by any initiate, and the mystery continues to puzzle scholars. Our only ancient sources are not very reliable. They are very late, and are nearly all Christian, polemical writings attacking the pagan cults. Several passages are included here, because modern interpretations of the Mysteries have been influenced by them. The Plato scholiast explicates the two sets of Lesser and Greater Mysteries, and preserves a ritual formula. Lactantius seems to be describing a feature of a sort of ceremonial passion play recalling the abduction of Persephone; his reference to lights is elaborated by Dio Chrysostom. Clement cites another ritual formula and "reveals" the contents of the sacred, secret chests [*kistai*], and Tertullian and Hippolytus both triumphantly expose the content of the great beholding [*epopteia*], the apparent climax of the initiation ceremony. They do not agree, however, whether the great mystery is the phallus or an ear of grain. Cf. Mylonas, *Eleusis*, pp. 258-278, and K. Clinton, *The Sacred Officials of the Eleusinian Mysteries* (Transactions of the American Philosophical Society 64, 3: Philadelphia, 1974).

(Scholiast on Plato, *Gorgias*, 497c.)

There were two sets of mysteries among the Athenians. One was called "Lesser," celebrated inside the city. The other was the "Greater," held at Eleusis. It was necessary to be initiated first into the Lesser, and then into the Greater; otherwise it was not proper to participate in the

Greater. These were celebrated in honor of Deo and Kore,
because Plouton carried off Kore, and Zeus slept with Deo.
Many base things were done in them, and these words were
spoken on the part of those being initiated: "I have eaten
from the drum, I have drunk from the cymbal, I have carried
the offering-dish [*kernos*], I have gone down into the
(bridal) chamber [*pastos*]."

(Lactantius, *Epitome* of the *Divine Institutes*, 23.7.)

     Similar to the other mysteries is that of Ceres
[Demeter]; in it Proserpina [Persephone] is sought with
lighted torches through the night, and when she has been
found the whole rite ends with expressions of joy and
brandishing of torches.

(Dio Chrysostom, *Orations* XII. 33.)

     ...It is as if someone would hand over a man, Greek
or barbarian, to be initiated in some inner sanctum of
exceptional beauty and size. He would see many mystical
sights, and hear many mystical voices. Darkness and light
would appear to him in alteration, and thousands of other
things would happen. It is furthermore like the initiating
personnel who, in the so-called "Enthronement," seat the
initiands and dance around them in a circle.

(Clement of Alexandria, *Protrepticus* II. 21-22; pp. 16-17
in the edition of O. Stählin, Leipzig, 1905.)

     The sacred formula of the Eleusinian mysteries is:
"I have fasted, I have drunk the *kykeon*, I have taken from
the chest, I have done my task and placed in the basket and
from the basket into the chest." ...The mystic chests are
such as these - for I must strip their sanctities naked and
speak aloud their ineffabilities--: are their contents not
sesame-sweets, cakes shaped like pyramids and balls, or
covered with navels, lumps of salt, and a serpent, the ritual
sign of Dionysus Bassaros? And are there not pomegranates
in addition, and sprigs of fig, fennel and ivy, and also
cheese-cakes and poppies? These are their sanctities!

(Tertullian, *Against the Valentinians*, 1.)

Even the famous Eleusinia, that heresy of Attic superstition, is a shameful thing about which they keep quiet,
in fact they impose torture before they certify the admis-
sion [of an initiate]. They start the *epoptai* off five
years before so that they may build up their expectation
by withholding knowledge and so that they may seem to reveal
something of a grandeur equivalent to the greed which they
have heaped up. Following this there is an obligation of
silence. This is kept assiduously because it is learned at
a late stage. However, the entire godhead in the innermost
sanctuary, the entire source of breathless adulation in the
epoptai, the entire secret token of their tongues, is revealed to be an image of the male organ.

(Hippolytus, *Refutation of All Heresies* V. 8.39.)

The Athenians, when they conduct the Eleusinian mysteries, reveal in silence to the *epoptai* the great, wonderful, most perfect initiation mystery, the *epoptikon*, an ear
of grain. This ear of grain is for the Athenians the great
initiatory light-bringer from that which is unformed
[*acharakteriston*], as when the hierophant himself ... at
night in Eleusis beneath a huge fire, celebrating the great
and unspeakable mysteries, cries aloud, "The Lady Brimo has
brought forth a holy son, Brimos."

C. The Cults of Dionysus

Ecstatic Worship of Dionysus

The classic treatment of Dionysiac religion is Euripides' tragedy the *Bacchae* ["Bacchant Women"]. It portrays the power of the secret rites in which the devout danced in Dionysus' honor, often in winter or mountain heights, and tore animals apart in order to consume their raw flesh and blood. Euripides' play conveys the abhorrence with which much of respectable society viewed these seemingly barbaric practices, but it also conveys the compelling appeal of this religion, especially to women - its promise of blessed happiness, of contact with elemental forces, of ecstasy, of possession by the gods. (The word *enthousiasmos* is often used to denote the in-dwelling of the god in his devotees.) On Dionysiac religion see M.P. Nilsson, *Greek Folk Religion;* W.K.C. Guthrie, *The Greeks and Their Gods* (Boston, 1950), pp. 145-182; E.R. Dodds' edition of Euripides' *Bacchae*[2] (Oxford, 1960), esp. the Introduction. The following passage from the *Bacchae* is a hymn of praise sung in honor of Dionysus *Bromios* ["Roarer"] by the chorus of Bacchant women, who congregate in a sacred band known as a *thiasos.*

(Euripides, *Bacchae* 64-168.)

From Asian land, passing by sacred Tmolos, I quickly ply for Bromios my pleasant toil, my easy-labored labor shouting *eua!* to Bacchus.

Who is on the road? Who is on the road? Who is in the palace? Let everyone come away, let every one consecrate his mouth with holy silence. For I shall sing a traditional hymn of Dionysus.

(72) O happy is he who with the god's blessing and knowledge of the rites of the gods leads a pious life and joins his soul to a *thiasos* and Bacchic revels in the mountains with devoted purifications, observing the ceremonies of the Great Mother Kybele, brandishing the *thyrsos,* and crowned with ivy, serves Dionysus.

Go, Bacchants; go, Bacchants, and bring Dionysus Bromios, divine son of God, back out of the Phrygian mountains into the broad streets of Greece. Bromios!

(88) He it is whom his mother carried and bore in
compulsive pangs of child-birth, casting him from her womb
when the lightning bolt of Zeus came flying at her, and she
departed the world at the stroke of the thunder. But then
Zeus the son of Kronos immediately received him in his
birthing-chamber, and enclosed him in his thigh and fastened
it with golden needles, to hide him from Hera.

.And he bore, when the Fates brought him to term, the
bull-horned god, and he crowned him with crowns of serpents,
which is the reason the maenads festoon their hair with
their beast-bred prey.

(105) O Theban nurses of Semele, crown yourselves with
ivy! Be laden with green bryony with its beautiful berries.
Play the Bacchant with branches of oak or pine, and deck
your garments of dappled fawn-skin with fillets of white
wool; be reverent in wielding the violent wands. Soon all
the earth will dance - he is Bromios, whoever leads the
thiasos [or "whenever Bromios leads the *thiasos*] - to the
mountain, to the mountain, where the crowd of women waits,
goaded from their looms and shuttles by Dionysus.

(120) O inner chamber of the Kouretes, O divine haunts
of Crete which gave birth to Zeus, where the Korybantes with
their triple crowns discovered in the caves this my round
drum of stretched hide. And in the tense strained Bacchic
dance they mixed it with the sweet-voiced breath of Phrygian
flutes, and they put it into Rhea's hand, an accompaniment
to the *eua*-song of the Bacchants. The raving Satyrs got it
from the goddess mother, and they attached it to the biennial dances in which Dionysus rejoices.

(135) He is pleasant on the mountains, when he falls
to the ground out of the swift-running *thiasoi*, wearing his
holy fawn-skin, tracking down the blood of the slaughtered
goat, the joy of flesh eaten raw, yearning for the Phrygian
mountains, the Lydian, and Bromios is the leader, *euoi!*

(142) The plain flows with milk, it flows with wine, it
flows with the nectar of bees; the Bacchic one holds up the
pine torch bright blazing like the smoke of Syrian incense

from his staff, and he darts at a run, with dances rousing
the stragglers and urging them on with his cries, tossing
his delicate locks in the air.

(151) And at the same time he roars out, with shouts
of *eua!*, thus: "O Bacchants, go; Bacchants, go! with the
glitter of Tmolos flowing with gold sing Dionysus to the
sound of deep-roaring drums, glorifying with *eua!* the god
of the *eua*-cry, in Phrygian shouts and cries, whenever the
sacred melodious flute plays its roaring sacred song, joining the pilgrimage to the mountain, to the mountain. Joyfully, then, like a colt at the manger with its mother, the
Bacchant moves her limbs in quick swift leaps.

This sort of nocturnal *oreibasia* ["Mountain-Processions"]
is also attested as early as the seventh century B.C. (though
it is not specifically Dionysiac) in the following fragment.

(Alcman, in Athenaeus, *Deipnosophists* XI. 498f-499a; frag.
56 in D. Page, *Poetae Melici Graeci*, Oxford, 1962.)

Often on the tops of the mountains when the gods took
delight in the festival with many torches you carried a large
(wooden) cup, like the ones shepherds carry, all golden; and
with your own hands you filled it with the milk of a lionness,
and you made a cheese, large, unbroken, to [Hermes] the
slayer of Argos.

The orgiastic nature of the Dionysiac rites is typified
by the musical instruments which accompanied the dance - in
this passage the geographer Strabo (who wrote in the late
first century B.C.) associates the cult of Dionysus with
similar cults in Phrygia (in Asia Minor) and Thrace (north-
east of Greece). Thrace was widely considered the land from
which Dionysus entered Greece.[31]

(Strabo, *Geography* X. 470-471.)

Among the Thracians (among whom the Orphic rites have
priority) the Kotyteia and the Bendideia are like the Phrygian
rites. Aeschylus in his tragedy "The Edonians" mentions
Kotyto and the instruments which accompany her, "they who
keep the sacred rites of Kotys [and her instruments]"; he

then alludes immediately to those who accompany Dionysus,
"The one holds in his hands bass flutes, worked on a lathe,
and fills it with fingered melody which brings on the in-
citement of madness; the other clashes bronze-bound hollow
cymbals." Again he says, "The lyre raises its cry, the
awesome bull-voiced mimes roar from some hidden place, and
the likeness of a drum, like subterranean thunder, comes
bearing deep-seated terror." These are like the Phrygian
ones, and it is not unlikely that, since the Phrygians are
colonists of the Thracians, they also transferred their
sacred rites there. In addition, by associating Dionysus
and Lycurgus the Edonian, they intimate the similarity of
their rites.

One of the gods from Thrace and Asia Minor whose cult
entered Greece in the fifth century and whose worship resembled that of Dionysus was Sabazios. The following excerpt is from a speech in which Demosthenes attacks his
opponent by emphasizing the degeneracy of the rites in which
he has participated. This passage alludes to some of the
cult practices, and also illustrates the suspicion with
which "respectable" elements regarded them.

(Demosthenes, *On the Crown*, 258-260.)

But you - the respectable man, spitting on everybody
else - consider the kind of fortune you have enjoyed....
[As a child you did menial service at your father's grammar
school], (259) and when you became a man you used to read
the texts and attend to the rest of the paraphernalia at
the initiation-rites your mother conducted - preparing fawn-
skins, mixing wine, purifying the initiates and wiping them
off with clay and bran, then after the purification bidding
them rise and say "I have escaped the evil, I have found the
better," and you thought it respectable that no one ever gave
out the shout as well as you. ...(260) During the days you
led your pretty *thiasoi*, garlanded with fennel and white
poplar, through the streets, and you would squeeze the
pareias-snakes and toss them above your head, and shout *Euoi
Saboi*, and dance around to *Hyes Attes! Attes Hyes!* greeted

by the old women as *Exarchos* [Leader], *Prohegemon* [Instruc-
tor], *Kittophoros* [Bearer of the Ivy], *Liknophoros* [Bearer
of the Winnowing-Fan], and such like, and you would get as
payment pastries - crumbled, twisted and fresh-ground.

When the Dionysiac mysteries became popular in Rome in
the second century B.C., the Romans translated their re-
actions against the cult into a general suppression of it.
The parts of Livy's account given here cast some light on
cult practices and the social class of the participants,
though the viewpoint is clearly that of a thoroughly hostile
witness.

(Livy, *History of Rome* XXXIX. 9.4, 10.5-7, 13.8-14.)

The mother told the young man that she had made a vow
on his behalf when he was sick, that as soon as he began to
recover she would have him initiated into the Bacchic rites,
and that she now wished to discharge the vow, as she was
obliged to do by the generosity of the gods. He must maintain chastity for ten days; on the tenth day he would partake
of a banquet and be washed with pure water, and then she
would conduct him into the sanctuary....

(10.5) [Then his mistress Hispala told him] that while
she was a slave she entered that sanctuary as an attendant
to her mistress, but as a free woman she had never gone near
it. She knew that it was the work-shop of every kind of
corruption, and it was well-known that for two years now no
one had been initiated there who was more than twenty years
old; as soon as a person was inducted, he was treated as a
victim for the priests. They would conduct him to a place
which resounded with screeches, chanting, music and the
crash of cymbals and drums, so that the voice of the initiate
could not be heard while the shameful act was perpetrated
upon him with violence....

(13.8) Hispala then expounded to the consul the origin
of the rites. At first that sanctuary belonged to the women,
and it was customary not to admit any man. They had three
days fixed each year in which initiations were held for the
Bacchants during the day. By custom the matrons were made

priestesses in turn. Paculla Annia of Campania changed
everything when she was priestess, in spite of a warning
from the gods. She was the first to initiate men, her sons
Minius Cerrinius and Herennius Cerrinius. Of the daytime
rite she made a nocturnal one; and for the three days each
year she established five initiation days each month. As
a result, the rites were in a state of promiscuity: men
mingled with women; the night added permissiveness; no crime,
no vice was neglected there. There was more debauchery on
the part of the men among themselves than with the women.
If some were less tolerant of the shame and more reluctant
to commit the crime, they were slaughtered as sacrificial
victims. To believe that nothing was illicit, among them
this was the most exalted faith. Men, as if their minds
had been taken from them, prophesied with frenzied tossings
of their bodies; women in the vestments of Bacchants, hair
in disarray, ran down to the Tiber with burning torches,
submerged the torches in the water and (because live sulfur
and lime were applied to them) brought them out with flame
still burning. People were reported to have been carried
off by the gods, when actually they had been tied to machines
which carried them out of sight into hidden caverns - these
were the ones who had refused to take the oath or take part
in the crimes or tolerate the abuse. They were an immense
group, and were now almost a second nation; several men and
women of the nobility were among the number. For the last
two years it had been the policy that no one over the age
of twenty be initiated - those of younger ages could be got
hold of and were more tolerant of error and vice.

Rites of Dionysus in Sikyon

This short passage describes the temple and worship of
Dionysus at Sikyon in the northern Peloponnese. The secrecy
of the Bacchic cult is here combined with a temple accessible
to the public.

(Pausanias, *Description of Greece* II. 7.5-6.)

After the theater is a temple of Dionysus. The god is
of gold and ivory, and beside him are Bacchants of marble.
They say that these women are sacred to the god and go into
a frenzy in his honor. There are other statues, but the
Sikyonians keep them in secret: these they bring on one
night a year into the Dionysion from the so-called *kosmeterion*
["vestry"], and they bring it accompanied by lighted torches
and native hymns; the one which they call Bakcheios goes
first - Andromadas the son of Phlias made it for them -
followed by the one called Lysios ["Releaser"], which Phanes
of Thebes brought from Thebes at the command of the Delphic
oracle.

The Anthesteria

The spring festival of the Anthesteria provides an
example of several types of rituals, public and private,
addressed to Dionysus. A fragment of the Hellenistic historian Apollodorus gives the names of each of the three
days of the festival, celebrated on the 11th, 12th and 13th
of the month Anthesterion. Cf. the discussion in M.P.
Nilsson, *Greek Folk Religion* (New York, 1962), pp. 32-36.

(Apollodorus of Athens, in the Scholia to Aristophanes,
Acharnians, 961; frag. 133 in *FGrH* 244.)

The whole festival held for Dionysus is called
"Anthesteria"; its parts are *Pithoigia* ["Opening of the
Wine Jars"], *Choes* ["Pitchers"] and *Chytroi* ["Pots"].

The ceremonies of the first day, *Pithoigia*, are briefly
described by Plutarch and by Phanodemus, a historian of the
fourth century B.C.

(Plutarch, *Table-Talk*, 655e.)

At Athens they inaugurate the new wine on the eleventh
of the month, and they call the day *Pithoigia*.

(Phanodemus, in Athenaeus, *Deipnosophists* XI. 465a; frag.
12 in *FGrH* 325.)

At the temple of Dionysus in Limnai ["The Marshes"]
the Athenians bring the new wine from the jars and mix it
in honor of the god and then they drink it themselves. Because of this custom Dionysus is called Limnaios, because
the wine was mixed with water and then for the first time
drunk diluted.

The second day of the festival, "Pitchers," was also
observed at the sanctuary of Dionysus in the Marshes. The
participants who conducted the rites in secrecy were a
group of priestesses called *gerarai*, the *Hierokeryx* [Sacred
Herald], and the *Basilinna*, the wife of the annual magis-
trate who was called the "King" because the office included
the priestly duties associated in very early times with the
King of Athens. The source for all this is a speech in
which Neaira, the wife of the "King" in one of the years in
the late 340's B.C., is accused of having profaned the secret
rites because she was not a full-blooded Athenian, and had
even been a prostitute before marrying her husband. The
passage also includes a reference to the ceremony, held
later in the day, in which the "Queen" became the bride of
Dionysus. The short selection from Aristotle describes the
location of this sacred mating, the Boukoleion in the Athenian
agora. On the Demosthenes passages see H.W. Parke, *Festivals
of the Athenians* (London and Ithaca, 1977), pp. 110-113.

(Demosthenes, *Against Neaira*, 73-76, 78.)

And this woman offered for you on behalf of the city
the unspeakably holy rites, and she saw what it was inappropriate for her, being a foreigner, to see; and being a
foreigner she entered where no other of all the Athenians
except the wife of the king enters; she administered the
oath to the *gerarai*[32] who serve at the rites, and she was
given to Dionysus as his bride, and she performed on behalf
of the city the traditional acts, many sacred and ineffable
ones, toward the gods. These are things which may not be
heard by everyone; how then is it pious for a passer-by to
do them, let alone for such a woman and one who has perpetrated such acts?

(74) ...In ancient times, Athenians, there was monarchy
in our city, and the kingship belonged to those who in turn
were outstanding because of being aboriginals. The king
used to make all the sacrifices, and his wife used to perform those which were most holy and ineffable - and appropriately, since she was queen. (75) But when Theseus cen-
tralized the city and created a democracy, and the city
became populous, the people continued no less than before
to select the king, electing him from among the most distinguished in noble qualities. And they passed a law that
his wife should be an Athenian who has never had intercourse
with another man, but that he should marry a virgin, in
order that according to ancestral custom she might offer the
ineffably holy rites on behalf of the city, and that the
customary observances might be done for the gods piously,
and that nothing might be neglected or altered. (76) They
inscribed this law on a *stele* and set it beside the altar
in the sanctuary of Dionysus in Limnai. This *stele* is
still standing today, displaying the inscription in worn
Attic letters. Thus the people bore witness about their
own piety toward the god and left a testament for their
successors that we require her who will be given to the god
as his bride and will perform the sacred rites to be that
kind of woman. For these reasons they set it in the most
ancient and holy temple of Dionysus in Limnai, so that most
people could not see the inscription. For it is opened once
each year, on the twelfth of the month Anthesterion. ...

(78) Now I wish to summon the sacred herald, who attends
the wife of the king when she administers the oath to the
gerarai with their baskets at the altar, before touching the
sacrificial victims, in order that you may hear the oath and
the formulas spoken, insofar as it is possible to hear them,
and that you may see how solemn and sacred and ancient the
traditional rites are:

Oath of the *Gerarai*: "I live a holy life and am wholly
pure from others who do not live a pure life and from rela-
tions·with a man; I serve as *gerara* at the Theoinia [feast

of the wine god] and the Iobakcheia to Dionysus in accordance
with ancestral custom and at the appropriate times."

(Aristotle, *Constitution of the Athenians*, 3.5.)

Not all the magistrates live together. The "King" kept
what is now called the Boukoleion near the *prytaneion* [town-
hall]. The evidence is that even now the mating and marriage
of the wife of the "King" with Dionysus takes place there.

In addition to these official ceremonies, private
drinking parties were held. In his comedy, The *Acharnians*,
Aristophanes shows us a man preparing to celebrate the ad-
vent of peace by observing the Pitcher-banquet. At this
banquet the host provided dessert, but each guest brought
his own wine and pitcher. The fragment of Phanodemus gives
an aetiological myth to explain this custom, as well as the
custom of taking the wreaths to the temple of Dionysus after
the party.

(Aristophanes, *Acharnians*, 1085-1093.)

Come quickly to dinner, bringing your hamper and your
pitcher, for the priest of Dionysus summons you. Hop to it
now - you've been holding up the banqueting long enough.
All the rest has been prepared - couches, tables, cushions,
spreads, wreaths, myrrh, sweets, whores, all kinds of cakes
(whole-wheat, flat, sesame, sesame-and-honey), and dancing-
girls, beautiful ones, the darlings of Harmodios. But hurry
as fast as you can.

(Phanodemus, in Athenaeus, *Deipnosophists* X. 437c-d; frag.
11 in *FGrH* 325.)

Demophon the King instituted the festival of the Pitchers
[*Choes*] at Athens. When Orestes arrived at Athens [after
killing his mother] Demophon wanted to receive him, but was
not willing to let him approach the sacred rites nor share
the libations, since he had not yet been put on trial. So
he ordered the sacred things to be locked up and a separate
pitcher of wine to be set beside each person, saying that a
flat cake would be given as a prize to the one who drained

his first. He also ordered them, when they had stopped
drinking, not to put the wreathes with which they were
crowned on the sacred objects, because they had been under
the same roof with Orestes. Rather, each one was to twine
them around his own pitcher and take the wreathes to the
priestess at the precinct in Limnai, and then to perform
the rest of the sacrifice in the sanctuary. The festival
has been called *Choes* ever since.

The third day *Chytroi* ["Pots"] was a day of relative
solemnity. Pots of food were set out for Hermes (as the
guide of the dead to the underworld). Theopompus, who wrote
in the fourth century, describes the ceremony and gives an
aetiological explanation for it.

(Theopompus, in the Scholia to Aristophanes, *Acharnians*,
1076; frag. 347 in *FGrH* 115.)

Those who had survived the great deluge [of Deukalion]
boiled pots of every kind of seed, and from this the festival gets its name. It is their custom to sacrifice to Hermes
Chthonios [Of the Underworld]. No one tastes the pot. The
survivors did this in propitiation to Hermes on behalf of
those who had died.

The *Chytroi* ended with a ritual cry usually interpreted
as an order to the souls of the departed to leave the land
of the living. Our source for the cry is a Christian writer
of the ninth century A.D., who gives another explanation
(cf. L. Deubner, *Attische Feste* (Berlin, 1932), pp. 94-96,
113-114).[33]

(Photius, *Lexicon*, s.v. "Thyraze Kares".)

"To the doors, Kares, it is no longer Anthesteria":
some authorities contend that this is what is said to the
crowd of Karian slaves, since at the Anthesteria they join
in the feast and do not do any work. Therefore, when the
festival is over, they send them back out to work with the
words, "To the doors, Kares, it is no longer Anthesteria."
But others contend that the proverb goes: "To the doors,
Keres, it is no longer Anthesteria," since the souls [*keres*]
wander about through the city at the Anthesteria.

The Rural Dionysia

Many of the demes of Attica had their own festivals of
Dionysus, held in the winter month of Poseideon. Our chief
source is this passage from Aristophanes' comedy The
Acharnians, in which Dikaiopolis makes a private peace
treaty with the Spartans, then celebrates with the bawdy
revelry of a phallic procession with the rest of his family.

(Aristophanes, *Acharnians*, 243-279.)

Dikaiopolis: Keep holy silence, holy silence!

Chorus: Quiet, everybody. Did you men hear that "holy
silence"? This is the one, the person we've been looking
for. Everybody out of the way - it looks as if the man is
coming out to make a sacrifice.

Dikaiopolis: Keep holy silence, holy silence! Girl, be
the Basket-bearer, come forward a little - Xanthias, hold
the phallus up straight. Now put the basket down, daughter,
so we can start.

Daughter: Here, mother, hand me the sauce-boat, so I can
pour the sauce on this cake.

Dikaiopolis: Well, that's fine. O Lord Dionysus, may it
be well-pleasing to you, that I conduct this procession,
make sacrifice with my household, and celebrate auspiciously
the country Dionysia, to observe my release from army duty.
And may my thirty-year truce be well concluded. Daughter,
be nice - and careful to carry the basket nicely - you look
like you've had a dose of bitter herbs. It'll be a lucky
man who marries you, and when he gets up, produces little
polecats that smell just as bad as you. Go on, and be very
careful in the crowd that nobody sneaks a nibble at your
baubles. Xanthias, you two hold the phallus up straight and
follow the Basket-bearer. I'll come along and sing the
phallus-song. Wife, you watch me from the roof. Let's go!
O Phales, comrade of Bacchus, wanderer in the night, adulter-
er, pederast: it has been six years since I have come in
joy to my deme to address you, to pour libations to make a
treaty for myself, discharged from business and battle and
Lamachos. Much more pleasant it is, O Phales, Phales, to

find that ripe and ready thieving wood-gathering Thracian
slave-girl of Strymodoros, the one from Phelleus, to grab
her waist, lift her up, toss her down, and get down to business, O Phales, Phales. If you join our drinking-party, at
dawn the morning after you will gulp down a cup of peace;
and the shield will hang on the fireplace.

The City Dionysia

The great Attic festival of Dionysus was held in the
spring month of Elaphebolion. After a procession on the
first day escorting the god's statue to the theater precinct,
the festival included three days of choral performances and
the production of tragedies and comedies. In the first
passage, Demosthenes the orator who as *choregos* or sponsor
of the boys' dithyrambic chorus in 349 B.C. was assaulted
by his enemy Meidias in the theater, here accuses Meidias
of sacrilege. In the process he cites some of the laws
and oracles regulating the festival.

(Demosthenes, *Against Meidias*, 51-54.)

Surely you know that you perform all these choral dances
and hymns to the god in accordance not only with the laws
concerning the Dionysia, but also with the oracles both from
Delphi and from Dodona, in all of which you will find it
enjoined upon the city to organize choruses according to
ancestral custom, to fill the streets with sacrificial savor
and to wear garlands. (52) Please take them and read the
oracles themselves.

> "Now I address you, the sons of Erechtheus, all who
> do dwell in
> Pandion's city, whose festivals follow the ancestral
> customs.
> Be ever mindful of Bacchus, and throughout the broad
> spacious roadways
> Set up the thanksgiving dances to Bromios for all the
> seasons,
> Cover your heads with thick garlands, set sweet smelling
> savor on altars."

"For good health, sacrifice and pray to Zeus Hypatos
[the Highest], and Apollo Prostaterios [the Guardian]. For
good fortune, to Apollo Agyieus [of the Streets], Lato,
Artemis; in the streets set bowls of wine and dances, and
wear garlands according to ancestral custom for all the
Olympian gods and goddesses, raising right arms and left;
and remember your donations."

(53) Oracle from Dodona: "The man of Zeus declares to
the Athenian people: whereas you have let pass the times
of sacrifice and the sacred embassy, he commands you to send
nine delegated envoys, and with dispatch. Make an auspicious
offering to Zeus Naios of three oxen and with each ox two
sheep, and to Dione an ox, and a bronze table for the dedication which the Athenian people have dedicated.

"The man of Zeus declares in Dodona: conduct a public
sacrifice to Dionysus, mix a bowl of wine and set up choruses;
sacrifice an ox to Apollo Apotropaios [the Averter]; both
free and slave are to wear garlands, and to be at leisure
for one day. A white bull to Zeus Ktesios."

(54) Athenians, these and many other fine oracles are
in the city's keeping. What then should you take to heart
out of them? - that they order us to offer sacrifices to
the gods indicated by each oracle, but in addition they also
enjoin us to set up choruses and to wear garlands according
to ancestral custom and all the oracles which come to us.

The following short passages illustrate the procession
with the statue of Dionysus from the suburban Academy to
the temple in the theater precinct, and also the conduct of
the performances themselves. For a detailed account of the
festival, see A. Pickard-Cambridge, *The Dramatic Festivals
of Athens* (Oxford, 1968), pp. 57-125; more briefly in Parke,
Festivals of the Athenians (London and Ithaca, 1977), pp.
125-136.

(Pausanias, *Description of Greece* I. 29.2.)

The Athenians also have shrines of gods and heroes and
tombs of men outside the city in the demes and along the
roads. The nearest is the Academy; it was once one man's

private property, but in my day is a gymnasium. ...There is
a temple there, not large, into which they bring the statue
of Dionysus Eleuthereus every year on certain fixed days.

(Alciphron, *Letters* IV. 18.16.)

May I always have the opportunity to garland myself
with Attic ivy and sing hymns to Dionysus each year at the
Hearth.

(*IG* II^2 1006, lines 12-14.)

[The youths of the city] accompanied Dionysus from the
Hearth to the theater with torches, and they sent to the
Dionysia a bull worthy of the god which they sacrificed to
the god at the procession.

(Philochorus, in Athenaeus, *Deipnosophists* XI. 464f; frag.
171 in *FGrH* 328.)

The Athenians, at the Dionysiac competitions, first had
breakfast and drank, and when they had finished they went
to the show. They wore wreathes to watch it, and during the
whole competition wine was poured for them and sweets were
brought around. They would pour out something for the
choruses to drink at their entrances, and when they were
through with the competition and were proceeding out, they
would pour some more for them.

D. The Mysteries of the Kabeiroi at Samothrace

On the island of Samothrace, off the coast of Thrace in the northern Aegean Sea, was an ancient cult of Thracian gods which became well-known to the Greeks. A mystery cult with initiation and some secret knowledge or experience is attested in the fifth century, and frequently alluded to in ancient literature. As with the Eleusinian and Dionysiac mysteries, the most explicit documents are from a very late period and are not necessarily very reliable. One such is the first selection, a list of the Thracian gods who were worshipped at the sanctuary, and the Greek gods with which they were at some point identified. The sanctuary on Samothrace has been excavated by the Institute of Fine Arts of New York University; the complete excavation report *Samothrace* edited by Karl Lehmann, is published in the Bollingen Series and includes as vol. I (New York, 1958), a complete collection of ancient testimonies edited by Naphtali Lewis.

(Ancient "Laurentine" Scholiast on Apollonius Rhodius, *Argonautica* I. 917.)

On Samothrace there are held initiations to the Kabeiroi, as Mnaseas says. Their names, four in number, are Axieros, Axiokersa, Axiokersos. Axieros is Demeter, Axiokersa is Persephone, and Axiokersos is Hades. Kasmilos, added as the fourth, is Hermes, as Dionysodorus relates. Athenion says that Iasion and Dardanos were born of Zeus and Electra. The title "Kabeiroi" seems to come from the Kabeira mountains in Phrygia, since they were transferred from there. Others say there are two Kabeiroi, the elder Zeus, and the younger Dionysus.

The historian Diodorus (first century B.C.) gives an account of the visit to Samothrace by the Argonauts. It connects Orpheus (himself a Thracian) with the cult, and presents a mythological prototype for the belief that the Samothracian gods protected their initiates from shipwreck.

(Diodorus, *Library of History* IV. 43.1-2.)

A great storm had come up and the leaders had despaired of safety, but they say that Orpheus, the only one of the Argonauts who had participated in the initiation rites, made

211

prayers for safety to the Samothracian gods. And as the
wind immediately subsided and twin stars fell above the
heads of the Dioskouroi [Kastor and Polydeukes], they were
all amazed at the unexpected event, and understood that they
had been rescued from their dangers by the gods' providence.
For this reason this reversal of fortune has been handed
on to succeeding generations, so that when in a storm sailors
offer prayers to the Samothracian gods, and they ascribe the
presence of the stars to the epiphany of the Dioskouroi.

In the next passage Diodorus gives the legendary account
of the origin of the mysteries. It constitutes a sacred tale
which may have functioned similarly to the Hymn to Demeter
at Eleusis (p. 171 above).

(Diodorus, *Library of History* V. 47.2-3, 48.2-49.4.)

Some say it [the island], called Saonnesos in ancient
times, was named Samothrace because of the settlers from
Samos and Thrace. The aboriginals had their own ancient
language, and many expressions from it have been preserved
until now in the sacrifices. ... (48.2) They say that among
the Samothracians were born three children of Zeus and
Electra, one of the daughters of Atlas - they were Dardanos,
Iasion and Harmonia. Of these Dardanos proved to be especially ambitious; he was the first to reach Asia on a raft, and
his first action was to found the city of Dardanos and to
establish what was later called Troy. ... But Zeus wanted
his other son also to attain some honor, and so he revealed
to him the initiation-rite of the mysteries, which had long
been on the island and were at that time handed on - though
it is not proper for anyone to hear them except the initiates.
He is supposed to be the first to initiate foreigners and
by this means to make the initiations prestigious.

After this Cadmus the son of Antenor arrived among them
during his quest for Europa. He participated in the initiation and married Harmonia, the sister of Iasion (and not, as
the Greeks tell the tale, the daughter of Ares). (49) This
marriage was the first at which the gods provided the banquet:

Demeter fell in love with Iasion and contributed the fruit
of the grain, Hermes gave a lyre, Athena the far-famed
necklace, a gown and flutes, and Electra the rites of the
Great Mother (as she is called) with their cymbals, kettle-
drums and ecstatic celebrants. Also, Apollo played the
lyre, the Muses the flute, and the other gods gave their
blessings and increase to the marriage. ...

Iasion married Kybele and fathered Korybas. After
Iasion departed for the gods, Dardanos, Kybele and Korybas
conveyed the rites of the Mother of the Gods into Asia and
took them away into Phrygia. ... Korybas called those who
in the rites of the Mother are inspired Korybantes, after
himself, and he married Thebe the daughter of Kilix. The
flutes were similarly transferred into Phrygia from there,
and the lyre of Hermes was taken to Lyrnessos. ... The myths
say that Ploutos [Wealth] was born of Iasion and Demeter,
though in fact it is the wealth of the grain, given at the
wedding of Harmonia because of her [Demeter's] relationship
with Iasion. ...

The details of the initiation are kept as one of the
ineffable things and are divulged only to the initiates.
But the epiphany of these gods is widely known, as is also
the unexpected help in dangers to those initiates who invoke
them. They say that those who have been in communion with
the mysteries become more reverent, more just, and in general
better than they had been. For this reason the most important of the ancient heroes and demigods were very eager to
take part in the initiation. Jason and the Dioskouroi, as
well as Heracles and Orpheus after they were initiated suc-
ceeded in all their campaigns, as a result of the epiphany
of these gods.

(Strabo, *Geography* X. 466.)

Some declare that the following are the same as the
Kouretes: the Korybantes, Kabeiroi, Daktyloi of Mount Ida,
and Telchines. Others say that they are relatives of each
other and make small distinctions among them. To speak

roughly and generally, during the ceremonies they are all
inspired and Bacchic and, vested as serving attendants
strike terror by means of war-dances with the din and clash
of cymbals, kettle-drums and weapons; as well as of flutes
and shouts. Thus these rites are in some way identified,
as are also those of the Samothracians, those in Lemnos and
several others, because their attendants are called the same.

Herodotus, who wrote in the fifth century B.C. and was
apparently an initiate of the Samothracian mysteries, here
hints at the symbolism and ritual of the initiation ceremony,
but without violating their secrecy. He is more concerned
with proving the antiquity of the cult, ascribing it to the
Pelasgians, who for him are the aboriginal, pre-Greek inhabitants of Greece.

(Herodotus, *The Histories* II. 51.)

The Greeks learned to make statues of Hermes with an
erect phallus not from the Egyptians, but from the Pelasgians;
the Athenians were the first Greeks to take them over, and
the others took them over from them. The Athenians had already long been counted as Greeks when the Pelasgians settled
with them in their country, and therefore they also began to
be considered as Greeks. Whoever has been initiated into
the rites of the Kabeiroi which the Samothracians celebrate,
having taken them over from the Pelasgians, that man knows
what I mean. For these Pelasgians who settled with the
Athenians used to inhabit Samothrace, and the Samothracians
took over their rites from them. Therefore the Athenians
were the first Greeks to make statues of Hermes with an erect
phallus, having learned it from the Pelasgians. The
Pelasgians told a sacred account about it, which is revealed
in the mysteries at Samothrace.

Another fifth-century source is this passage from
Aristophanes, which shows that Samothracian initiates expected the continuing protection of the gods. The passage
from Aristophanes is followed by a commentary on it compiled
in later antiquity, which makes explicit the rewards of
initiation.

(Aristophanes, *Peace*, 276-279, 285-286.)

Gentlemen, what's going to happen to us? Now the fight gets serious. If any of you happens to have been initiated at Samothrace, now's the time to make a good prayer to turn aside the onslaught of - the guy's two feet. ... [after the prayer is answered:] Well done, well done, Dioskouroi! Maybe it will come out all right! Take courage mortals!

(Scholiast on Aristophanes, *Peace*, 277-278.)

In Samothrace were certain rites of initiation which seem to have been celebrated as a kind of prophylactic charm against dangers. In Samothrace were the mysteries of the Korybantes and those of Hecate. The cave Zerinthos was also renowned: there, it is said, they held ecstatic rites to Hecate, and certain initiations in her honor, and sacrificed dogs. The poet of the "Alexandra" mentions it: "Leaving the cave Zerinthos of the dog-slaying goddess and Saos the stronghold foundation of the Kyrbantes." When they are in danger they invoke the *daimones* to whom they are supposed to be initiated, to make an epiphany and to ward it off.

Those who are initiated into the mysteries of the Kabeiroi are supposed to be just and to be saved from terrors and storms.

The following passage, attributed in various versions to several important Spartans of the classical period, attests that moral purity and a confession of sin were part of the rites at the sanctuary.[34]

(Plutarch, *Laconic Sayings*, 217c-d.)

When Antalkidas was being initiated at Samothrace he was asked by the priest what was the most terrible thing he had done in his life. He said, "If such a thing has been done by me, the gods will know by themselves."

The Christian writer Hippolytus gives his version of the secret doctrine taught in the Samothracian cult. As usual, this late and biased testimony must be used with caution.

(Hippolytus, *Refutation of All Heresies* V. 8.9-10.)

This is the great and unspeakable mystery of the
Samothracians, which it is permitted only to us initiates,
he says, to know. For the Samothracians explicitly convey
to those undergoing initiation that Adam is among them the
primal man. Two statues stand in the *Anaktoron* [Palace] at
Samothrace, of nude men holding both arms stretched up to
heaven, and their pudenda turned up, as does the statue of
Hermes on Kyllene. The statues just mentioned are images
of the primal man and of the regenerating spirit consub-
stantial in every way with that man.

CHAPTER VI. DEATH AND AFTERLIFE

A. Views of Death; Burial Rites

The following selections demonstrate the range of
Greek views on the important question of human mortality.
Like contemporary man, the Greeks had a wide variety of
opinions on the subject. The selections are arranged in
approximately chronological order, to illustrate how these
views developed, became more complex, and were affected by
changes in the political and social fabric of Greek civi-
lization. For further reading, see H. Wagenvoort, "The
Journey of the Souls of the Dead to the Isles of the Blest,"
Mnemosyne 24 (1971) 113-161; B.C. Dieterich, *Death, Fate
and the Gods* (London, 1965); J. Boardman and D. Kurtz,
Greek and Roman Burial Customs (Ithaca, 1971); W.K.C. Guthrie,
Orpheus and Greek Religion (London, 1935), pp. 148-193;
M.P. Nilsson, *Minoan-Mycenaean Religion* (Lund, 1950).

Homer's Iliad

This passage describes, at the conclusion of the *Iliad*,
the funeral of the Trojan hero Hector. His body has just
been begged from Achilles by Hector's father Priam, and as
the episode opens Priam returns with the body inside the
walls of Troy. As so often, Homer provides a prototypical
account of an important Greek institution, in this case an
elaborate funeral of a distinguished person.

(Homer, *Iliad* XXIV. 707-745, 776-804.)

No man was left there in the city, nor woman either,
for an unbearable grief came upon them all. Near the gates
they met Priam as he carried home the corpse. First Hector's
wife and lady mother wailed as they hurled themselves on the
light-running wagon and touched his head. Around them the
crowd milled and wept. And now for the whole day until the
setting of the sun they would have shed tears of lament for
Hector before the gates, had not the old man spoken from his
chariot amid the crowd, "Let the mules pass through; you may
fill yourselves with weeping, when I have brought him home."

So he spoke, but they stood apart and yielded to the
wagon. When the others had brought him to his glorious house,
then they placed him on a corded bed, and by his side sat

217

singers, leaders of the dirge, who sang the lament. The
man chanted the dirge, and the women responded with the
lament. Among them white-armed Andromache led the wailing,
holding in her hands the head of man-slaying Hector, "Husband, you are young to have perished, and you leave me a
widow in the palace, and your child is still an infant, the
son which we bore, you and I, in our misery. I don't think
he will reach adulthood, for this city will be utterly destroyed before then. You have perished, its guardian, you
who defended it and protected its noble wives and helpless
children. They will soon be riding in the hollow ships,
and I with them. But you, my child, either will follow me
to a place where you must perform unfitting tasks and toil
for an ungentle master, or some Achaean will snatch you by
the arm and hurl you from the tower, a woeful death, in his
anger because Hector killed his brother or father or son,
since very many of the Achaeans have bitten the vast earth
with their teeth at the hands of Hector. For your father
was not a gentle man in grievous war. The folk now wail
for him in the city and unspeakable grief and pain have you
brought to your parents, Hector; for me especially shall
grievous woes be left. For when you died you didn't stretch
out your hands to me from the bed, nor speak to me any wise
word, upon which I might have pondered night and day as I
shed my tears." ....

But old Priam said to the people, "Come on now, Trojans,
bring wood, and do not in your hearts fear any clever ambush
of the Argives. For Achilles sent me from the black ships
with this promise, that he would not harm us until the
twelfth dawn came."

So he spoke, and they yoked oxen and mules, and then
quickly gathered before the city. For nine days they gathered
countless amounts of wood, but when the tenth dawn arose,
giving light to mortals, then they carried out bold Hector,
shed tears, and placed the corpse on the top of the pyre,
and cast fire on it.

When early-born, rosy-fingered dawn appeared, the
people gathered around the pyre of glorious Hector. When
they were assembled together, first they quenched the pyre
with fiery wine, all of it, as far as the strength of the
fire had reached. His brothers and his companions gathered
the white bones, mourning and shedding warm tears down their
cheeks. They took the bones and placed them in a golden urn
and covered it with soft purple robes. They placed the bones
in a hollow grave and covered it over with great close-set
stones. Then they heaped up the mound and watches were
placed all around, lest the well-greaved Achaeans should attack before the appointed time. When they had piled the
mound they went back and gathered together and enjoyed a
glorious feast in the house of Priam, the Zeus-nurtured
king. So they were busy about the funeral of Hector, the
tamer of horses.

Homer's Odyssey

   In the course of his travals, Odysseus went, at Circe's
instructions, to the entrance of the underworld to consult
the dead, specifically the seer Teiresias, about his return
home. The picture of the dead given here agrees with that
in the *Iliad*: they are weak, wavering phantoms, unable to
speak without drinking the blood of the animals Odysseus
sacrifices on their behalf. The sacrificial procedure is
described in detail; apparently its ceremonies were also
practiced at an oracle of the dead at Ephyra in Thesprotia,
northwestern Greece, as late as the second century B.C. See
S.I. Dakaris, "The Dark Palace of Hades," *Archaeology* 15
(1962) 85-93. For a fifth-century painting inspired by this
passage in Homer, see p. 231 below.

(Homer, *Odyssey* XI. 21-50, 139-149.)

We went along the stream of Ocean until we reached the
land of which Circe had spoken. There Perimedes and
Eurylochos took hold of the sacrificial victims, and I drew
a sharp sword from my thigh and dug a trough about a cubit
long on this side and that. Around it I poured a libation
to all the dead, first with a mixture of honey and milk, then
with sweet wine, and third with water. Then I sprinkled white
barley on top. Repeatedly I besought the wavering heads of

the dead, promising to offer them, on my return to Ithaca,
a barren cow, the best of the herd, and to fill up the
altar-pyre with good things for them, and also to offer
separately to Teiresias a black sheep, an outstanding one
among our flock. When I had prayed to the tribes of the
dead with prayers and supplications, I took the sheep and
slit their throats; into the trough the dark blood flowed,
and the souls of the departed dead flocked up from Erebos
- brides, god-like youths, old men who had endured much,
innocent maidens who had only just put on grief, and many
wearing the wounds of bronze spears, men slain of Ares, with
armor all gory. Many of them roamed one by one about the
trough with much loud screaming, and pale fear seized me.
Then I urged and commanded my companions to flay and burn
the sheep which had been slaughtered with pitiless bronze
and were lying there, and I told them to pray to the gods,
mighty Hades and awesome Persephone. I drew the sharp sword
from my thigh and sat down, to keep the wavering heads of
the dead from coming close to the blood before I had made
my inquiry of Teiresias.... [Before Teiresias comes Elpenor,
a companion of Odysseus who has just died; since his body
has not yet been cremated, he can speak without drinking the
blood in the trough, and he asks for a proper burial. Then
Odysseus sees his mother's ghost, but keeps her away from
the blood until Teiresias approaches and tells him of his
future adventures and return home. Odysseus then addresses
him.] "Teiresias, the gods themselves have decreed it so.
But now tell me this: I see the soul of my deceased mother,
and she is sitting silently near the blood, and dares neither
to look her son in the face nor to speak to him. Tell me,
sir, how may she know who I am?" So I spoke, and he replied,
"I will tell you this easily, and let you know. Any one of
the departed dead whom you allow to come near the blood, he
will speak to you clearly. Any whom you deny, he will go
back again."

Odysseus then speaks to his mother, Antikleia, then to a series of heroic women; later, he encounters several heroes of the Trojan War, several ghosts who are being punished, and Heracles. Among the heroes is Achilles, and the following excerpt includes, after Odysseus' summary of the traditional Greek view of heroic glory, a much more gloomy and skeptical comment from Achilles on the lot of the dead.

(Homer, *Odyssey* XI. 478-491.)

"Achilles, son of Peleus, by far the mightiest of the Achaeans, I come because I have need of Teiresias, if he would tell me some way to return to rugged Ithaca. I have not yet come anywhere near Achaea, nor yet have I come to my land, but I always have difficulties. Still, no man before was more blessed than you, Achilles, nor shall be in the future. When you were alive we honored you like the gods, we Argives, and now here you rule mightily among the dead. Do not be sad, Achilles, because you are dead."

So I spoke, but he in turn replied, "Do not speak lightly to me of death, shining Odysseus; I would be willing, if I could live on earth, to serve another man, a man without an estate of his own, who had no great livelihood, rather than to be the lord over all the departed dead."

The Lyric Poets

Mimnermus of Colophon (fl. 632-629 B.C.) and Simonides of Ceos (c. 556-468 B.C.) offer in their elegiac poetry powerful witness to the transitory nature of human life and the imminance of death.

(Mimnermus, in Stobaeus, *Eclogae* IV. 34.12; frag. 2 in M.L. West, *Iambi et Elegi Graeci* II, Oxford, 1972.)

We are like the leaves that the hour of spring, rich in flowers, shoots forth, which suddenly bloom in the rays of the sun. Like them we take our pleasure in our span of youth, not knowing whether evil or good shall come from God. For dark Fates stand beside us, the one contains the end of painful old age, the other the end of death. For the bloom of youth is short lived, so long as the sun spreads over the earth. And when this hour passes by, then death is better

than life. Many woes are born for the soul. At one time
a household is worn out, and the painful works of poverty
appear. Another man longs for children, and though he longs
for them he goes beneath the earth to Hades. Another has
pain which destroys the soul. There is no man for whom Zeus
does not have many woes.

(Simonides, in Stobaeus, *Eclogae* IV. 41.9; frag. 16 in D.
Page, *Poetae Melici Graeci*, Oxford, 1962.)

If you are a mortal, never talk about what may happen
tomorrow, nor when you see a happy man talk about how long
he will be so. Change is swift, nor is the change in the
course of a wide-winged fly so swift.

(Simonides, in Plutarch, *Letter to Apollonius*, 107b; frag.
15 in Page.)

Little is the strength of men, and his duties unavail-
ing. Toil upon toil in a short life. Death hovers about
nevertheless, a death that cannot be avoided. Both good
and bad men take an equal share of it.

(Simonides, in Diogenes Laertius, *Lives of the Philosophers*
I. 89; frag. 76 in Page.)

Kleoboulos composed poems and riddles to the total of
three thousand lines. Some say that he composed the epitaph
for Midas, "I am a brass marker, and I live on the tomb of
Midas. So long as water flows, and tall trees grow green,
the sun rises and shines, the moon gives light, rivers flow
and the sea washes the shore, I will remain on this much-
lamented tomb and tell those who pass by that Midas is buried
here." A poem of Simonides supports this identification,
where he says, "Who, relying on his understanding, would
praise Kleoboulos, the native of Lindos, who placed the might
of a gravestone against the ever-flowing rivers, the flowers
of spring, the flame of the sun, the golden moon and the waves
of the sea? All these are less than the gods, but a stone
even mortal hands may shatter. This is the wisdom of a fool."

Death and the Family

In their tragedies, the fifth-century dramatists frequently treated death and its aftermath, especially in its
domestic impact. The first two passages portray the usual
rites which relatives paid to the dead after the burial,
though in each of these cases the emotional force is
heightened by the tragic circumstances of the plot. In
Aeschylus' *Libation Bearers* [*Choephoroe*], Electra brings
offerings to the tomb of her father Agamemnon, recently
murdered by her own mother Clytemnestra in collusion with
Aigisthos, Clytemnestra's paramour, and she prays that her
brother Orestes will return to avenge the murder.

(Aeschylus, *Libation Bearers*, 123-149.)

Electra: O thou most great herald of those above and those

below, Hermes Chthonios [Of the Underworld], make proclamation

for me to the *daimones* below the earth, the guardians of my

ancestral home, to heed my prayers, and also to Earth her-

self, who giveth birth and breeding to all things, and taketh

their yield again. I, pouring these lustral waters to the

dead, call upon my father: "Take pity on me, and kindle

thine own Orestes as a light to the house. For we have now

been sold, and sent to wander by our mother, who hath ex-

changed us for her man Aigisthos, him who had his share in

thy murder. I am even as a slave, and Orestes is an exile

from his possessions, while they go vaunting in the luxury

thy labor hath earned. I beseech thee, may Orestes come back

here with some good stroke of luck, and do thou hear me,

father. Grant to me to be much more reverent than my mother,

and to have a more respectful hand.

"These are my prayers for us; for our enemies, I ask

that thy champion appear, father, and that those who killed

thee die in justice for their crime. In the central place

I put these words of a curse, uttering it upon them. For

us, however, let there be a procession of blessings from be-

low, in company with the gods, with Earth and with Justice

the bringer of victory." To such prayers as these, I add

the pouring of libations.

By the opening of Euripides' *Orestes*, Clytemnestra has
been killed by Orestes, and Clytemnestra's sister Helen
here sends her daughter to perform the ritual libations at
her tomb.

(Euripides, *Orestes*, 112-123.)

Helen [to her daughter Hermione]: Now do exactly what I
say. Take this libation and these clippings of hair, and
go to Clytemnestra's grave. Stand there and pour this mixture of honey, milk and wine over the grave and, as you
pour, repeat these words: "Your loving sister Helen, prevented by fear of the Argives from coming to your grave in
person, sends you these gifts." Then implore her to be
gracious to us all, to my husband and me and these poor
children whom Apollo has destroyed. Promise her besides
that I will labor to perform, like a good sister, all the
dues and rites of the gods below.

One of the ways in which the extended Greek family, so
important in the political and social fabric of the city-
state, demonstrated its coherence and identity was by a
common burial plot on its ancestral lands. This passage
from Demosthenes describes the burial plot of the clan of
the Bouselidai.

(Demosthenes, *Against Macartatos*, 79.)

There is a burial place common to all those who are
descended from Bouselos. It is called the burial place of
the Bouselidai, a large area, enclosed, as the ancients
prescribed. In this burial place all the other descendants
of Bouselos, for example Hagnias and Euboulides and Polemon,
lie, and all the others who similarly are kinsmen, and descended from Bouselos. All hold in common this place of
burial.

The necessity of burying the dead, and its crucial importance to the family of the deceased, forms the basis of
Sophocles' *Antigone*. In the following brief excerpt, the
blind seer Teiresias describes in brilliant detail the effect that Kreon's refusal to bury Polyneikes has had upon
the state religion.

(Sophocles, *Antigone*, 1016-1030.)

Teiresias: For our altars and hearths have been completely
infected by the birds and the dogs with the carrion from the
wretched fallen child of Oedipus. Therefore no longer do
the gods receive prayers and sacrifices from us, nor the
flames of thigh-bones. Nor does a bird shriek forth clear
cries, happy, clear cries, for it has glutted itself with
the blood and flesh of the slain man. ... Be gracious to
the dead, do not stab the dead. What glory is it to kill
the dead again?

   Euripides in the *Alcestis* offers an eloquent testimonial
to the love of a wife for a husband, even an unworthy one.
Alcestis is willing to die for him, yet this sacrifice is
made more poignant in the scapegoat's awareness of what her
actions will cost her. Life is still the most precious
commodity for a Greek.

(Euripides, *Alcestis*, 152-197.)

Handmaiden: How is she not most excellent? Who will deny
it? What must the woman become who would surpass her? How
could anyone show greater honor to her husband than to be
willing to die on his behalf? The whole city knows these
things. You will be amazed to hear what she has done in
the house. When she realized that the fated day had come,
she washed her white skin with water from the river; from
her cedar chests she took clothes and adorned herself hand-
somely, then stood before the hearth and prayed: "Mistress,
I now go beneath the earth, and for the last time do I pros-
trate myself before you in supplication. Take care of my
children. To my son join a loving wife, to my daughter a
noble husband. May they not die before their time, as I
who nurtured them do, but happy in their fatherland may they
fill out a happy life."
   Then she went to all the altars which are in the house
of Admetus, and decked them with garlands, and prayed before
them, cutting off tufts of myrtle from the branches, not
crying or groaning, nor did the incipient danger change the

natural beauty of her skin. Then she went back to her
chamber, fell on the bed, and there cried and spoke as follows: "O Bed, where I gave up my virginity to this man, for
whom now I perish, farewell. I don't hate you, but you have
slain me alone. I hesitated to betray you and my husband,
so I die. You some other woman will have, no wiser, perhaps,
but luckier."

Falling forward on the bed she kissed it; all the spread
was moist from the flood of her tears. But when she had had
enough crying, she fell back from the bed and walked out,
face down. Again and again she left the room, then turned
around and fell again upon her marriage bed. The children
clung to their mother's gown and were crying. She took them
into her arms and embraced one and then the other, as a
dying woman would. The entire household staff were crying
throughout the house, in pity for their mistress. She gave
to each her right hand. There was no one too low whom she
did not call and speak to and receive a reply. Such are
the woes in the house of Admetus, and he would have escaped
them, if he died, but by escaping death he has gained this
pain which surely he will not forget.

Death and the State: Thucydides

Thucydides the son of Olorus wrote a masterful account
of the Second Peloponnesian War (431-404 B.C.). His writings
are among the most precious legacies of Greek thought, and
have long inspired scholars, politicians and statesmen.
Perhaps Thucydides' greatest achievement was to portray the
effects of prolonged, total war upon society. The following
selections describe the Athenian custom of celebrating those
who had fallen in defense of their country; Pericles was
chosen to give the oration over the dead, and we have selected that portion of the speech which seems best to explain
how this kind of death might be seen as a perfect sacrifice
for civic virtue. We follow with Thucydides' description
of the plague which afflicted Athens in the early years of
the War, and the breakdown in morality and virtue that it
caused.

(Thucydides, *History of the Peloponnesian War* II. 34, 43, 52.)

(34) In the same winter [431 B.C.] the Athenians followed the customs of their fathers and buried at public expense those who had first died in the war. The ceremony was as follows: the bones of the departed are displayed for three days in a tent made for this purpose, and each person brings to his own dead whatever he might wish. When it is time for the funeral, wagons bring up cypress coffins, one for each tribe, and the bones of each man rest in the coffin of his tribe. One bier is left empty, and is carried covered in the procession. This is a memorial for those missing who could not be found for interment. Anyone who wishes, citizen or alien, may join in the procession, and the women related to the dead are present and sing songs of lamentation. They place the coffins in the public gravesite, which is located in the most beautiful quarter of the city [the outer Kerameikos, outside the Dipylon gate]. There the Athenians bury all those who have fallen in battle except for the men at Marathon, whose valor they judged to be so extraordinary that they buried them on the spot where they fell. When they have covered the bodies with earth, then a man selected by the city, whose judgment seems best and who is most highly esteemed, speaks the appropriate praise for the dead. After this they go home. So they bury the dead, and they employed this practice throughout the war, whenever the opportunity arose....

(43) "And these men were of such a character as to benefit the city. It is necessary for the rest of you to pray, to be sure, for a safer conclusion, but with a purpose no less fixed to meet the enemy; you must analyze the benefit of such an attitude not merely by the words of a speaker, for a speaker could spend no little time in enumerating the benefits of defeating the enemy to you who know it clearly yourselves. Rather you must day by day contemplate the power of this city and become her lovers, and when you have thoroughly digested her greatness, become mindful that men who were bold

and knew what was necessary and in the execution of deeds
were moved by a sense of honor - these were the men who acquired this city. If they failed in an attempt, they thought
it right that the city should claim their bravery, and sacrificed to her their fairest offering. They gave their bodies
to the state and for themselves won a praise which is ageless and the most distinguished of tombs, not the one in
which they are in fact buried, but the one in which their
glory survives forever and is commemorated on every occasion
of speech or deed. For the whole world is the tomb of famous
men, and the epitaph of the *stele* in their own land not only
commemorates them, but also in foreign lands for each man
there is an unwritten memorial of them planted in the mind
rather than written on a tombstone. Seek to emulate these
men, judge freedom to be happiness, and courage to be freedom, and do not be too concerned about the dangers of war.
It is not the wretched who have the best justification for
tossing away their lives, for they have no hope of improve-
ment; but rather those in the opposite condition, who might
lose all if they live and those for whom it is very important whether or not they suffer a loss. To a man with spirit
the embarrassment associated with cowardice is more bitter
than death when it comes unanticipated, in the middle of
the fight and when the hopes of the people are still high."...

(52) Over and above the troubles already pressing upon
them, the Athenians suffered because people from the country
crowded into the city. This situation particularly affected
the refugees. There was no housing available for them, but
they had to live in huts that were stifling in the summer;
there they perished chaotically. Body lay on body, and half-
dead people rolled in the streets and near all the fountains,
for they longed for water. The temples in which they stayed
were full of corpses of those who had died there; so over-
whelming was the disaster that men, not knowing what might
happen, became neglectful of divine and human law equally.
All the customs they had formerly followed were thrown into
chaos, and each buried his dead as he could. Many turned to

disgraceful modes of burial because they lacked proper
materials, for so many of their kinsmen had already perished.
They used the pyres of other people, sometimes anticipating
the builders, and would place their own dead on them and
light the fire. Others would hurl the body they were carrying onto an already lighted pyre and go away.

The Orphic View of the Afterlife

The following passages constitute our major sources on
the ideas of the Orphic teachers about death and the afterlife. Pindar and Plato, writing in the early fifth and mid
fourth centuries respectively, offer the chief early testimony to a belief in post-mortem punishment and rewards, and
in some sort of metempsychosis, as well as to a view of the
soul as imprisoned in the body. More systematically, the
late Hellenistic writer Diodorus describes the role of Orpheus
in forming Greek beliefs about the geography of the underworld.

(Pindar, *Olympian* II. 63-88.)

...If the man who has it [wealth studded with virtues]
knew the future - that the hearts of the dead who act reck-
lessly *here* straightway undergo their punishment; but the
sins committed in this realm of Zeus receive sentence in the
underworld from one who renders his sentence in accord with
dreadful necessity. Good men receive a life without toil,
with ever-equal rights, enjoying equal sun in their days;
they never disturb the earth with strength of arm, nor water
of the sea for hollow livelihood; rather, those who have taken
pleasure in oaths well kept live out an age without tears
in company with the honored of the gods. The others - they
endure toil which is terrible to behold.

As for those who have managed to endure three cycles in
both places without making their souls partake of crime, they
complete the way of Zeus and arrive at Kronos' bastion, where
the breezes, born of Ocean, blow over the island of the
Blessed: the golden flowers blaze, both on shining trees
on land, or nourished by the water; they entwine their arms
with garlands and crowds, to the just designs of Rhadamanthys
- he it is whom the great father, the spouse of Rhea who holds

the highest seat of all, keeps ready in his place beside
him. Peleus and Kadmos are among them, and Achilles, whom
his mother brought when she had persuaded Zeus with her
supplications.

(Pindar, in Plato, *Meno*, 81b; frag. 127 in C.M. Bowra,
Pindari Carmina, Oxford, 1935; frag. 133 in B. Snell and
H. Maehler, *Pindarus*, Leipzig, 1975.)

For some Persephone will accept the punishment of
ancient sorrow; their souls she sends back in the ninth year,
to the sunlight above, and therefrom noble kings, mighty in
strength, most great in wisdom, take their increase; for
the rest of time they are called saintly heroes by men.

(Plato, *Cratylus*, 400b-c.)

[On the word *soma*, "body"]: It can be analyzed in a
number of ways, if one changes it a bit, even a very little
bit. Some say that the body (*soma*) is the tomb (*sema*) of
the soul, as if the soul were buried in the present time.
And because the soul indicates by means of the body whatever it means, for this reason it is called "sign" (*sema*).
However, it seems most likely that the Orphic poets give
this name on the grounds that the soul was making reparations
for past misdeeds. The soul has an enclosure in order that
it might be safe (*sozetai*) like a prison - and that is, as
the name itself suggests, the safe (*soma*) of the soul until
it pays back the penalty; and not even a letter of the word
needs to be changed.

(Diodorus, *Library of History* I. 96.4-6.)

Orpheus brought back from Egypt most of his mystic
rituals, the orgiastic rites concerning his own journey and
the mythic account of his adventures in Hades. The rite of
Osiris is the same as that of Dionysus, that of Isis similar
to that of Demeter; only the names were changed. The punishments of the wicked in Hades and the Fields of the Pious and
the fantastic imaginings common to the many, all were introduced by Orpheus in imitation of the funeral rites of Egypt.

Hermes, the conductor of souls, according to ancient Egyptian
custom brings up the body of the Apis to a certain point and
gives it to one wearing the mask of Cerberus. After Orpheus
introduced this insight among the Greeks, Homer totally followed it when he composed the lines,

> Cyllenian Hermes called forth the souls
> Of the suitors; he had his wand in his hand.[35]

And a little later he sings,

> They went past the stream of Ocean and the Leucadian
>   Rock,
> And by the gates of the sun and the land of dreams,
> And now they have come to the meadow of Asphodel.
> There dwell the souls, the shades of worn-out men.[36]

Polygnotus' Picture of the Underworld

A foremost artist of the fifth century was the painter
Polygnotus, who in the middle of the century was commissioned
by the people of Cnidus to decorate a club house they were
constructing in the sanctuary at Delphi. The theme of one
of these paintings was the visit of Odysseus to the underworld (cf. p. 219 above), and in the following description
of the mural as seen by Pausanias, we can reconstruct a
fifth-century view of the topography of the realm of the
dead. Orphic influences may be present, and there are explicit references to the Eleusinian mysteries as a means to
a happy afterlife. Cf. C. Robert, "Die Neikyia des Polygnot,"
Hallisches Winckelmannsprogram 1892; W.K.C. Guthrie, Orpheus
and Greek Religion (London, 1934), pp. 162-163, 187-190.

(Pausanias, Description of Greece X. 28-31.)

Half the painting shows Odysseus after his descent into
Hades in order to ask the soul of Teiresias about the safety
of his homecoming. The scenes in the painting are as follows. There is water, clearly the river Acheron; reeds grow
in it, with obscure forms of fish which resemble shadows more
than fish. There is also a boat in the river, with the ferryman at the oars. Polygnotus, it seems, has followed the poem
called the Minyad, which says of Theseus and Peirithous that
"they did not find the boat which carried the dead, which
the old ferryman Charon steered, within its mooring." On
the same basis Polygnotus has painted Charon as an old man

already at an advanced age. The passengers on the boat are
not particularly well known: Tellis is shown as a young
man, and Kleoboia is still a maiden; she holds on her knees
a chest of the sort they usually make for Demeter. I have
heard of Tellis that the poet Archilochus was his grandson;
of Kleoboia they say that she introduced the rites of Demeter
to Thasos.

On the bank of the Acheron it is especially noteworthy
that beneath the boat of Charon is a man who had been unjust
to his father: he is being strangled by his father, for
in those days they valued their parents very highly....
Near the man who behaved outrageously to his father and as
a result has his fill of woe in Hades, there is a man who
has violated sacred things and has suffered the consequences;
the woman who is punishing him is expert in agony-producing
drugs. Men were then still strongly devoted to piety, as
the Athenians demonstrated when they captured the sanctuary
of Olympian Zeus at Syracuse and removed none of the dedications, but let the Syracusan priest stay to guard them.
Datis the Persian showed the same thing in his speech to
the Delians and also in his actions when, having discovered
a statue of Apollo in one of his Phoenician ships, he returned it to the Tanagraeans at Delion. At that time, then,
all men held the divinity in such reverence, and for this
reason Polygnotus has included the vignette of the violator
of sacred things.

Above what has been described there is Eurynomos. The
guides at Delphi say that Eurynomos is one of the *daimones*
in Hades, and that he devours the flesh of the dead, leaving
them only their bones. Now, the poems of Homer, as well as
the *Minyad* and the *Returns* (which mention Hades and the hor-
rors there) do not know of any *daimon* Eurynomos. Nevertheless, I will describe Eurynomos and the way he has been
represented: his complexion is between blue and black,
like that of the flies which gather around meat; he shows
his teeth, and a vulture's skin is spread for him to sit
upon.

Immediately after Eurynomos are Auge of Arcadia and
Iphimedeia: Auge came to the house of Teuthras in Mysia;
they say that of all the women with whom Heracles slept,
she bore the son who most resembled his father. As for
Iphimedeia, she has received great honors from the Carians
in Mylasa.

(29) Above the figures I have already discussed,
Perimedes and Eurylochos, Odysseus' companions, are carrying sacrificial victims. Behind them a man is seated, and
a label says that he is Oknos. He is represented plaiting
a cord, but a she-ass standing beside him keeps eating the
part of the cord he has plaited. This Oknos was, they say,
a diligent man, with a spendthrift wife, and as much as he
earned by his work, she would spend without much delay.
Thus, they maintain that Polygnotus symbolized the wife of
Oknos in this vignette.... Right next to the man twisting
the string is Ariadne. She sits upon a rock and looks toward
her sister Phaedra, who is using a rope as a swing, holding
the rope in each hand. The design, though it is very grace-
fully executed, makes us recall the manner of Phaedra's
death.... Below Phaedra is Chloris, reclining on the knees
of Thyia. It would be accurate to say that these women, as
long as they were alive, had great affection for each other.
Chloris was from Orchomenos in Boeotia, Thyia was a daughter
of Kastalios from Parnassos....Poseidon had intercourse with
Thyia, and Chloris married Neleus, the son of Poseidon.

Next to Thyia stands Prokris the daughter of Erechtheus;
with her is Klymene, who turns her back to her. According
to the poem *Returns*, Klymene is a daughter of Minyas; she
married Kephalos the son of Deion; their son was Iphiklos.
Everybody tells the tale of Prokris, and how she was killed
by her husband.

More toward the middle of the painting you will see
Megara, who was from Thebes. Heracles took this woman and
in time divorced her, alleging that he had lost the children
she had borne him and that he believed he had married her
under an unfavorable *daimon*.

Above the heads of the women I have discussed is the
daughter of Salmoneus sitting upon a rock, and Eriphyle
standing beside her. She is extending her fingers along
the neck of her dress and in the folds she is presumably
holding the famous necklace.

Above Eriphyle he has painted Elpenor, then Odysseus
crouching down, holding his sword over the trench. Teiresias
the seer is approaching. Behind Teiresias, on a rock, is
Odysseus' mother Antikleia. In place of clothing, Elpenor
wears a kind of mat, the usual garb of sailors. Further
down than Odysseus, sitting on chairs, are Theseus, holding
his own and Peirithoos' swords in both hands, and Peirithoos,
looking at the swords, presumably grieving over the useless-
ness of the swords and the fact that they had been no help
in their exploits....

(30) Next, Polygnotus has painted the daughters of
Pandareos. According to Homer, in one of Penelope's
speeches,[37] while they were still maidens their parents
were killed by the wrath of the gods; orphaned, they were
brought up by Aphrodite, and from other goddesses also received gifts: from Hera intelligence and beauty, from
Artemis stature, and from Athena women's skills; Aphrodite
went up to heaven, intending to find a happy marriage for
the girls with Zeus' help, but while she was gone the girls
were seized by the Harpies and given to the Furies. Such is
their story as Homer tells it; Polygnotus has painted the
girls crowned with flowers and playing at knucklebones, and
identified them as Kameiro and Klytie.... After the daughters
of Pandareos is Antilochos; one foot is on a rock, and he
holds his face and head in his hands. Behind Antilochos is
Agamemnon; he is leaning on a scepter under his left shoulder,
and is holding up a staff. Protesilaos is sitting there,
looking toward Achilles....Beyond Achilles stands Patroclus.
These, except for Agamemnon, do not have beards.

Painted above them are Phokos as a young boy and Iaseus
with a full beard; he is removing a ring from the left hand
of Phokos. The story goes like this: Phokos (the son of

Aiakos) crossed from Aegina to what is now Phokis, intending
to gain power over the population on the mainland and to
dwell there; when he arrived Iaseus developed a very great
affection for him and among other gifts gave him, as was
appropriate, a ring-seal set in gold. A little later Phokos
returned to Aegina, where Peleus started to plot to kill
him. To commemorate this affection Iaseus in the painting
is shown desiring to look at the seal, and Phokos is letting
him take it.

Above these is Maira, seated upon a rock. According
to *Returns*, she was still a maiden when she died, a daughter
of Thersander and grand-daugher of Sisyphus. Next is
Aktaion....and his mother, holding in their hands a fawn
and seated upon the skin of a fawn; a hunting dog lies beside them, attesting Aktaion's life and how he died.

As you look back at the lower parts of the painting,
next to Patroclus there is Orpheus seated upon a ridge; he
holds a harp in the left hand, and touches a willow tree
with the other. It is the branches that he touches, as he
leans back against the tree. The grove is apparently that
of Persephone, where black poplars and willows grow, according to Homer.[38] Orpheus is represented as a Greek; neither
his clothing nor his cap is Thracian. Leaning up against
the other side of the tree is Promedon. Some authorities
think that Promedon's name is an innovation of Polygnotus',
but others think he was a Greek who loved music, especially
the singing of Orpheus. In this part of the painting is
Schedios, the leader of the Phokian forces at Troy. After
him is Pelias seated in a chair; his hair and beard are
white, and he is looking at Orpheus. Schedios holds a dagger
and wears a crown of long grass. Thamyris is sitting near
Pelias; his eyes have been destroyed, and he is represented
in total dejection, with long hair and beard; a lyre lies
fallen at his feet, its horns and strings broken. Above him
is Marsyas, seated upon a rock, and Olympus is beside him,
represented as a handsome youth learning to play the flute....

(31) If you look back again to the upper part of the
painting, there is, next to Aktaion, Ajax (the Salaminian)
and also Palamedes and Thersites playing dice, the invention
of Palamedes. The other Ajax [the son of Oileus] is watching
them play; his complexion is like that of a man who has been
shipwrecked, with the salt still encrusting his skin.
Polygnotus has deliberately gathered the enemies of Odysseus
into one place.... Meleager the son of Oineus is higher up
in the painting than Ajax the son of Oileus, and he seems to
be looking at Ajax. All of these have beards, except
Palamedes.... In the lower part of the painting, after
Thamyris of Thrace, Hector is seated. He holds both his
hands around his left knee, displaying the appearance of
someone in grief. After him is Memnon, seated on a rock,
and Sarpedon right next to Memnon. Sarpedon has buried his
face in both hands, and one of Memnon's hands is resting on
Sarpedon's shoulder. All these have beards. Memnon's cloak
has birds embroidered on it.... Beside Memnon a nude
Ethiopian boy is represented, because Memnon was king of
the Ethiopian race.

The Above Sarpedon and Memnon is Paris, without a beard.
He is clapping his hands, as if he were a farm-hand, and it
looks as if he is calling Pentheseleia with the clapping.
Pentheseleia is there, too, looking at Paris, but the position of her head seems to show her disdain for him, and her
lack of respect. Pentheseleia is represented as a maiden
with a bow like the Scythian ones, and with a leopard skin
on her shoulders.

The female figures above Pentheseleia are carrying water
in broken pots. One still has a fresh appearance, but the
other is already getting on in years. Individually these
women have no inscription, but both together are identified
as representatives of women who have not been initiated.
Above them is Kallisto the daughter of Lykaon, and Nomia,
and also Pero the daughter of Neleus. Kallisto is using a
bearskin for a pallet, and has her feet resting on the knees
of Nomia. The Arcadians contend that Nomia is one of their

local nymphs. The poets' version about them is that the
nymphs live a great many years, but are not completely im-
mune to death.

   After Kallisto and the women with her is the representa-
tion of a cliff, and Sisyphus the son of Aiolos, straining
to push the rock to the cliff. There is also a storage jar
in the painting, and an old man, a child, a young woman under
the rock, and another woman beside the old man, apparently
the same age as he. The others are carrying water, but you
can see that the old woman's jug has broken, and the water
that is left in the sherd she is pouring back into the jar.
The evidence suggested to us that these also were among those
who neglected the ceremonies at Eleusis. In earlier times
the Greeks considered the Eleusinian initiation to be more
honorable than any other, as much so as gods are more eminent
than heroes. Under this jar is Tantalus, with all the suf-
ferings which Homer has given him in his poetry,[39] and besides these there is also the terror of the stone hanging
above him. Clearly Polygnotus has followed the version of
Archilochus; I am not sure whether he learned the part about
the stone from others or whether he introduced it into the
tale himself.

Plato on the Afterlife

   The following selections, including allusions to Orphic
and Pythagorean doctrines, demonstrate the range of Plato's
thinking on the questions of death and the afterlife.

(Plato, *Phaedo*, 107d-108c.)

   The tale is as follows. When someone dies, his *daimon*,
who took charge of him while he was alive, tries to lead him
to a place where it is necessary for them to be brought together and offer their cases for judgment. Then they must
go to the house of Hades with that spirit as guide who has
the assignment of conveying them from here to there. When
they have been there as long as necessary and experienced
what they experienced, another guide brings them back after
many long passages of time.

This journey is not as Aeschylus' Telephos describes it.
He says that the path to the house of Hades is straight, but
it is not so in my judgment nor is it even a single path.
For otherwise there would be no need of a guide. No one
would lose his way if there were only one road. It seems
more likely that it has many forks and crossroads, and I
cite as my evidence the ceremonies and rituals of this world.
The wise and disciplined soul follows its guide and is aware
of its environment, but the soul which clings closely to the
body, as I said before, and hovers around it and the visible
world for a long time, and resists much and suffers much, is
at last and only by force led away by its guardian spirit.
When it comes to the place where the rest of the souls are
gathered, the soul which is impure and has done an impure
deed, either by perpetrating an unjust murder or some other
such deed, which are kindred crimes and the work of kindred
souls, then all the others flee and shun this soul, and none
wish to be its companion or guide it. It wanders in utter
confusion until some time passes; when that time has passed
it is carried off by necessity to the place proper to it.
But the soul which has lived its life purely and moderately
enjoys the company and guidance of the gods, and each dwells
in its proper place. There are many wonderful regions in
the earth, and the earth is itself neither of the quality
nor of the size supposed by the geographers.

(Plato, *Republic* II. 363c-e.)

Musaeus and his son [Eumolpos] have a more positive view
of the blessings that the gods give the just. They lead them
to the House of Hades in their song and make them recline and
arrange a drinking party for the holy ones and cover them
with wreaths. They use the rest of the time for drinking,
thinking that the lovliest payment for justice is eternal
drunkenness. Others extend the rewards of the gods still
further. For they say that the children of the children of
the pious man who keeps his oaths, and his race thereafter,
survive successfully. Such and such are the praises they

give to justice. But the impious and unjust they bury in
the mud in the House of Hades and compel them to carry
water in a sieve and bring them into bad repute while they
still live and all the things which Glaukon enumerated as
mistreatments for the just who are thought to be unjust;
all these very things they attribute to the unjust, but have
nothing more to say. Such is the praise and blame for just
and unjust.

(Plato, *Phaedo*, 113d-114c.)

When the dead reach the place where their *daimon* con-
ducts each one, first they are judged, both those who lived
a good and holy life, and those who did not. Those who are
judged to have lived moderately proceed straight to Acheron,
and embark on the vessels waiting for them there, and then
go down to the lake, and there they dwell and are purified
of their sins, if they have done anything wrong, and receive
their rewards for good deeds, according to each's merits.
But those who seem to be incurable because of the greatness
of their sins, whether many great sacrileges or unjust mur-
ders or violations and any other such unjust acts, these
their own appropriate destiny hurls into Tartaros, from
which they never return.

Others have been judged guilty of sins which, while
great, are curable, such as offering violence to father or
mother in a passionate state, but have spent the rest of
their life in repentance, or have committed acts of manslaughter in some such fashion. These will fall down into
Tartaros by necessity, but when they have fallen down and
been there for a year, then the wave hurls them out, the
manslayers by Kokytos and the parricides and matricides by
Pyriphlegethon. While they are being carried along and when
they come by the Acherusian Lake, then they will call out
and cry out, some to those they have killed, others to those
they have mistreated, and as they call out they beg and plead
for permission to leave the stream and come into the lake and
be received. If they persuade them, then they come out and

put an end to their troubles; if not, they are conveyed back
into Tartaros and then back into the rivers, and they cannot
put an end to this endless circle until they convince those
whom they have wronged, for this is the punishment passed
on them by the judges.

But those who are judged to have lived a life outstanding in its holiness, these are released from these places in
the earth and are set free as from a prison. These pass up
to their pure home and dwell on the surface of the earth.
Of these the ones who have purified themselves sufficiently
by philosophy live thereafter without bodies, and come to
still more beautiful places, which are more difficult to
describe, and which time does not permit. But on what
grounds we must direct our lives to leave nothing undone
which might help us attain virtue and wisdom, O Simmias, is
clear. For the prize is lovely and the hope great.

Epitaphs

As we do, the Greeks often chose to commemorate the
deceased with an identifying marker, a *stele*, which was the
equivalent of our gravestone. It is our custom to give the
name of the departed, dates of birth and death and, occasionally, a scriptural verse or other quotation alluding
to some unusually positive feature of the individual's life.
Greek practice varied; the grave inscription might be limited
to the name of the deceased; or the words on the stone might
speak of the nature of death or the afterlife, in terms
ranging from simple faith to aggressive scepticism. Often
the stone itself would speak to passers-by and call upon
them to read and learn. Occasionally the deceased would
speak in the first person to a loved one. The first example
given here is the epitaph composed by the great poet Simonides
on behalf of the three hundred Spartans who died defending
the pass of Thermopylae against the Persian invaders in 480
B.C. This is followed by a longer encomium on these same
Spartans, and by four other epitaphs, also by Simonides:
on the Athenian dead at the battle of Plataea (also against
the Persians, in 479 B.C.), on the Spartan dead at the same
battle, on a crusty old Timocreon of Rhodes and a merchant
from Crete. All the other examples date from the Hellenistic
and Roman periods, and have been selected from R. Lattimore,
Themes in Greek and Latin Epitaphs (Urbana, Ill., 1962).

(Simonides, in Herodotus, *The Histories* VII. 228; frag. 22
in E. Diehl, *Anthologia Graeca* II, Leipzig, 1924.)

> Stranger, announce to the Lacedaemonians that here
> We lie, obedient to their commands.

(Simonides, in Diodorus Siculus, *Library of History* XI. 11.6;
frag. 26 in D. Page, *Poetae Melici Graeci*, Oxford, 1962.)

> To those who died at Thermopylae is a glorious fortune
> and a wondrous destiny. Their grave is an altar. Instead
> of lamentations, they have remembrance. Their wine is praise.
> Such a burial neither mold makes obscure nor time, which
> conquers all things. This shrine of brave men has taken as
> its guardian the glory of Greece. Leonidas the king of
> Sparta offers witness, for he has left behind a great orna-
> ment of courage and perpetual glory.

(Simonides, in the *Palatine Anthology* VII. 253; frag. 118
in Diehl.)

> If dying well is the greatest part of virtue,
> Fate has apportioned it to us of all men.
> For we, hastening to bestow freedom upon Hellas,
> Lie here enjoying a good repute that will never grow old.

(Simonides, in the *Palatine Anthology* VII. 251; frag. 121
in Diehl.)

> These men bestowed unquenchable glory upon their dear
>   country
> And took upon themselves the dark mist of death.
> They have died, but are not dead, since their virtue
> Glorifies them and leads them up out of Hades' home.

(Simonides, in the *Palatine Anthology* VII. 348; frag. 99
in Diehl.)

> I've drunk much, and eaten much, and said much that
>   was bad
> About men; and I lie here, Timokreon of Rhodes.

(Simonides, in the *Palatine Anthology* VII. 254a; frag. 138
in Diehl.)

> A Cretan by birth, I, Brotachos of Gortyn, lie here;
> I came for merchandise, not for this!

(F. Preisigke and F. Bilabel, *Sammelbuch Griechischer
Urkunden aus Aegypten*, Strassburg, 1915-   , #4314;
Lattimore, p. 176; from Alexandria, 3rd c. B.C.)

> No longer does your mother take you in her hands,
>   Philoxenos,
> And cast them lingeringly about your lovely neck.
> Nor do you go to the famous city with the young men,
> Or rejoice in the shaded hall of the gymnasium.
> Your father Kaunos brought your strong bones here and
>   buried them,
> When he touched the flesh with the fire that consumes
>   everything.

(*IG* XII. 1.141, lines 1-6; Lattimore, p. 51; from Rhodes,
2nd c. B.C.)

> A secretary. This man taught for fifty years
> And two more in addition. Now the plain of the Pious
>   holds him,
> For Plouton and Kore have given him a place to dwell;
> Hermes and Hecate the torch-bearer have made him beloved
> Of all, and supervisor of the mysteries,
> Because of his faithfulness.

(*IG* XII. 5.310; Lattimore, p. 270; from Paros, 2nd c. B.C.)

> Neikandros was my father, Paros my country.
> My name is Sokrateia. When I died Parmenion
> My husband buried me, granting me this gift,
> That it be a memory of a seemly life, and that it be
> At hand even to men of the future. The Fury
> Of Childbirth (which cannot be guarded against)
> Destroyed my pleasant life through a hemorrhage.
> By my pains I could not bring the child into the light,
> But he lives among the dead in my own womb.

(G. Kaibel, *Epigrammata Graeca*, Berlin, 1878, #67; Lattimore, p. 211; from Athens, Hellenistic.)

> Under the walls of this tomb the earth conceals
> Kydimachos,
> Who was rich and well along in years before he sailed
> into the harbor.
> He saw his grandchildren, and his old age was free of
> care.
> Now, dead, he shares our common fate.

(J. Geffcken, *Griechische Epigramme*, Heidelberg, 1916, #209; Lattimore, p. 129; from Astypalaea, late Hellenistic.)

> Do not bring me anything to drink; when I was alive
> I drank.
> Do not bring me anything to eat; I have enough. All
> is nonsense.
> If for the sake of remembrance of the life I lived
> with you
> You bring saffron or frankincense as a gift, friends,
> You give these things appropriately to those who have
> received me.
> These things belong to the gods below. Dead have
> nothing to do with the living.

(*IG* XII. 8.449, lines 12-14; Lattimore, p. 58; from Thasos.)

> I pray you, husband, I will receive you
> Even when late, Theodoros, and we shall both
> Share this bed and forget our misfortunes.

(*IG* IX. 2.640, lines 8-9; Lattimore, p. 77; from Larisa.)

> There is nothing more - nothing remains to the dead -
> Than to afflict the mind of passers-by. There is nothing
> else.

(Kaibel, *Epigrammata Graeca*, #648, lines 9-12; Lattimore, p. 36; from Rome.)

> This plain must surely be the isles of the blessed. Here
> Pious men live, most just and gentle.
> While they lived they treated all men
> With decency, wisdom, justice and respect.

(*IG* XII. 9.1179; Lattimore, p. 116; from Chalcis, 2nd c. A.D.)

> I proclaim to those who become owners of the property:
> Let him who shall not spare this work or image which has been
> set up, and who shall dishonor it or move it from one place
> to another or in outrage defile it or injure it or break it
> either in whole or in part or overturn it and scatter it and
> obscure it; this man may God attack with distress, fever,
> chills, itch, blight, madness, blindness and disorder of his
> mind. May his possessions disappear, may he not walk on the
> land or sail on the sea or beget children. May his house
> not increase; may he not enjoy produce of his house, nor
> light, nor the use and possession of anything. May he have
> the Furies as his protectors. If anyone tends me or guards
> me and helps to protect me, may he fare very well and be
> praised by his people. May his house increase by the number
> of his children and by the benefit of crops. May grace and
> health protect him.

(Kaibel, *Epigrammata Graeca*, #243, lines 5-6; Lattimore, p. 29; from Pergamum, 2nd c. A.D.)

> Your soul has flown from the bones to other *daimones*
> And now you dwell in the plain of the blessed ones.

(Kaibel, *Epigrammata Graeca*, #646a; Lattimore, p. 75; from Rome, 3rd or 4th c. A.D.)

> Do not pass by my epitaph, wayfarer,
> But stand, listen, and when you have heard, go on your
>   way.
> There is no boat in Hades, no ferryman Charon,
> No Aiakos, keeper of the keys, no dog Cerberus.

All of us who have died and gone below
Are bones and ashes, nothing else.
I have spoken to you truthfully. Go away, traveler,
Lest I appear to you, though dead, to be an idle talker.

B. The Nature of the Soul: Ghosts

The Greeks were concerned from earliest times with the
question of the nature of the soul. Homer in Book XXIII of
the *Iliad* describes the soul as a sort of double, similar
in all physical manifestations, *e.g*. height, eyes, voice,
and dressed in the same garments that the person might have
worn during life. This notion survived in Greek thought
until the fourth century, as can be seen in Plato's *Phaedo*.
The following selections offer a representative sample of
Greek attitudes towards apparitions of the dead and, if we
may believe Pliny, the ancients, both Greek and Roman, loved
a good ghost story.

(Homer, *Iliad* XXIII. 62-107.)

When Sleep seized Achilles and loosened the concerns
of his heart and poured around him sweetly - for his shining
limbs were weary from chasing Hector to windy Ilium - then
the spirit of unlucky Patroclus came to him, in everything
like to himself in height, in fair eyes and in voice, and
similar clothes covered his skin. He stood by Achilles'
head and said to him: "You sleep, and have forgotten me,
Achilles; you did not neglect me when I was alive, but you
do so now that I am dead. Bury me quickly, so that I may
enter the gates of Hades. The spirits keep me far away, the
phantoms of men who are exhausted; they will not allow me
to join them beyond the river. But I wander just as I am
through the house of the dead. Give me your hand, I beg you,
for never again shall I come out from Hades, when you have
given me what I desire from the fire. Never more in life
will we sit apart from our comrades making plans, but for
me bitter fate has opened her jaws, which was my lot since
birth. And you too have a doom, Achilles like to the gods,
to die by the wall of the wealthy Trojans. But I will tell
another thing and I will give you a task, if you are willing.
Do not put my bones away from yours, but together, as we
were brought up in your home, when Menoitios brought me from
Opoeis to your country when I was still a child, driven by
the grief over manslaughter, on the day when I killed the

247

son of Amphidamos in my folly, unwillingly, over the dice.
There the horseman Peleus received me into his home, reared
me kindly and named me your squire. So let one coffer hold
our bones, a golden one with twin handles, the one your
queenly mother gave you."

Then in answer spoke swift-footed Achilles: "Why, my
dear head, do you come here and give me orders about each
of these matters? I will complete these tasks, and I will
do as you say. Stand nearer. Let us embrace if only for a
moment and take our fill of bitter tears."

So he spoke and reached out with his hands. But he
could not hold him. The spirit like smoke passed beneath
the earth with a faint cry. Achilles jumped up in amazement,
clapped his hands, and spoke a mournful word: "Alas, even
in the house of Hades there is a spirit and phantom, although
there is no mind at all. All night long the spirit of
wretched Patroclus has stood over me, weeping and wailing
and giving commands about each and every thing, and it was
wonderfully like him."

(Aeschylus, *The Persians*, 607-632, 681-692.)

Atossa: ...For this reason I direct my path here from my
house again, without my chariot and without my former luxury,
bringing propitiating offerings to the father of my son,
gifts which soothe the dead, white sweet milk from an unblemished cow, and bright honey, honey from the bee who works
in the flowers, with lustral water from a virgin spring, and
an unmixed drink from an ancient vine, its rustic mother.
There is at hand the fragrant fruit of the pale-green olive,
which always lives in the thick foliage, and flowers made
into garlands, the children of fruitful earth.

But, my friends, chant the hymns while I offer these
libations to the dead, and call forth the *daimon* of Darius,
while I send ahead these offerings to the gods below which
the earth will drink.
Chorus: Royal Lady, Queen of the Persians, send these libations to the chambers beneath the earth; we by our hymns will

request the conductors of the dead beneath the earth to
hear our prayers favorably.

Holy *daimones* of the world below, Earth and Hermes and
you, O Lord of the Dead, send from below a spirit [*psyche*]
to the light. If he knows of some remedy for our misfortunes,
he alone of mortals can say how to do it. ...
Ghost of Darius: O Faithful ones among the faithful, comrades
of my youth, elders of Persia, what trial tries the state?
It groans, the ground is struck, and gapes open. I am
alarmed to see my wife near the tomb, and yet I receive her
kindly offerings. But you stand by my tomb and groan and
with cries and shrieks to rouse the dead you call upon me
pitifully. It is not an easy ascent from the land of the
dead, most importantly because the gods beneath the earth
are better able to take than to release. Nevertheless,
because I rule among them, I have come. Hurry up, so that
I may incur no blame for the time I spend here. What unanticipated misfortune burdens the Persians?

(Herodotus, *The Histories* IV. 14.)

I will tell a story concerning Aristeas which I heard
at Prokonnesos and Cyzicus. They say that Aristeas, being
of no less nobility than his fellow townsmen, went into a
fuller's shop and died; the fuller shut his workshop and
went to tell the kinsfolk of the man what had happened. The
story was now spreading through the city that Aristeas was
dead when a man from Cyzicus, who had just arrived from the
town of Artaca challenged those who were reporting his death.
He said that he had stumbled upon him as he was going to
Cyzicus and spoken to him. The man was absolutely insistent
on the story, but in the meantime the relatives of the deceased had come to the fuller's shop with all the appropriate
equipment to prepare him for burial; when the shop was opened,
no Aristeas, either dead or alive! In the seventh year after
this he appeared at Prokonnesos and composed the poem which
the Greeks call "The Tale of the Arimaspians" and vanished
again.

(Herodotus, *The Histories* VI. 117.)

At the battle of Marathon six thousand four hundred
Persians fell, one hundred and ninety-two Athenians. These
are the numbers which fell on both sides. A marvelous event
took place: a certain Athenian, Epizelos the son of
Kouphagoras, while fighting in the encounter and acquitting
himself well, lost the sight in his eyes, though he was not
wounded or stabbed in any part of the body. He remained
blind for the rest of his days. I heard that he told this
tale about his misfortune: it seemed to him that a large
hoplite stood before him, whose beard covered his whole
shield; this apparition went past him, but slew the man
standing next to him. This was Epizelos' tale as I learned
it.

The following is an epigram on the Athenians who died
fighting at Potidaea in 432 B.C. Its reference to the soul
[*psyche*] returning to the aether, the fiery upper air is
explained by E.R. Dodds, *The Greeks and the Irrational*
(Berkeley, 1956), p. 174, n. 112: "It seems to be based on
the simple idea that *psyche* is breath or warm air..., which
will tend to float upwards when released at death into the
atmosphere."

(*IG* I^2 945; *SEG* X. 414; Kaibel, *Epigrammata Graeca*, #21,
lines 6-9.)

The aether has received their souls, the earth their
        bodies;
They were undone at the gates of Potidaea.
Of their enemies, some have their portion of the grave,
        while others fled
And reckoned the wall their surest hope for life.

This same notion of the soul as an airy substance imprisoned in the body (cf. p. 230 above) also lies behind
the following passage from Plato, with its speculations on
the results of metempsychosis.

(Plato, *Phaedo*, 81c-d.)

Socrates: My friend, it is necessary to believe that the corporeal is heavy and weighty and earthly and visible. The soul having such a quality is weighed down and dragged back into the visible world from fear of the unseen or Hades, as is said, and hovers around tombs and graveyards; concerning whatever shadowy phantasms which have been seen, they are the manifestations of such souls, souls which have not yet completely disappeared but retain part of the visible, and therefore can be seen.

Cebes: That seems likely, Socrates.

Socrates: Yes, Cebes. These are not the souls of the good, but of the wicked, and are compelled to wander about these places to give recompense for their former bad actions. They wander until out of zeal for the corporeal, which seeks after them constantly, they are imprisoned again in a body. As is fitting, they cling to the same sort of natures which they developed during life.

Cebes: What do you mean, Socrates?

Socrates: For example, those who were gluttons or selfish or drunkards, and who cultivated these vices rather than try to avoid them, they are likely to become donkies or some other such animal, don't you agree?

Cebes: Yes indeed!

Socrates: Those who preferred injustice and tyranny and roberry should become wolves and hawks and kites, unless we can suggest more suitable beasts for them to become?

Cebes: Indeed these are just right.

Socrates: Therefore it is easy to imagine into what sort of animals all the other souls will go, in accordance with the kind of actions they pursued during life.

(Pausanias, *Description of Greece* VI. 6.7-10.)

They say that Odysseus was wandering after the capture of Troy and was carried by the winds to a number of cities in Italy and Sicily, and he came with his ships to Temesa. One of his sailors got drunk and raped a maiden, and as a punishment for this crime was stoned to death by the citizens. Odysseus did not care at all about his loss and sailed away, but the ghost of the stoned man took every opportunity to kill without distinction the people of Temesa, and he preyed on all age groups, until the Pythian priestess forbade them to leave Italy, as they had resolved to do, but ordered them to propitiate the Hero and assign him a sanctuary and build him a temple and give to him each year the loveliest of the maidens in Temesa to wed. They did as the god commanded and there was no further terror from the ghost. Euthymos happened to come to Temesa at the time when the people were placating the ghost as usual and learned what was going on. He wished to enter the temple and also take a look at the girl. When he saw her he at first pitied her, then came to love her. The girl swore to marry him if he saved her, and Euthymos put his armor on and waited for the ghost to come. He conquered him in battle, and the Hero was driven from the land, dove into the sea and disappeared. Euthymos had a glorious wedding and the citizens were free of the ghost from that time on.

(Pliny the Younger, *Letters* VII. 27, to Licinius Sura.)

Leisure provides time for me to learn from you, and you to instruct me. Therefore I am very eager to know whether you think that ghosts exist and have their appropriate shape and some sort of power, or whether they have no substance or reality and take shape only from our fears. I am inclined to believe that they do exist, chiefly on the basis of what I heard happened to Curtius Rufus. He was still new and unknown, and was attached to the staff of the governor of Africa. One afternoon he was walking in the portico of his home when there appeared to him the figure of a woman, who was in size and beauty beyond the normal. He was terrified, but she told him that she was the guardian spirit of Africa and had come to reveal his future. She said that he would return to Rome and hold further offices, and would return again to this same province with supreme power, and there die.

Everything came true. Furthermore, when he came to Carthage
and was disembarking from his ship, the same figure is said
to have accosted him on the shore. He himself, when he fell
ill, interpreted his future by his past, and misfortune by
previous successes, and gave up all hope of recovery, although
none of his staff expected the worst.

The following story, which I will tell you as I heard
it, seems more terrifying and no less marvelous, don't you
agree? There was in Athens a large and comfortable house,
but with the reputation of causing danger to anyone who
lived there. In the silence of the night one could hear the
sound of iron and, if you paid special attention, the rattle
of chains, at first far away, and then close at hand. Soon
there appeared a ghost, an old man worn out and filthy, with
a long flowing beard and hair standing on end; around his
legs were chains, and he wore chains on his wrists and shook
them. The inhabitants passed fearful nights, for they lay
awake in terror; disease followed the lack of sleep and as
fear grew death soon followed. For even during the day, when
the image was absent, the recollection of it flashed before
their eyes, and the terror remained longer than the cause of
the terror. The house was deserted and abandoned to empti-
ness and entirely left to the disposal of the monster; nevertheless it was advertised in case someone unaware of its
evil reputation might want to buy it or rent it.

The philosopher Athenodorus came to Athens. He read
the advertisement and when he learned the price, became
suspicious. On inquiring he learned the whole story, but
he was no less eager to rent it, in fact, more so. When it
began to grow dark he ordered that a couch be prepared for
him in the front part of the house, and asked for notebooks,
pen and a lamp. He sent all his servants into the inner rooms
of the house, he concentrated mind, eyes and hands upon his
writing, lest an idle mind invent the ghost or other imaginary
fears. At first there was only the usual nightime silence,
then he heard iron rattling and chains being dragged along.
He did not lift his eyes or stop writing, but strengthened

his mind and shut his ears. Then the noise grew louder,
came nearer, was in the doorway, then was heard within the
room. He looked about and saw and recognized the ghost
described to him. It stood and beckoned to him as if calling him. He on the other hand indicated by a sign that it
should wait a little and he bent again to his tablet and pen.
The ghost shook its chains over his head while he wrote.
Then he turned around and saw it beckoning as before; he
did not delay but picked up his lamp and followed. It
stalked along with a slow gait as if weighed down by chains.
After it turned off into the courtyard it suddenly disappeared and abandoned its companion. He plucked some leaves
and plants to mark the spot. Next day he went to the magistrates and urged them to order that the spot be excavated.
They found bones trussed with chains, which the body, rotted
away by time and the earth, had left bare and corroded by
the chains. The bones were collected and buried at public
expense. After the ghost had been properly laid to rest
the house was free of it.

These stories I believe on the evidence of others; this
story I can support myself. One of my freedmen, an educated
man, was sleeping in the same bed as his younger brother.
The latter seemed to see someone sitting on the bed and ap-
plying shears to his head and cutting off some hairs from
the top of his head. When it grew light, he found his hair
shorn at the top and the hairs lying on the floor. A short
time passed and a similar occurrence confirmed the first one.
A slave boy was sleeping with others in the young slaves'
quarters. Two men clad in white came through the windows
(so he said), cut his hair as he lay in bed, and departed
in the same way they had come. Daylight revealed that this
boy's hair had been cut and the hairs scattered about.
Nothing worthy of note followed, save the fact that I was
not summoned to trial, which would have been the case had
[the emperor] Domitian lived longer, in whose reign these
things happened. In his desk was found a charge laid against
me by Carus; from this it could be conjectured, because it

is the custom of the accused to let their hair grow, that
the cutting of my slaves' hair was a sign that my imminent
danger was removed.

I beg you to apply your knowledge to this matter, for
I think it is worth your long and careful reflection, nor
am I an unworthy beneficiary of your expertise. If you
choose to argue both sides of the question in your typical
fashion, that is quite acceptable, but I hope you will put
your most persuasive arguments on one side, lest you should
leave me in suspense and confused, although I am consulting
you to remove my doubts. Farewell.

[1]Hesiod derives the name "Aphrodite" from *aphros,* meaning "foam." Cf. n. 3 below for another etymology.

[2]Homer, *Iliad* I. 527-530. Cf. p. 2.

[3]*Aphron* means "foolish," "senseless." Cf. n. 1 above.

[4]Another translation: "Phoebus must be brought to account: what ails him?"

[5]Cf. Damascius, *On First Principles,* 55 (frag. 70 in O. Kern, *Orphicorum Fragmenta,* Berlin, 1922); "Orpheus said, 'Then great Chronos [Time] fashioned a silver egg for the divine Aether.'"

[6]For some typical hero-shrines, see H.A. Thompson, "Some Hero Shrines in Early Athens," in *Athens Comes of Age: From Solon to Salamis* (Princeton, 1978), pp. 96-108.

[7]The text is corrupt here, but Nilsson suggested that this is the name of the first day, on which Heracles was worshipped as an Olympian god.

[8]The "companions" refers to their fathers or guardians who have assembled to present their sons to the other members of the phratries. Exactly what a phratry was or did is a complicated and obscure question, but it had a religious function and membership in a phratry was obligatory for enrollment as a citizen in Athens. Cf. p. 139.

[9]Homer, *Iliad* IV. 193-194.

[10]Cf. D. H. Gill, "Trapezomata, a neglected aspect of Greek sacrifice," *Harvard Theological Review* 67 (1974) 117-137.

[11]A similar deme calendar, from Erchia, has been published by G. Daux in *Bulletin de Correspondance Hellénique* 87 (1963) 603-638, with further discussion by E. Vanderpool, *ibid.* 89 (1965) 21-26; M. Jameson, *ibid.* 154-172; S. Dow, *ibid.* 180-213.

[12]Spread with meats and offerings. See D.H. Gill, "The classical Greek cult table," *Harvard Studies in Classical Philology* 70 (1965) 265-269.

[13]A goddess of initiations, perhaps. The daughter of Dionysus and Nikaia.

[14]Meaning unknown.

[15]An epithet of Persephone.

[16]The Hellotion was probably the shrine of Athena Hellotis, an important goddess at Marathon.

[17]An epithet of Demeter.

[18]A festival of Demeter, held on the 12th of the month.

[19]Ancestors of the clans.

[20]The Tetrapolis was a vestigial religious consortium of Marathon and three neighboring demes.

[21]For a translation and commentary on a fourth-century Zeus festival on the island of Kos, see D.R. Smith, "The Coan Festival of Zeus Polieus," *Classical Journal* 69 (1973) 21-25.

[22]The amount was originally one drachma [6 obols], but this has been erased and the higher fee inserted.

[23]Whether the "house" refers to the whole phratry or to some smaller group within it is unclear; see Andrewes, *op. cit.*, p. 4.

[24]Perhaps the phrase should be translated "for instruction."

[25]Hesiod, *Works and Days*, 287-289.

[26]Paraphrased from Homer, *Iliad* IX. 497-500.

[27]The Greek text is unintelligible at this point.

[28]The text says "pictures."

[29]The text adds "or with a puppy."

[30]For the mysteries of Andania in Messenia, see Pausanias, *Description of Greece* IV. 26-27 and *SIG*³ 736; *LGS* 62; quoted in part in F. Grant, *Hellenistic Religions*, pp. 31-32.

[31]Cf. also the mysteries of Thracian gods on Samothrace, pp. 210-216.

[32]The late lexicographer Pollux (*Onomastikon* VIII. 108) gives the following definition of the *gerarai*: "These offered to Dionysus the ineffably holy sacrifices, along with other sacred functions. There are fourteen of them, appointed by the *basileus*." And the *Etymologicum Magnum* quotes Dionysius of Halicarnassos: "The *gerairai* are holy women among the Athenians, whom the *basileus* appoints in equal numbers to the altars for the purpose of honoring [*gerairein*] the god."

[33]Cf. R. Ganszyniec, "Thyraze Kares," *Eranos* 1947, 100-113; M. van der Valk, "Thyraze Kares or Keres," *Revue des Études Grecques* 76 (1963) 418-420; J. ter Vrugt-Lenz, "Thyraze Keres," *Mnemosyne* 15 (1962) 238-247.

[34]Cf. Plutarch, *Laconic Sayings*, 229d, and in N. Lewis' collection, *op. cit.*, #239 and #240.

[35]Homer, *Odyssey* XXIV. 1-2.

[36]Homer, *Odyssey* XXIV. 11-14.

[37]Homer, *Odyssey* XX. 66-78.

[38]Homer, *Odyssey* X. 510.

[39]Homer, *Odyssey* XI. 582.

GLOSSARY OF TRANSLITERATED WORDS
AND TECHNICAL TERMS

agora -- a public market place.

ambrosia -- traditionally, the food of the gods; as an
offering to Zeus Ktesios, it was made of water, oil
and fruit.

Anthesterion -- see: months.

archon -- lit. "ruler"; one of the ten chief magistrates
at Athens.

athlothetai -- commissioners in charge of competitions.

basileus, pl. *basileis* -- lit. "king"; at Athens, the *archon*
with jurisdiction over the state religious observances;
elsewhere, certain other kinds of chief magistrates.

Boedromion -- see: months.

choinix -- a dry measure, 4 *kotylai*.

chous, pl. *choes* -- a liquid measure, 12 *kotylai*.

daimon, pl. *daimones* -- a spirit or divinity, a more general
word than *theos*, which is here translated "god."

deipnophoroi -- lit. "dinner-bearers"; cult officials.

deme -- one of the local administrative units of the
Athenian city-state.

drachma -- monetary unit, worth six obols; in the fifth
century B.C., it was the equivalent of a day's pay for
a skilled workman.

Eleusinion -- a shrine of the Eleusinian deities near the
agora in Athens.

embateres -- pastures (? -- meaning doubtful).

epistates, pl. *epistatai* -- official; at Athens, the presiding officer of the council and the assembly.

epoptes, pl. *epoptai* -- an initiate into the highest grade
of the Eleusinian mysteries; the word refers to one
who has "beheld" the sacred things.

eranos, pl. *eranoi* -- sacred banquet; also, an association
devoted to sacred meals.

eua!, *euoi!* -- cry of Bacchic enthusiasm.

261

exegetes -- lit. "interpreter"; a cult official who interprets the omens.

genos, pl. *gene* -- kinship group, clan.

gerara, pl. *gerarai* -- priestesses of Dionysus at Athens;
  see note 32.

Hekatombaion -- see: months.

hieromnemones -- lit. "sacred recallers"; cult officials
  at Epidauros.

hieropoioi -- lit. "sacred doers"; commissioners of the
  Athenian state cults.

hierosyna -- honorarium to an officiating priest.

kalathephoroi -- lit. "basket-bearers"; participants in a
  sacrificial procession.

kanephoroi -- lit. "basket-bearers"; participants in a
  sacrificial procession.

kore -- lit. "girl," "daughter"; Kore is the proper name of
  Persephone's daughter.

kotyle, pl. *kotylai* -- a dry and liquid measure, about a
  cup (1/4 liter).

koureion -- a sacrifice to commemorate a son's coming of age.

kykeon -- the sacred porridge drunk by Eleusinian initiates;
  made of barley, water and pennyroyal.

libation -- a liquid offering poured to the gods.

Maimakterion -- see: months.

medimnos, pl. *medimnoi* -- a dry measure (192 *kotylai*), about
  12 gallons (45 liters).

meion -- lit. "lesser"; a sacrifice to commemorate a son's
  birth.

mina -- monetary unit, worth 100 drachmas.

Metageitnion -- see: months.

months -- the Athenian year began about midsummer with the
  month Hekatombaion, which included the Panathenaic festival; it was followed in order by Metageitnion, Boedromion
  and Pyanepsion; the winter months (approximately coin-
  ciding with November, December and January) were
  Maimakterion, Posideon and Gamelion; the early Greek
  spring began in Anthesterion ("month of flowers"), followed by Elaphebolion, Mounichion, Thargelion and
  Skiraphorion.

Mounichion -- see: months.

neokoros -- temple attendant.

neopoioi -- superintendants of temple administration.

obol -- monetary unit, 1/6 drachma.

oreibasia -- lit. "mountain-treading"; nocturnal ceremony
of the Bacchic women.

orgeones -- members of a cult association.

orgia -- general term for sacred rites, often with special
reference to secret rites.

oschophoroi -- lit. "vine-bearers"; participants in a
sacrificial procession.

pareias -- a snake sacred to Sabazios.

pelanos -- a porridge of barley and wheat flour.

peplos -- a woolen dress worn by women and girls; a new
peplos was woven every year by a special team of maidens
and presented to Athena at the Panathenaia.

prytaneion -- town hall; the headquarters of the *prytaneis*
during their term of office, and the central hearth-
shrine of the city-state.

prytaneis -- executive board of a city-state's council and
assembly.

stade -- a measure of distance, about 1/7 mile (200 meters).

stater -- a coin, often worth two or four drachmas.

stele, pl. *stelai* -- a stone slab displaying a commemorative
inscription or relief sculpture.

talent -- as a monetary unit, worth 6000 drachmas; as a
measure of weight, equivalent to about 55 pounds (25
kilograms).

theokolos -- lit. "god-tender"; a cult official.

thiasos, pl. *thiasoi* -- an association for religious purposes.

thyrsos -- a staff or wand topped with a pine cone and decked
with fillets.

INDEX OF ANCIENT SOURCES

Aelian. *The Nature of Animals* VII. 13 (p. 80). *Varia Historia* II. 19 (pp. 67-68); III. 43 (p. 99). Frag. 99 Hercher (p. 72).

Aeschylus. *Agamemnon*, 160-182 (p. 26), 750-781 (pp. 89-90). *Libation Bearers*, 123-149 (p. 223). *The Persians*, 607-632, 681-692 (pp. 248-249). *Prometheus Bound*, 160-168, 188-193, 199-205, 528-535 (pp. 26-27).

Alciphron. *Letters* IV. 18.16 (p. 209).

Alcman. Frag. 56 Page (p. 197).

Anaxagoras. Frag. 12 Diels-Kranz (pp. 32-33).

Antiphon. *Orations* I. 14-20 (pp. 145-146).

Apollodorus of Athens. Frag. 133 Jacoby (p. 201).

Apollodorus. *Library* II. 7.7 (p. 61).

Apollonius Rhodius. *Argonautica* I. 494-511 (pp. 39-40); scholia on I. 917 (p. 211).

Aristophanes. *Acharnians*, scholia on 961 (p. 201), scholia on 1076 (p. 205), 1085-1093 (p. 204). *Birds*, 688-702 (p. 41). *Frogs*, 324-336, 340-353, 369-413, 440-459 (pp. 187-188), 1030-1036 (p. 161). *Peace*, 276-279, 285-286 (p. 215), scholia on 277-278 (p. 215). *Ploutos*, 594-597 (p. 133), 654-695, 707-747 (pp. 73-75), scholia on 768 (p. 144), scholia on 1153 (p. 133).

Aristotle. *Constitution of the Athenians*, 3.5 (p. 204), 54.6-7 (p. 118), 55.2 (pp. 139-140), 60 (pp. 118-119). *Metaphysics*, 1072b25-31 (pp. 49-50). *Nicomachean Ethics* VIII. 1160a19-30, 23-28 (p. 135). *Physics*, 258b10-259a13 (pp. 48-49). Frag. 15 Rose (p. 190).

Arrian. *Anabasis of Alexander* VII. 23.2 (p. 67), 23.6 (p. 67).

Athenaeus. *Deipnosophists* X. 437b (p. 133), 437c-d (pp. 204-205); XI. 462b-c (p. 134), 464f (p. 209), 465a (p. 202), 473b-c (p. 144), 494f (p. 63), 498f-499a (p. 197).

Clement of Alexandria. *Protrepticus*, scholia on II. 11 (pp. 103-104); II. 21-22 (p. 192). *Stromateis* III. 3.17 (p. 191).

Critias. *Sisyphus*, frag. 1 (p. 35).

273

Homer *(continued)*
478-491 (p. 221); XIV. 418-436 (p. 108); XXII. 205-210, 236-240
(p. 154); XXIV. 1-2 (p. 231, n. 35), 11-14 (p. 231, n. 36).

Homeric Hymn to Apollo, 146-164 (p. 117).

Homeric Hymn to Demeter (pp. 171-183).

Hyperides. *Against Demosthenes*, 31 (p. 68).

IC III. 2.2 (pp. 29-30).

IG I^2. 6, B and C (pp. 184-185), 76, lines 1-46 (pp. 185-187), 408,
422, 436, 444, 467, 473, 485, 487, 499, 503, 606 (p. 150), 625, 631,
643, 650, 658, 684, 706 (p. 151), 784, 785, 788 (p. 152), 945, lines
6-9 (p. 250).

IG II^2. 204 (pp. 105-106), 334 (pp. 119-120), 1006, lines 12-13 (p. 209),
1237 (pp. 140-143), 1358, col. ii, lines 1-53 (pp. 113-115), 1362
(p. 125), 1533, lines 1-18 (pp. 78-80), 2311 (pp. 120-121), 4547
(p. 152), 4548 (pp. 151-152), 4960 (p. 78), 4962 (p. 75).

IG IV^2. 1.40 and 41 (p. 75).

IG VII. 235 (pp. 127-128).

IG IX. 2.640, lines 8-9 (p. 243).

IG XII. 1.141, lines 1-6 (p. 242); 5.310 (p. 242); 7.2 (p. 124);
8.449, lines 12-14 (p. 243); 9.1179 (p. 244).

Isaeus. *Orations* VIII. 15-16 (pp. 144-145).

Isocrates. *Panegyricus*, 28-29 (p. 189).

Kaibel. *Epigrammata Graeca* 21, lines 6-9 (p. 250), 67 (p. 243), 243,
lines 5-6 (p. 244), 646a (pp. 244-245), 648, lines 9-12 (p. 244).

LGS. 17 (pp. 140-143), 18 (p. 75), 34 (p. 125), 43 (pp. 125-126), 65
(pp. 127-128), 95 (p. 124), 96 (p. 124).

LSAM. 24(A), lines 25-38 (p. 76).

LSCG. 77 (p. 129), 85 (pp. 126-127).

Lactantius. *Divine Institutes*, Epitome, 23.7 (p. 192).

Livy. *History of Rome* XXXIX. 9.4, 10.5-7, 13.8-14 (pp. 199-200).

Lycurgus. *Against Leocrates*, 93 (p. 104).